FROM PROBLEMS TO PROFITS

The Madson Management System for Pet Grooming Businesses

Revised and Updated Edition

Madeline Bright Ogle

Publisher
THE MADSON GROUP, INC.
Sonora, California

ISBN No. 1-878795-25-2

Library of Congress Catalog Card No. 97-072659

Manufactured in the United States of America

Library of Congress Cataloging-in-Publication Data

Oggle, Madeline Bright, 1926-
    From problems to profits: the Madson Management System for pet grooming business / [by Madeline Bright Ogle]. -- Rev. and updated ed.
      p. cm.

    1. Pet grooming salons--Management. 2. Dog grooming industry--management. I. Title. II. Title: The Madson Management System for pet grooming businesses.

SF427.55.045 1997   636.7'08'33
ISBN 1-878795-25-2   QBI97-40553

Printing History
Original Edition © 1989, Madeline Bright Ogle
Published by Manor House Publishing, Santa Rosa, California

Published by

THE MADSON GROUP
1067 Mono Way, Suite 230
Sonora, California 95370
800-556-5131
E-mail: madsongroup@earthlink.net
Web: http://www.petgroomer.com/madson.htm

TABLE OF CONTENTS

LIST OF ILLUSTRATIONS

INTRODUCTION

ACKNOWLEDGEMENTS

1   THE HERITAGE OF PET GROOMING

2   INTRODUCING THE MADSON MANAGEMENT SYSTEM

3   STEP ONE OF THE BUSINESS PLAN

4   STEP TWO OF THE BUSINESS PLAN

5   STEP THREE OF THE BUSINESS PLAN

6 THE PET GROOMING SALON MANAGER

7 CREATING A SUCCESSFUL SUPPORT STAFF

8 HIRING THE SUPPORT STAFF

9   AN EFFECTIVE SUPERVISORY SYSTEM FOR THE SUPPORT STAFF

10   DEVELOPING A SAFETY PROGRAM

11   CLIENT RELATIONS THAT BRING THEM BACK AGAIN AND AGAIN

12 THE PEOPLE AND PET MARKETING PROGRAM

13 DAILY BOOKKEEPING AND RECORD KEEPING PROCEDURES

14 FINANCIAL MANAGEMENT TO INCREASE PROFITS

15 PLANNING FOR THE FUTURE

APPENDIX A FORM COMPLETION INSTRUCTIONS

APPENDIX B   PERSONNEL FORMS

APPENDIX C   TELEMARKETING PROCEDURES FORM

LIST OF ILLUSTRATIONS

INTRODUCTION

Good management is the key to a successful and prosperous business. Adequate capitalization is important, but without sound management it is a waste of money. When originally published in 1989, *From Problems To Profits* was the industry's first comprehensive system of management training for the pet grooming business. Now several years later the manual is more useful and popular than ever.

The reason is simple. Sound principles of management rarely become out-of-date, and that holds true for our original edition of *From Problems To Profits*. However, we have made some pertinent revisions in this revised and updated edition for your convenience.

Over the years many readers have reported greater financial success by applying the information in *From Problems To Profits*. Yet, there are many pet grooming businesses that have not yet gained the advantages of the knowledge that awaits them in this manual. Perhaps that is why so many pet grooming salons continue to struggle along barely surviving and giving their owner life-shortening stress. The thought of a comfortable retirement for the pet grooming owner is a joke. Most pet grooming salons will never have the equity to fund a retirement plan, they're too busy just trying to survive!

Now it can be different! *From Problems To Profits* – The Madson Management System empowers pet grooming salons to become prosperous through a proven management system. It is a benchmark in the pet grooming trade and long overdue!

After thirty-six years in the pet grooming field I have shown that with the right management system any one can succeed. Using the management system I developed and perfected over those many years I annually earned a six-figure income. I had over 3,500 regular clients. I sold my business—not the building—just the business—for well over $300,000.00. I can teach you to do the same, or better! I want you to have the success I enjoyed.

From Problems To Profits is your road map, read it over and over again. Apply the principles faithfully. You will discover financial success and personal satisfaction.

A crucial characteristic of a successful manager is motivation. The term motivation means **the energized pursuit of goals.** The key words are, energized, pursuit, and goals. Effective motivation requires a purpose, a plan to achieve that purpose, and the energy to carry out the plan.

The Madson Management System provides a set of goals and a systematic plan to achieve those goals. As rest stops on a highway refresh you, so does the accomplishment of each goal in the business plan. It provides the inspiration you need to continue your financial journey. Each goal you achieve will stimulate you to get on the road and achieve the next one.

I remember the wonderful feelings when I was first able to reach one of my goals. I was finally able to purchase something really special for my family's Christmas holiday. The feelings of success made the hard work worthwhile and the work ahead an agreeable challenge. There are always new goals to achieve for the motivated manager. Simple acknowledgments by clients stating that it was apparent the business was really growing was enough to make my day. Whatever your business goals, the Madson Management System will help you achieve them.

Yours in being the best!

Madeline Bright Ogle

ACKNOWLEDGEMENTS

My gratitude to Stephen A. Mart for his graphic design and illustrations that are so easy to identify with, and for hours of data processing. I feel blessed to have these capable men providing valuable input at every turn.

Kudos to Spiros Bairaktaris for his cover art. Thanks to Kate Fabian for the pen and ink art, and Joyce Bacci for illustration type. All of these people are special artists in their own right and I am grateful to have their assistance.

Thanks to friends and colleagues for their prayers and support. Special thanks to those who allowed me to read page after page to make certain the information had clarity.

THE HERITAGE
OF PET GROOMING

CHAPTER

1

Many reference materials attest to man's fondness of pets, but no books trace the origins of pet grooming. However, there are occasional references that shed light on the art of pet grooming. Ferdinand Mery, authored The Dog (London, 1970). In it, he established that dogs were first perceived as useful to man as early as 4240 B.C. Mery mentions unusual religious totems with dogs depicted in their sculpture. As centuries passed the dog eventually became commonly accepted as a pet, and is now considered "man's best friend."

In past centuries, pets have lived comfortably in the castles of Kings and Queens. They have served as working dogs in the marketplace and traveled with entertainment groups. Art from the fourteenth through the eighteenth century depicts small dogs and cats near the footstools of ladies of the Court. In other paintings small pets sit with their masters on lounges and chairs. Another shows a young man standing next to his spaniel. Frequently, the images depict larger breeds sitting on the floor next to their masters.

The Elizabethan era reveals some of the earliest historical evidence of pet grooming activity. While the method of grooming is unclear, the pets are clean and well-groomed. Perhaps groomers in the marketplace cleaned them. One such grooming in a lithograph shows a dog being sheared while sitting on a lady's lap. Women shearing dogs is also the subject of etchings.

In 17th century France, the poodle was the official dog at court. The era of King Louis XV of France reveals the first official records of dog grooming parlors. Rare books of the 19th century mention dog grooming in Europe. The Book of the Dog (Vero Shaw, 1879) refers to the existence of pet grooming in England. Specific grooming recommendations such as washing, grooming, and coat conditioning occur in Ashmont's Kennel Secrets, (Boston, 1893). Pet groomers have a historical tradition of which they can be proud.

Over the years, attitudes have been changing toward many animals. Animals that provided carriage for thousands of years, such as horses, mules, and camels, are now replaced by advanced developments in transportation. Many of these animals have different uses presently and maintain a special relationship with man. However, none are more beloved as pets than dogs and cats. And what man loves, he cares for and protects.

I hope you appreciate and admire, our heritage as groomers. You've chosen a field whose history shows it as both an occupation and an art. Similarly, the practice of medicine provides a necessary function for man's existence, yet the practice of medicine is an art. Unless you know the history of your profession and the revolutions taking place in your field, you are unlikely to succeed. Too many of today's pet grooming salons are as outmoded as a horse replaced by an automobile.

THE EVOLUTION OF PET GROOMING SALONS

The roots of today's salon lie in the marketplaces and palaces of the past. This is where groomers were first advancing our chosen field. Pet grooming salons as we know them today simply did not exist. More recently, kennels offer grooming services so pets return to their owners clean and smelling fresh. Also, many veterinarians have added grooming services so their client's pets are clean and fresh when picked up. Some neighborhood pet shops have also expanded into the service business by offering pet grooming services.

Before the 1940's, "doggie barbershops" went into business. These shops had very little room. The entire operation consisted of three or four cages, a table, and a bathing and drying area. Pedestal stand blow dryers, such as the Bonet "fluff-drier," were not yet introduced. Some doggie barbershops still exist though their number is decreasing. The burgeoning pet population demands modern and professional pet grooming services.

Kennels provided grooming in much the same manner using unsafe and ineffective cage driers. Lacking air conditioning, these "sweat shops" were already hot. With the introduction of pedestal stand blow dryers in the 1940's they became nearly unbearable for employee and pet. Trimming was laborious without electric clippers and modern supplies. No more than eight dogs a day can be in this environment and owners can only earn a limited income.

The late 1940's introduced new grooming tools. Yet, the biggest contributing factor to today's vast pet grooming market occurred in the middle 1950's. This is when the population explosion of dogs and cats began. The opportunity for pet grooming to become a viable profession had arrived. Pet grooming began to move out of the back room and away from the edge of town in rundown buildings. It moved downtown, to main street.

Through the centuries the pet dog and cat became an integral part of the family. When the United States zero birthrate became actuality, Americans brought more pets into their homes than ever. The population, especially of smaller breeds like the Poodle, Pomeranian, Sheltie, Lhasa Apso, Shih-Tsu and Pekinese, exploded. People loved the furry cuddliness of their little friends. With the movement toward town homes and condominiums, the smaller breeds fit better in the confined spaces of the new homes. They took up minimal space and were well-mannered travellers in automobiles. Perhaps the preference for smaller breeds is a functional necessity for today's lifestyle. The question is, will grooming salons make the adjustment demanded by the changes in our modern day clients and their pets?

A goldsmith's workshop by Alessandro Fei (1543-92). Look closely and you will find three well-groomed pets. Over four hundred years ago owners were taking care of their pets.

Photo: Scala/Art Resource, N.Y.

PET GROOMING SALONS CIRCA 1980-2000

The poor conditions of early grooming salons are simply not suitable for the years 1980 to 2000. Think about your current operation or the salon you are considering. Compare it to this vision of the state-of-the-art salon.

The ideal salon has stainless steel tubs with special drain traps designed specifically to catch the pet's hairs. It has an automatic lift to set the larger pets in the bathing tub and a washer and dryer for towels. It includes ceiling-mounted blow dryers. No more hairballs in the dryer's wheels and enough blowing power on medium heat to dry pets efficiently. The clippers have special wiring that boost amperage and yet operate at cooler temperatures. It has the latest design in cages from famous American and Japanese designers. Improved lighting enables employees to inspect the quality of their work. An emergency generator for power outages allows business activities to continue uninterrupted. The tiled bathing department has maintenance procedures posted. The advanced sanitation procedures include a "potty-walking" area.

These are just a few of the attributes of the state-of-the-art salon. You will learn more about it in the chapters ahead and eventually use the ideas in your own salon.

In a recent census, the estimated population of dogs and cats in America was 57 and 58 million respectively. These numbers are still growing and will continue to grow. By the year 2000 there will be 3.1 pets per household. Houses are becoming smaller and the number of apartment dwellers increases. Pets often eat and sleep in the same room with their owners. Never have so many pets been living so closely with us. Being this close to their pets, people want them to be clean and well-groomed more than ever.

INTRODUCING THE
MADSON MANAGEMENT SYSTEM

CHAPTER 2

Without a sound business plan backed by an effective management system a business cannot survive, let alone make substantial profits. Even with adequate capital a poorly managed operation will drain your reserves. You are not in business to spend money but to make money.

Think of the management system as the engine of your automobile. You, the owner, have the key to turn on the engine, but the engine does the work. Your job is to steer the auto to its destination. Likewise, as the driver of your salon, you need to steer your management system to higher profits.

Your expertise as a pet groomer is a valuable asset. However, it is not enough to guarantee the success of your business. You are first a businessperson and secondly, a pet groomer. This misunderstanding of priorities is an unprofitable fact in nearly every salon today. You are selling services not products. Your product is your grooming skill. Yours is a service business and service businesses have special challenges that require a specialized management system. Your skills plus the Madson Management System equals success.

Your goals are many. They are to increase your support staff, client base, and number of appointments. You must train groomers to duplicate your style, and pay salaries — not expensive commissions. To steer your way to this goal requires management skill.

If you are unskilled at management, the Madson Management System will be invaluable to you.

AN OVERVIEW OF
THE MADSON MANAGEMENT SYSTEM

The Madson Management System contains all the resources necessary to develop a successful pet grooming salon. The core of the system is the business plan. It is a road map to guide you along your route to financial success. Without a business plan you are like a ship without a course and no possibility of reaching your destination.

The business plan consists of three steps. Complete each step before moving to the next one. Each step contains objectives and an action plan to help you accomplish them. It also details the minimum number of staff members needed to carry out the action plan. Remember, the business plan is a proven system. It will work! All that it needs is your commitment and perseverance. There is no such word as success without "U".

Following, is a brief description of what you will learn from each successive chapter.

Chapter Three contains Step One of the Business Plan. Step One will give you an overview of the first objectives you are to establish. It will provide a step-by-step Action Plan to accomplish those objectives. It will describe the multiple responsibilities of the two staff members of Step One; the owner/manager/trimmer and the pet bather. Chapter Three will describe how to implement Step One using current staff members for salons with more than two staff members.

Chapter Four describes the objectives of Step Two and the Action Plan to complete those objectives. The objectives are two-fold. The addition of two crucial staff members and the installation of the "assembly line" method of operation.

Chapter Five describes the objectives of Step Three and its Action Plan. Upon completion of Step Three your salon will be a full-service salon. It will have a full staff, a manager, and be capable of supporting you as an absentee owner. In addition, you will have the option to expand into a Pet Center.

Chapter Six discusses the pet grooming salon manager. In Steps One and Two that will usually be the owner. It also describes what the manager needs to employ the Madson Management System successfully.

Chapter Seven will teach you the foundation for creating a successful support staff. It entails the setting up of a personnel department with appropriate job descriptions. It provides instruction in training, employee pay schedules, and personnel policies and procedures.

Chapter Eight discusses personnel management techniques in more detail. It explains the hiring process that finds job candidates and assists you in selecting the most qualified person. It also describes legal employment agreements to protect your business.

Chapter Nine presents a supervisory system for the support staff to maximize employee productivity. It includes how to run a staff meeting, make job performance evaluations, and resolve performance problems. It also contains valuable methods for employee discipline and termination which legally safeguard the employer.

Chapter Ten makes the pet grooming salon a safe environment for people and pets. By following its safety program a pet salon will gain a valuable reputation for professional, humane pet care services.

Chapter Eleven will teach you how to increase your business through client relations. It describes an extensive number of promotional techniques and materials which will become indispensable to you. It will help you gain the maximum profit from your current client base.

Chapter Twelve compares the difference between passive and active marketing. It gives you the specific resources for increasing your client base.

Chapter Thirteen explains effective daily bookkeeping procedures. It also includes detailed methods to organize written records supporting an efficient operation.

MADSON MANAGEMENT SYSTEM FORMS

Purchasers of **From Problems to Profits** may make copies of the following copyrighted forms included in the business manual to implement the Madson Management System.

- Cash Reserve Journal Sheet
- Employment Questionnaire
- Effective Management Checklist
- Employee Handbook
- Weekly Employee Timekeeping Record
- Daily Response Report (Telemarketer)
- Manager's Advance Planning Schedule
- Supplies Control Log Sheet
- Job Descriptions (all seven titles)

- Ad Response Record
- Emergency Report
- Client Base Goal Worksheet
- Annual Profit/Loss Projection
- Action Plans
- Daily Response Report (Receptionist)
- Manager Performance Evaluation
- Evaluation Checklist
- Telemarketing Procedures Form

- Client Relations Department Performance Evaluation
- Trimming Department Performance Evaluation
- Bathing Department Performance Evaluation
- Letter of Request for Advertising Information
- Weekly Summary of Complete Trim and Bath-only Services
- Letter of Request for Tax Identification Number

The legal agreements listed below are included in **From Problems to Profits** as samples only. Do not copy them for use in your business. Legal agreements used in your salon should be prepared by your attorney.

- Job Applicant Practical Exam Agreement
- General Introductory Period Agreement
- Manager Introductory Period Agreement
- Employee Confidentiality Agreement
- Job Agreement–Client Relations Department
- Job Agreement–Bathing and Trimming Departments
- Manager Job Agreement
- Tutorial Training Agreement
- Release and Hold Harmless Agreement

The forms listed below are **Madson Business Forms** available for purchase separately from The Madson Group. Samples of each form are included in the business manual.

- Client and Pet History Filecard
- Pet Care Services Brochure/Mailer
- Pet Sympathy Card
- Pet Birthday Card
- Pet Sitter's Information Record
- Client Response Postcard

- Daily Caging and Payment Register
- Pet Groomer's Report and Health Alert
- Get Well Card for Pets
- Client Service Questionnaire
- Manager's Daily Summary Report of Services and Sales

Chapter Fourteen offers financial management methods that allow you to turn your bookkeeping records into a profit center.

Chapter Fifteen provides resources for the pet salon owner with an insatiable appetite for advancement. It details procedures for establishing a state-of-the-art pet grooming salon. As an extra, it teaches the beginning steps for converting your salon into a Pet Center. When retirement or lifestyle change is contemplated Chapter Fifteen explains profitable options.

MADSON MANAGEMENT SYSTEM FORMS

Several chapters discuss Madson Management System forms provided for your use in selected illustrations. They will be invaluable to the successful operation of your salon. The illustrations also include samples of Madson Business Forms. You can order more Madson Business Forms from The Madson Group, Inc.

Succeeding chapters will describe both Madson Management System forms and Madson Business Forms. Detailed instructions will assist you to organize and complete all forms.

STEP ONE
OF THE BUSINESS PLAN

CHAPTER

3

The number one enemy preventing your success is the tendency to focus on "just maintaining." You can earn a six-figure income in pet grooming, but not if your only concern is maintaining the status quo. Increasing the value of your salon will supplement your retirement portfolio. It can be worth three times or more what you invested. This is not possible however, if you are happy to simply maintain. If you do, your salon's value will also remain idle.

Every pet grooming business needs a business plan if it is to grow and prosper. The explanation of the business plan begins with this chapter and continues through chapters four and five. Chapters six through fifteen provide specific details for implementing the general objectives of the business plan. The explanations are in plain, easy to understand English.

The business plan has three divisions, or steps. After fulfilling the objectives of Step One move on to Step Two and complete its objectives. Finally, after meeting the goals of Step Two, advance to Step Three. This step signals a major achievement.

Your finest investment is in yourself. You are the business. You are also an ethical businessperson with a responsibility to your community. Examine the Code of Ethics in illustration 3-1 and the Business Plan. These are the best resources to return to when making successful business decisions.

To carry out this management system successfully your second best investment is in your staff. It is precisely here that the average owner falls short. The salon owner is accustomed to wearing many hats; owner, trimmer, manager and even receptionist. This will not produce success. It is vital to create a professional staff if you want to be profitable.

THE OBJECTIVES OF STEP ONE

Step One of the Business Plan has objectives for the owner/manager to achieve. Each is a measurable goal. To achieve the objectives you will use the resources of this manual. Before you begin working on the objectives of Step One, review the entire manual. Management decisions will become easier if you are familiar with the entire business plan. By reading Step One each working morning the goals and tasks stay fresh in your mind. There are four objectives in Step One.

Objective 1.
Build a minimum cash reserve of $10,000.00.

The cash reserve is the most important of the four objectives of Step One. The minimum reserve is $10,000.00. This cash reserve will subsidize the costs of hiring two new staff members when you reach Step Two. Many owners will not need to use the entire $10,000.00. This is because new employees soon "pay their way" by allowing the grooming of additional pets. Though you may not need the entire amount, don't proceed to Step Two until you have saved it.

Objective 2.
Increase appointments and open for business one extra day each week.

You will accomplish this by implementing the Madson Management System's People and Pet Marketing Program.

Objective 3.
Increase the client base.

Every pet grooming salon has a client base which is measurable. Step One requires an increase in the salon's client base. For rural areas, the increase is 100 new clients. For pet salons in and around urban areas the increase is 200. The Action Plan provides guidance to measure accurately, and increase, your salon's client base.

Objective 4.
Prepare a budget for Step One.

It is essential to use sound financial planning methods. That means having a budget for your salon. The Annual Profit and Loss Projection enables you to accomplish this. It projects reasonable revenue and overhead expenses expected in the coming year. Owners who manage pet salons without budget projections have only a vague notion of their salon's financial standing. The Action Plan will assist you in preparing the Annual Profit and Loss Projection.

THE ACTION PLAN FOR STEP ONE

Detailed methods to achieve the objectives of each step of the business plan are in the Action Plans. They provide step-by-step details to guide you in achieving the objectives. By having

Code of Ethics

It is the company's objective:

To promote a professional reputation for the pet grooming industry by striving for excellence in our services.

To conduct all business in an honorable and fair manner.

To believe that long-term success is produced by adhering to ethical and moral business standards.

To achieve total client satisfaction.

To provide employees with job security and above-average conditions of employment.

To ensure that the highest level of humane pet care is provided to every pet.

To encourage management and staff to successfully implement and fulfill our Code of Ethics.

and maintaining a clear picture of the actions necessary to achieve your objectives you are more likely to attain them. Begin with the Action Plan for Step One to start construction of the management system in your pet grooming salon. Use the Action Plan for the entire period of your involvement with Step One.

With every instruction on the Action Plan, there are chapter references to find pertinent details. Whenever the Action Plan refers to a form there are chapter references showing the location of detailed instructions in its use.

Post a copy of the objectives of Step One and its Action Plan in your private office. You are now ready to begin your first assignment.

Action 1.
Actions for building the minimum cash reserve.

Step One requires the owner to continue to operate as the manager/trimmer. Open your salon one extra day each week and book the overflow of appointments for that day. Instead of hiring a new trimmer for the extra day, do the work yourself and save that day's income in an interest-bearing savings plan. By following this savings procedure you will build a substantial cash reserve. Even if you have never saved this amount before it is possible if you are willing to work the extra day. This savings is needed to fund expansion and the additional staff required in Step Two.

Faithfully save the extra day's gross receipts to accumulate a minimum of $10,000.00 in your cash reserve. If you trim twelve pets on the extra day at an average fee of $22.00, you will gross $264.00 each week. At this rate, you can save the minimum cash reserve of $10,000.00 in thirty-eight weeks.

Further details on saving the cash reserve are in illustration 3-4. Salons already operating seven days a week can implement swing shifts (Chapter Twelve) and put the earnings in the cash reserve.

Make several copies of the Cash Reserve Journal Sheet in illustration 3-5. Bind them together to form a Cash Reserve Journal. Keep the journal with your bank records for the cash reserve savings account. Even though your bank will provide you with records, record all deposits and interest in the Cash Reserve Journal for later use. Instructions on completing the journal are in Appendix A. The account balance shown in the journal should reconcile with your monthly bank statement.

Continue to live modestly even though your income increases and invest the new income in a savings plan. Within a few months, the accumulated earnings will allow you to expand and invest in additional staff.

Action 2.
Actions for increasing appointments.

Begin accomplishing the first objective by investing in a phone answering machine. Use it after business hours. On the recording, encourage callers to leave their number so you may return their calls and secure their business. Reply to all calls by noon the next business day. Select an answering machine with remote message pick-up capability. This feature allows you to call your business from another phone and listen to caller's messages.

Begin using the Madson People and Pet Marketing Program described in Chapter Twelve and you will find your appointments increasing.

Objectives

Step One

of the

BUSINESS PLAN

Objective 1   Build a minimum cash reserve of $10,000.00.

◆

Objective 2   Increase appointments and open for business one extra day each week.

◆

Objective 3   Increase the client base.

◆

Objective 4   Prepare a budget for Step One.

ACTION PLAN

MANUAL   FORMS

STEP ONE OF THE BUSINESS PLAN

PREPARATION

Before beginning to accomplish the actions thoroughly read
the entire manual at least once.   all

Post a copy of the Objectives for Step One of the Business Plan
(illustration 3-2) and this action plan at your desk.   3

ACTION 1.

Complete *Action 1. Actions for building the minimum cash reserve.*   3
Follow the instructions in *Building a Cash Reserve* (illustration 3-4).   3
Make copies of the Cash Reserve Journal Sheet (illustration 3-5).   3

ACTION 2.

Complete *Action 2. Actions for increasing appointments.*   3
Begin using a telephone answering machine.   3
Implement the Madson People and Pet Marketing Program.   12
Delegate receptionist and telemarketing duties following the
instructions in *The Receptionist and Telemarketer at Step One.*   3
Make copies of the Manager's Planning Schedule (illustration 12-1),
the Daily Response Report-Receptionist (illustration 11-4), and
the Daily Response Report-Telemarketer (illustration 12-5).   11/12
Make every customer a loyal client with the client relations
program and encourage them to join the Preferred Client Program.   11

ACTION 3.

Complete *Action 3. Actions to increase the client base.*   3
Follow the instructions to measure your salon's client base
in *Using the Client Base to Measure Achievement.*   12
Make copies of the Client Base Goal Worksheet (illustration 12-3).   12

ACTION 4.

Complete *Action 4. Actions to prepare a budget for Step One.*   3
Prepare monthly financial statements and track profit and loss
operating ratios.   14
Follow the supportive procedures for daily bookkeeping and
record keeping.   13
Make copies of the Annual Profit and Loss Projection
(illustration 14-1), the Weekly Employee Timekeeping
Record (illustration 13-1), and the Weekly Summary of
Complete Trim and Bath-Only Services (illustration 14-2).   13/14
Read *Comprehensive Business Insurance.*   14

ADDITIONAL ACTIONS

Complete the instructions in *The Support Staff at Step One,*
Introducing Your Staff to the Madson Management System, and
Guidelines for Three or More Employees (as needed).   3
Complete the instructions in *Creating a Successful Support Staff.*   7
Consult your attorney to prepare employment agreements.   8   8
Have your attorney also prepare client relations agreements.   11   11
Implement the supervisory system.   9
Implement the safety program.   10
Construct the Information Center and use it daily.   13
Read *The Pet Grooming Salon Manager* at least once each week.   6
Make copies of the Effective Management Checklist and
complete one each day.   6
Read *Step Two of the Business Plan* at least once each week.   4

BUILDING A CASH RESERVE
A GOAL OF STEP ONE OF THE BUSINESS PLAN

1. **Open for business one extra day each week.**

   Consider Sundays, experience has shown them to be as busy as Saturdays. Follow the Action Plan for Step One to market more appointments to fill the extra day. Be sure to encourage new clients to book an advance appointment, especially on the new day of the week your business is now open. Adjust employee work schedules for the extra work day and add a part-time pet bather as needed.

   > **Hint:** When you reach your trimming capacity, market the extra day with special incentives for bath-only pets. Employ a part-time bather to complete the overflow.

2. **Announce the expansion of the salon's services to present clients.**

   Post a sign in the reception area announcing that you are open one extra day each week. Make your announcement look and sound exciting. Emphasize the benefit to the client to capture client attention. The sign should clearly state the day of the week and hours of operation. Have photocopies of the sign made and distribute them to every client.

   > **Hint:** Consider offering clients incentives for referrals, especially for referrals booked on the new day of operation.

3. **Faithfully deposit net receipts into your cash reserve weekly.**

   Open an interest-bearing savings account exclusively for the cash reserve at your bank or savings and loan institution. Do not deposit the extra day's net receipts directly into the cash reserve. Instead, first deposit the net receipts into your regular business checking account; then write a check in the same amount and deposit it into the cash reserve account. It is a sound bookkeeping practice to always deposit all revenues into your business checking account first, and then distribute revenues to other accounts. This process creates an effective audit trail, record of gross revenue, and greatly assists your bookkeeper/accountant.

   > **Hint:** Market-interest accounts generally earn higher interest although they usually have a minimum opening deposit. When your cash reserve account accumulates enough funds to meet the minimum deposit requirements, transfer your funds to a market-interest account.

4. **Maintain a cash reserve journal.**

   A blank Cash Reserve Journal sheet is provided with the business manual. Make copies and bind them together to form your cash reserve journal. Fill in the blanks on each line indicating all deposits, withdrawals, and interest earned. Use the space provided for notes describing reasons for any necessary withdrawals, extra "seed-money" deposits, or other reminders.

   > **Hint:** When a monthly bank statement reconciliation is completed for the cash reserve account, ensure the resulting account balance is equal to the balance shown in the cash reserve journal. Both account balances will be identical if you have properly entered all account activity into the cash reserve journal.

Train your employees in the client relations policies and procedures as described in Chapter Eleven. Upon completion of training immediately begin using these techniques and the accompanying forms. Emphasize the importance of the Preferred Client Program (Chapter Eleven) to your employees. Give all clients a copy of the Pet Care Service Brochure explaining the program.

Post a notice for your clients that you will be open one extra day each week. Don't worry if bookings are slow at the start. By following the marketing procedures in Chapter Twelve appointments will increase. In my salon, we closed Mondays and opened Sundays. Sunday clients preferred to have their pet groomed on a day they were home from work. Many even dropped the pet off on their way to church. By working an extra day and answering the phone whenever it rings, you are expanding.

Action 3.
Actions to increase the client base.

You will begin to increase the client base by using the Madson Management System's marketing and client relations procedures. There is still more to do. Part of increasing your client base is the accurate measurement of it. Follow the instructions in Chapter Twelve, *Using the Client Base to Measure Achievement.*

Action 4.
Actions to prepare the budget for Step One.

Thoroughly review the budget instructions under the heading *The Annual Profit and Loss Projection* in Chapter Fourteen. Prepare your Annual Profit and Loss Projection following the instructions contained in Appendix A. Supportive procedures for daily bookkeeping and organizing records are in Chapter Thirteen. Learn them and use them.

THE SUPPORT STAFF AT STEP ONE

The support staff at Step One consists of the owner/trimmer and the pet bather(s). It is advisable to conform your current employees to the recommendations of Step One.

While working to achieve the objectives of the business plan, most owners will trim as well as manage. In these cases the owner will assume, or delegate, duties later required of added staff. For example, the owner will be the manager, master pet trimmer, receptionist, and telemarketer. The job descriptions contained in Appendix B will explain the duties of each position.

The owner of a small, growing business has the most responsible position, and works longer hours than the staff. However, with the Madson Management System, there is a light at the end of this seemingly unending tunnel. Eventually, by diligent application of the Madson Management System, you will be free to hire a manager and continue trimming. Or, you may choose to continue managing and hire a master pet trimmer. You can also hire a manager and master pet trimmer and become an absentee owner. To achieve this success you must complete the steps of the business plan.

As you can see, the responsibilities of the owner are almost limitless. To assist you in performing these duties review Chapter Six.

Review Chapters Seven, Eight, and Nine to familiarize yourself with the methods for creating and supervising a successful support staff.

CASH RESERVE JOURNAL

My goal is to save $ _____ , _____ .00 ($10,000 minimum).

DATE	DESCRIPTION	(+) DEPOSIT	(+) INTEREST	(−) DRAWS	BALANCE
	Balance brought forward				

Page _____

The Pet Bather

The support staff at Step One consists of only an owner/manager/trimmer and pet bather. Most pet grooming salons are one or two employee operations. Their average client base is about 300 to 600 patrons. Until demand requires it, you don't need the expense of additional staff. You will hire additional staff in Step Two and the cash reserve you build in Step One will pay for it.

Salon owners typically employ one or two pet bathers. They also assist with front counter and phone duties, so it is easy to conform to the staff structure of Step One. The Madson job description for a pet bather is in Appendix B. There are also six other job descriptions eventually employed by the management system. Review the pet bather job description and compare its duties to the duties performed by your pet bather(s). Assign additional duties listed in the pet bather job description to your pet bather(s).

THE RECEPTIONIST AND TELEMARKETER AT STEP ONE

There are more duties required in Step One than that of owner/manager/trimmer and pet bather. Divide these extra responsibilities between the existing staff. Two crucial responsibilities are that of receptionist and telemarketer. Complete these duties faithfully to achieve the objectives of Step One.

Train yourself and your pet bather(s) in the duties of receptionist and telemarketer. If you don't personally complete these duties, delegate them to someone every business day. The person covering these duties may have to work some overtime, but it's worth it to get the added business.

If you have two or more pet bathers, have one pet bather assume phone duties in the afternoon. For example, a pet bather may bathe from 10 a.m. to 4 p.m. and handle phones from 4 to 7 p.m. With a one-hour lunch break, the pet bather works eight hours. This avoids costly overtime.

The delegation of extra duties to the pet bather(s) provides the opportunity to develop additional professional skills. The process of delegation also encourages the pet bather(s) to improve client relations skills and learn how to market services. Note that each job description says the owner may assign extra duties at his discretion. Naturally, you will pay for any overtime worked to complete the extra duties.

INTRODUCING YOUR STAFF TO THE MADSON MANAGEMENT SYSTEM

Thoroughly review the Madson Management System manual. Next, call a staff meeting of your employee(s). Inform them of your decision to start using the system. Explain to them the responsibilities and rewards that it creates. Encourage your employees to adapt to the new management system because of mutual benefit. There is good reason for employees to get excited about the new management system. As the business grows and profits increase, they will get increases in salary. They will also derive enhanced self-esteem by being a part of a professional salon. The Madson Management System motivates employees by offering potential for advancement and reducing deficiencies in productivity caused by boredom.

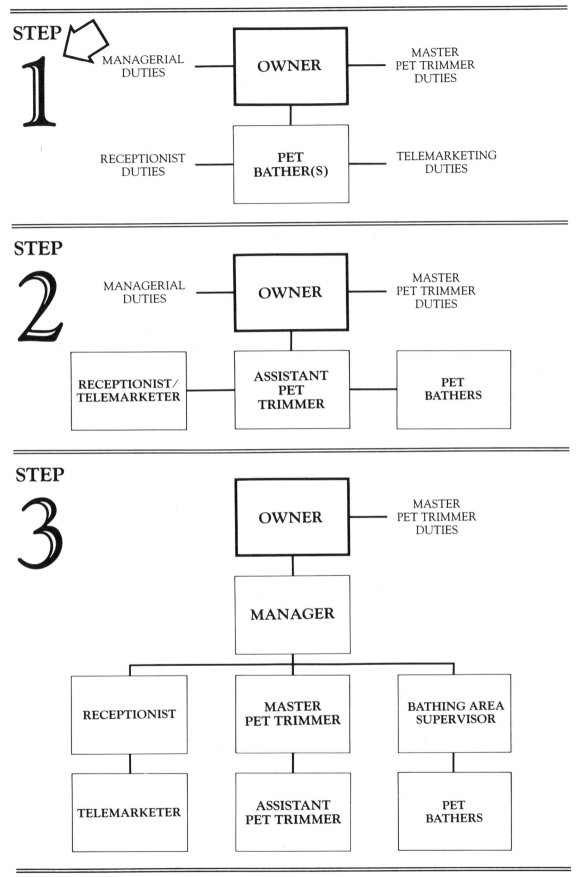

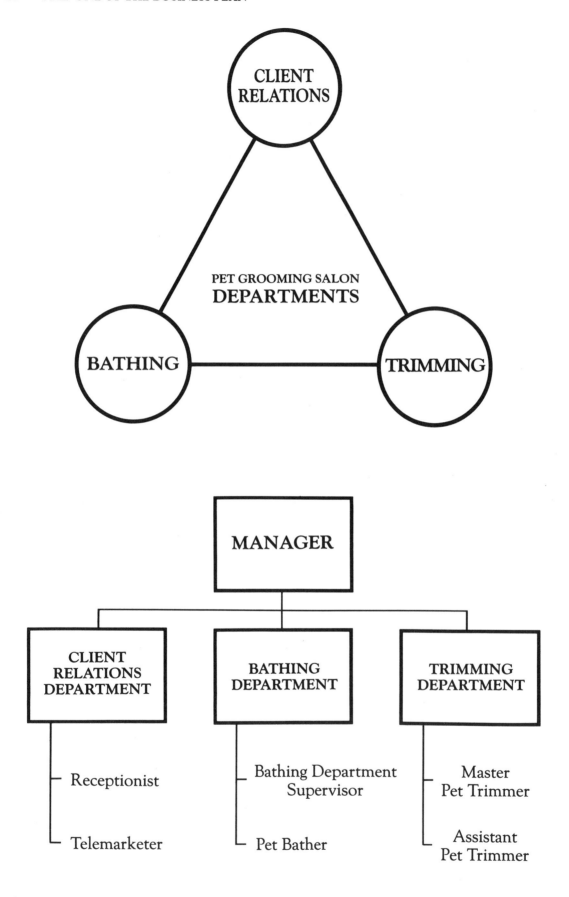

EVALUATION CHECKLIST
FOR STEP ONE OF THE BUSINESS PLAN

*You must answer "YES" to every question
before implementing Step Two of the Business Plan.*

YES NO **Have you re-read Chapter Four, Step Two of the Business Plan, and studied the Action Plan for Step Two until you are completely familiar with its purpose and instructions?**

If you answered NO, do not move to Step Two. Read Chapter Four and locate its Action Plan for Step Two of the Business Plan. Review every action instruction and reading references listed on the Action Plan for Step Two.

YES NO **Have you completed the Action Plan for Step One of the Business Plan?**

If you answered NO, return to the Action Plan for Step One and finish all instructions.

YES NO **Have you accumulated a minimum $10,000.00 cash reserve?**

If you answered NO, continue saving an extra day's net receipts until you reach the cash reserve goal. Review the illustration titled "Building a Cash Reserve" and make sure you are using a Cash Reserve Journal.

YES NO **Have you increased the size of the client base (100 new clients in rural areas, 200 new clients urban/suburban areas) since first beginning Step One?**

Refer to your Client Base Goal Worksheet (see Action Plan for Step One of the Business Plan).
If you answered NO, increase marketing efforts described in Chapter Twelve.

YES NO **Have you prepared an Annual Profit and Loss Projection for the next twelve months?**

If you answered NO, refer to the instructions for preparing an Annual Profit and Loss Projection in Chapter Fourteen.

3-8

At the first staff meeting with your current employee(s), give a copy of the pet bather job description to each bather. Let them study it and then answer any questions. The Madson job description may be similar to your present pet bather duties. However, the pet bather(s) will see a difference in your commitment to staff a professional pet grooming salon.

If you are now paying bathers by a piecework method, stop it. Salaries are a better method for both owner and employee. Review the information under the heading Salaries in Chapter Seven. Inform them of the date you will begin to pay them by salary. State the amount in writing on the job description distributed at the meeting. Pet bathers performing the same duties as before should see little difference in their gross pay.

Distribute the Madson Employee Handbook to the pet bather(s). Review the employee policies and procedures at this first meeting.

GUIDELINES FOR THREE OR MORE EMPLOYEES

Most pet grooming salons today consist of owner/manager/trimmer and pet bather(s). However, there are exceptions. Some salons already have more staff than required in Step One. Conforming to the staff structure prescribed by Step One requires some adjustments and decisions. Even though you have more employees than recommended you must still achieve the objectives of Step One. Do this before moving to Step Two.

If you have more employees than described by Step One, provide each of them with a job title. Use job descriptions from Step Two and Step Three of the Business Plan as needed. For example, if you have a front counter person, assign them the duties of receptionist and telemarketer. If you now employ a very experienced full-charge trimmer give them the title of master pet trimmer. If you employ an inexperienced trimmer, assign them the duties of assistant pet trimmer.

If your new staff structure performs so efficiently that you have a surplus employee, use them for telemarketing. The primary objectives for support staff is to generate new business and to handle the increased demand for pet care services.

THE CHECKLIST BEFORE BEGINNING STEP TWO

Accomplish every objective of Step One before moving to Step Two. As directed in the Action Plan, measure the results before proceeding with the next step. Proceed to the checklist evaluation and answer all the questions.

If you answered "YES" to every question, you are ready to move forward to Step Two of the Business Plan. However, if even one answer is "NO," do not to continue to Step Two. Notice there is an alert on the evaluation checklist next to each question. If there is a "NO" response to a question, the alert tells you how to change that answer to a "YES." Only when you have replied "YES" to every question are you ready to start Step Two of the Business Plan. The corrective evaluation checklist is a fail-safe indicator of the appropriate time to begin Step Two. It alerts you to a problem, offers a solution, and prompts you to continue with Step Two.

The time it takes to complete the first Action Plan provides time for management's skills to grow from experience. You are on your way to becoming the chief representative of a professional pet grooming salon. Get ready to send up trial balloons and start on the way to more money in your pocket and an exciting future. Work hard, stay motivated, and be responsible to your objectives. After completing Step One of the Business Plan, you are ready for the real excitement about to happen in your salon.

STEP TWO
OF THE BUSINESS PLAN

CHAPTER
4

Your salon at Step One is like a caterpillar spinning a cocoon. It is certain to burst free as a butterfly able to reach new heights. Step Two sees the fulfillment of that dream with increased profit and potential.

You are not the same owner as when you first started Step One of the Business Plan. You've become more effective as a manager and your salon operation is more professional. Your cash reserve offers the necessary financial resources to accomplish the objectives of Step Two. The hard work caused by adding an extra day allows further expansion. The People and Pet Marketing Program will enlarge your client base and you will be proud of your salon's growing reputation.

THE OBJECTIVES OF STEP TWO

The owner/manager must achieve five objectives in Step Two of the Business Plan. Each is a measurable goal and the manual furnishes instructions in achieving the objectives.

Objective 1.
Add an assistant pet trimmer and receptionist.

By following the procedures of Step One your business will have grown. Step Two continues that process. It transforms salon operations to not only accommodate the expansion of the client base but to increase it. Creating more business is almost always a preferred alternative to raising prices and an increased number of pets warrants additional staff.

There is nothing new about hiring additional staff, grooming more pets, and making more money. You knew the concept before studying the management system, but the main barrier was the expense. However, the cash reserve built in Step One will allow the hiring and training of additional staff. Don't be anxious about using it to build your business. The alternative is to increase revenue by raising prices. A price raise is not an effective technique for raising revenue. It is best used as a hedge against inflation and increases in overhead. The salon would have to double its fees to equal the revenue from grooming twice as many pets. You can imagine the clamor from your clientele if you tell them that prices are being doubled!

Objective 2.
Increase appointments.

Typically, an owner/trimmer completes an average of twelve trims per day. A trained assistant working with the owner/trimmer as a team can easily accommodate an increase to twenty trims daily. This increase of 66% more trims obviously requires an equal increase in trim appointments. You can accomplish this through the telemarketing activities of the receptionist and increased attention to the marketing program.

Objective 3.
Install the "assembly line" grooming method of operation.

This is the most efficient method of increasing trims. The description of it is in part three of the Action Plan.

The assembly line method using an assistant pet trimmer allows the addition of eight pet trims daily. At an average grooming fee of $22.00 this creates sizable increases. The return is $176.00 daily, $1,056.00 weekly, and an annual increase of $54,912.00. An increase of almost $55,000.00 annually may seem significant. It a conservative projection, however, if you faithfully follow the Madson Management System.

Objective 4.
Increase the client base.

Step Two requires the owner/manager to increase the client base. The increase is 200 for pet salons in rural areas, and 500 for those in or around urban areas. The increase is significant, but reasonable, for a pet grooming salon using the Madson Management System.

Objective 5.
Prepare a budget for Step Two.

The Action Plan will assist you in preparing an Annual Profit and Loss Projection. This will allow you to prepare the budget for Step Two.

THE ACTION PLAN FOR STEP TWO

The format of the Action Plan for Step Two is the same as the Action Plan for Step One. It provides chapter references to find applicable instructions and forms necessary to accomplish the

Objectives
Step Two
of the
BUSINESS PLAN

Objective 1	Add an assistant pet trimmer and receptionist.
	◆
Objective 2	Increase appointments.
	◆
Objective 3	Install the "assembly-line" (grooming) method of operation.
	◆
Objective 4	Increase the client base.
	◆
Objective 5	Prepare a budget for Step Two.

objectives. Replace the posted copy of the Step One Action Plan with the one for Step Two. You are ready to begin your first assignment.

Action 1.
Actions for hiring the assistant pet trimmer and receptionist.

Refer to Chapter Eight for complete instructions on the hiring process for all positions on the support staff. You can promote an experienced pet bather to assistant trimmer because it is advisable that the assistant have some pet bathing experience.

Use only the minimum necessary from the cash reserve to acquire the additional staff. They will soon be paying their own way and you do not want to deplete the cash reserve any more than necessary. Working capital is an essential ingredient for a successful business. Always rebuild your cash reserve to the minimum $10,000.00 after using for expansion. Drawing Funds From the Cash Reserve, in this chapter has instructions in using the cash reserve correctly.

Action 2.
Actions for increasing appointments.

Begin another increase in appointments by training the receptionist in client relations (Chapter Eleven) and telemarketing (Chapter Twelve). During Step One you and the pet bather(s) performed these duties. In Step Two delegate the telemarketing aspect to the receptionist. The receptionist can devote more time to this activity, and properly trained and supervised will significantly increase appointments. Use the time freed from reception and telemarketing to focus more attention on the People and Pet Marketing Program (Chapter Twelve). As a team, the owner/manager and receptionist can achieve the objective to increase appointments by 66%. You can even exceed it.

Action 3.
Actions to install the "assembly line" grooming method.

This method of operation is the key to increased profits and prepares you for Step Three. It requires the use of an assistant pet trimmer and the application of the pre-clipping concept.

The assistant pet trimmer's main responsibility is the pre-clip of dogs. This term is what some pet groomers call "rough-out" work. The change in terms is not gratuitous. The term pre-clip is consistent with the concept of assembly line grooming and connotes a sense of professionalism. A pre-clip consists of trimming face, feet, tail, pattern, and stomach. In some instances it involves the complete removal of a pet's coat. The pre-clipped pet then goes further down the assembly line to the bathing department. Lastly, it goes to the owner/master pet trimmer for the finish trim work.

During the early part of the day the Master Pet Trimmer may assist in pre-clips to initiate the assembly line method. When the first bathed pet is finished he does nothing but finish trims.

Assistant pet trimmers also complete bath-only dogs. This means scissoring around the feet, eyes, stomach, and anus. They then do the bunning or bowing. They also serve as back-up pet bathers. The goal for assistants is eight trims and four baths a day. As the assistant gains competency through hands-on experience with several breeds they are ready to learn finish trimming. This can begin at the end of the day after finishing pre-clips.

Call a staff meeting and explain the assembly line method to the entire staff. Make copies of illustration 4-3 depicting the method and distribute them at the meeting. This method

ACTION PLAN
STEP TWO OF THE BUSINESS PLAN

PREPARATION
Before beginning to accomplish the actions you must answer | 3
yes to every question on the Evaluation Checklist For Step One.
Post a copy of the Objectives for Step Two of the Business | 4
Plan (illustration 4-1) and this action plan at your desk.

ACTION 1.
Complete *Action 1. Actions for hiring the assistant pet trimmer* | 4
and receptionist.
Read *Creating a Successful Support Staff.* | 7
Complete the instructions in *The Support Staff at Step Two.* | 4
Prepare job descriptions, employee handbooks, personnel files, | 7 | B
employment agreements (from your attorney), and the training
program for the assistant pet trimmer and receptionist.
Follow the instructions in *Drawing Funds From the Cash Reserve.* | 4
Include the assistant pet trimmer and receptionist in the | 9
supervisory system.
Include the assistant pet trimmer and receptionist in the | 10
safety program.

ACTION 2.
Complete *Action 2. Actions for increasing appointments.* | 4
Fully-implement the Madson People and Pet Marketing Program. | 12
Make every customer a loyal client with the client relations | 11
program and encourage them to join the Preferred Client Program.
Read *Telemarketing at Step Two.* | 4

ACTION 3.
Complete *Action 3. Actions to install the "assembly line"* | 4
grooming method.
Make copies of the Assembly Line Method of Operation (illustration 4-3). | | 4

ACTION 4.
Complete *Action 4. Actions to increase the client base.* | 4
Follow the instructions to measure your salon's client base | 12
in *Using the Client Base to Measure Achievement.*

ACTION 5.
Complete *Action 5. Actions to prepare a budget for Step Two* | 4
Prepare monthly financial statements and track profit and loss | 14
operating ratios.
Follow the supportive procedures for daily bookkeeping and | 13
record keeping.

ADDITIONAL ACTIONS
Read *The Pet Grooming Salon Manager* at least once each week. | 6
Complete an Effective Management Checklist each day. | | 6
Read *Step Three of the Business Plan* at least once each week. | 5

requires a team effort so encourage their active participation. Emphasize the opportunity for an employee to advance in responsibility and salary by using this method.

Action 4.
Actions to increase the client base.

The additional time spent by the owner/manager implementing the People and Pet Marketing Program will increase the client base. Remember, an important part of increasing the client base is measuring it. Follow the instructions in Chapter Twelve under the heading *Using the Client Base to Measure Achievement*.

Action 5.
Actions to prepare the budget for Step Two.

Thoroughly review the budget information under the heading *The Annual Profit and Loss Projection* in Chapter Fourteen. Prepare your Annual Profit and Loss Projection following the instructions contained in Appendix A. Supportive procedures for daily bookkeeping and organizing records are in Chapter Thirteen. Learn them and use them.

THE SUPPORT STAFF AT STEP TWO

Step Two emphasizes support staff teamwork. The goal is to build a team that works together efficiently to reduce costs. Step Two of the Business Plan follows a formula corporations have used for decades. Large-scale operations increase production and profitability through teamwork. Each team member performs specialized job duties. The use of assembly lines in factories is an example of the formula. The net result is higher production, minimum expense, and better quality. The pet grooming salon needs to become more like an assembly line yet maintaining the ambience of a small service business. This method of operation results in large profits. Too many pet grooming salons ignore methods used by other segments of the business world. Good management practices are similar for any business and your product and service is not an exception.

The new employees hired to work with the existing staff create an effective team if the owner/manager is an effective coach. The new team depends on the owner's management for guidance. The successful coach creates a compatible staff by emphasizing teamwork. Each team member must feel excitement about the possibilities inherent in the new team formation. Encourage the concept of mutual success. The team in your salon will be aware of your attitude toward them. Be aware of your team's perception of the concern you project for their success as individuals and as a team. View them as people with their own feelings and ambitions and not as tools performing a function. Their contributions can move you from an old-fashioned inefficient salon operation toward a profitable new business method.

You continue to be both manager and master pet trimmer for the duration of Step Two. When you hire a manager in Step Three, he will take over many of your management tasks.

PRE-CLIP → BATH → FINISH TRIMMING
Asst. Pet Trimmer   Master Pet Trimmer

Madson Team Trimming Operations

formerly "Assembly Line Operations"

GOAL: The Assistant Pet Trimmer pre-clips enabling the Master Pet Trimmer to complete up to eight or more additional trims daily.

SCORE: A win-win proposition. The Assistant Pet Trimmer earns a good salary and the opportunity for promotion to Master Pet Trimmer, the Master Pet Trimmer earns a good income with promotion to Manager a possibility, and the salon dramatically increases gross revenue.

KEY: The **Pre-clip.** The Assistant Pet Trimmer trims the pet's face, feet, tail, pattern, stomach, or complete removal of a pet's coat prior to reaching the Master Pet Trimmer.

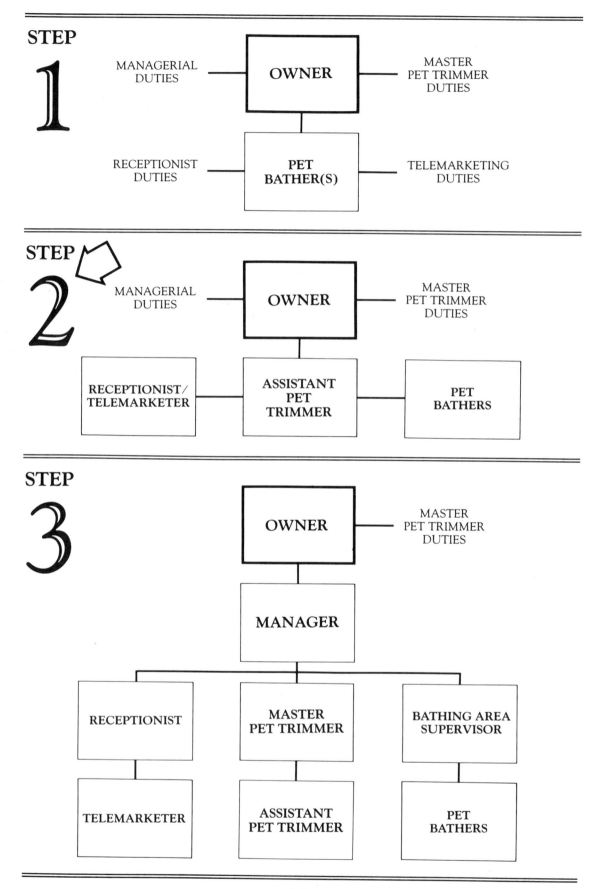

EVALUATION CHECKLIST
FOR STEP TWO OF THE BUSINESS PLAN

*You must answer "YES" to every question
before implementing Step Three of the Business Plan.*

YES NO **Have you re-read Chapter Five, Step Three of the Business Plan,
and studied the Action Plan for Step Three until you are completely familiar with its purpose and instructions?**

If you answered NO, do not move to Step Three. Read Chapter Five
and locate its Action Plan for Step Three of the Business Plan. Review
every action instruction and reading references listed on the Action
Plan for Step Three.

YES NO **Have you completed the Action Plan for Step Two of the
Business Plan?**

If you answered NO, return to the Action Plan for Step Two and
finish all instructions.

YES NO **Have you reimbursed the cash reserve for any draws taken maintaining the account balance at a minimum $10,000.00?**

You should have no less than the minimum cash reserve requirement
before implementing the expansion of Step Three. If you answered
NO, faithfully seed extra savings into the cash reserve until you have
reimbursed all draws and the balance is no less than $10,000.00.
Review the illustration titled "Building a Cash Reserve" and make
sure you are using a Cash Reserve Journal.

YES NO **Have you increased the size of the client base (200 new clients in
rural areas, 500 new clients urban/suburban areas) since first
beginning Step Two?**

Refer to your Client Base Goal Worksheet (see Action Plan for Step
Two of the Business Plan).
If you answered NO, increase marketing efforts described in Chapter
Twelve.

YES NO **Have you prepared an Annual Profit and Loss Projection for the
next twelve months?**

If you answered NO, refer to the instructions for preparing an
Annual Profit and Loss Projection in Chapter Fourteen.

The Assistant Pet Trimmer

A signal is being flashed when demand for services exceeds the capability of the owner/trimmer. It is time to hire additional staff in the trimming department. The assistant pet trimmer is the unique solution. This addition to the pet grooming support staff marks the inauguration of the "assembly line" grooming method.

The assistant pet trimmer learns finish work to the owner's standards allowing the owner to clone his trimming style. The clients will see no difference in the quality of grooming services even though many more pets are being groomed each day. The growth of the business does not need to result in a reduction of quality.

The assistant pet trimmer is a key factor in the future of the pet grooming salon. Eventually the demand for trims will grow. This is the time to hire an additional master pet trimmer. An experienced assistant is the best candidate for this position. He has familiarity with the salon's operation and the ability to trim in the style of the owner. A pet trimmer hired from outside cannot imitate the owner's style as quickly or even be receptive to the requirement. Avoid these problems by taking the time to hire and train an assistant pet trimmer.

If you do not have a candidate on your present staff, then seek an outside applicant. If you do, make certain they have some previous experience handling and bathing pets. Alternatively, seek someone with training from a reputable grooming institute. Follow the instructions in Chapter Eight when hiring staff members.

The Receptionist

A receptionist is the second position filled when you begin Step Two of the Business Plan. The primary functions of the receptionist are client relations duties. These duties include; maintenance of the appointment book, booking and confirming advance appointments, keeping the front counter area clean and supplied with promotional materials, and providing a liaison between clients and salon management. The duty of filling in vacancies left by cancellations will alone justify the receptionist's salary.

The most important function of the receptionist is to provide effective client relations. The front counter location makes the receptionist the first staff member the client meets upon entering the salon. This affords the finest opportunity to promote the salon. Some clients may only deal with the receptionist on their visit to the salon. Because of this involvement with clientele, receptionists need advanced training in client service techniques.

When you begin Step Two hire the receptionist as a part-time employee. The hours for the receptionist are about 1 p.m. to closing during the week and eight hours on Saturdays. Assign more hours to the receptionist as business expands. An alternative is to hire and train a second part-time receptionist.

Receptionists make a significant contribution to the achievement of the objectives of Step Two. Whenever the receptionist is absent from work someone else must assume the duties.

DRAWING FUNDS FROM THE CASH RESERVE

The cash reserve makes the addition of new staff possible. You may feel this is money you cannot afford to spend. Perhaps you believe you could have done the work of the assistant pet trimmer and receptionist yourself. By doing this you would avoid paying the new salary. Still, you cannot grow without a trained staff. It is not just an expense, it is an investment, and it is always wise to invest in your future.

The cash reserve provides back-up protection for the salon's cash flow. If the new employee's salary is higher than their contribution to the salon's revenue, there is a deficit. If business increases by $400.00 in a given week and salaries increase by $425.00, there is a deficit of $25.00. Do not use the reserve to pay the salary, use it only to cover the $25.00 deficit. The extra overhead is temporary and will soon disappear as revenues increase from the additional staff.

Within a few weeks the income contributed by the new employees will offset their salary. In subsequent weeks you will show an increasing net profit. Even allowing several weeks for the new employees to develop efficiency should not substantially reduce the cash reserve.

Record and explain draws from the reserve on the Cash Reserve Journal Worksheet (Chapter Three). Be sure the Cash Reserve Journal Worksheet always coincides with the bank statement. Except for emergencies use the cash reserve only for hiring new staff. Before completing Step Two, return the cash reserve to the minimum $10,000.00.

TELEMARKETING AT STEP TWO

During Step Two of the Business Plan, the receptionist assumes the duties of telemarketer. Telemarketing will add ten or more appointments daily when performed as recommended. At an average of $22.00 per booking the minimum weekly increase from ten bookings daily is $1,100.00. Even if the part-time salary is a generous $175.00 weekly the net profit is an attractive $925.00 weekly. In my salon, the telemarketing receptionist averaged eighteen new appointments daily. In addition, the number of no-show clients dropped dramatically as a result of confirming appointments. The receptionist is a valuable contributor to the salon when performing the Madson Management System's client relations and telemarketing duties.

THE CHECKLIST BEFORE BEGINNING STEP THREE

Follow the same procedure in completing the checklist for Step Two as you did in Step One.

STEP THREE
OF THE BUSINESS PLAN

CHAPTER

5

Step Three of the Business Plan involves the transformation of a pet salon into a full-service pet grooming operation.

There are over 115 MILLION pet dog and cats in the United States and about 20,000 pet grooming salons. That calculates to a potential 5,750 pets for every pet grooming salon. Whatever the potential is in your area the Madson Management System enables you to achieve the highest possible percentage of that total.

Your location does not limit the need for progressive and professional management. Whether marketing for clients in a rural or urban area, the objectives and potential for success are the same. The client base of a rural pet grooming salon may never be as large as an urban salon. The primary difference is in the characteristics of the clients. The goals of the management system remain the same.

THE OBJECTIVES OF STEP THREE

Step Three has four measurable objectives.

Objective 1.
Add a bathing department supervisor, telemarketer, and master pet trimmer.

Meeting the increased demand for services and quality control requires additional employees. They are also necessary to provide for continued growth. Step Three expands the trimming and bathing departments and adds a full-time telemarketer.

Objective 2.
Increase appointments.

The addition of a master pet trimmer (capable of 12 complete trims daily) increases the pet trimming volume to an average thirty-two pet trims daily. Compared to the team of Step Two this is an increase of 31% more pet trims. It also requires a corresponding increase in trim appointments. You can accomplish this through the People and Pet Marketing Program.

Objective 3.
Hire a manager.

The increasing responsibility of the salon owner demands the addition of a salon manager. In Step Three the client base usually increases to about 1,500. This is the point to hire a full-time manager. Not hiring a manager at this point causes the growth and quality of pet care services to plateau. A full-time manager provides the impetus to rise above this plateau to even greater profits.

Objective 4.
Prepare a budget for Step Three.

The budget for Step Three accounts for expected increases in expenses and gross revenues. The Action Plan provides assistance in preparing an Annual Profit and Loss Projection for Step Three using the resources of Chapter Fourteen.

THE ACTION PLAN FOR STEP THREE

The format of the Action Plan for Step Three is similar to the plans for Step One and Two. It provides chapter references to find related instructions and forms needed to accomplish the objectives of Step Three. Replace the copy of the Action Plan for Step Two in your private office with the one for Step Three. You are ready to begin your first assignment.

Action 1.
Actions for hiring the telemarketer, bathing department supervisor, and master pet trimmer.

Refer to Chapter Eight for complete instructions on the hiring process for all positions on the support staff. When qualified, promote your assistant pet trimmer to master pet trimmer and hire a new assistant. Promote your most qualified pet bather to bathing department supervisor. Guidelines for these two promotions are under the heading The Support Staff at Step Three in this chapter.

Action 2.
Actions for increasing appointments.

Train and schedule the telemarketer according to the instructions in Chapter Twelve. An experienced telemarketer will add an average of twelve appointments per three-hour shift.

Objectives
Step Three
of the
BUSINESS PLAN

Objective 1   **Add a bathing department supervisor, telemarketer, and master pet trimmer.**

◆

Objective 2   **Increase appointments and client base.**

◆

Objective 3   **Hire a manager.**

◆

Objective 4   **Prepare a budget for Step Three.**

The receptionist, now freed from covering the telemarketing duties, will concentrate efforts on client relations promotions (Chapter Eleven).

The owner and the new manager will increase appointments by fully implementing the People and Pet Marketing Program (Chapter Twelve). The manager will supervise the support staff's completion of client service and telemarketing duties. Be sure to use every marketing method in Chapter Twelve to secure more appointments.

Action 3.
Actions to hire a manager.

The characteristics required of a pet grooming salon manager are in Chapter Six and the job description is in Appendix B. Refer to Chapter Eight for complete instructions on the hiring process.

Action 4.
Actions to prepare a budget for Step Three.

Thoroughly review The Annual Profit and Loss Projection (Chapter Fourteen) and prepare your budget by the instructions contained there. Review the rest of Chapter Fourteen to be sure you have implemented all instructions. Prepare a new Annual Profit and Loss Projection whenever each preceding budget expires.

In objective four the manager assists in preparation of the budget, achieving projections, and keeping actual expenses within the budget.

THE SUPPORT STAFF AT STEP THREE

Hire the remaining four positions of the support staff in Step Three.

1. Telemarketer
2. Bathing Department Supervisor
3. Master Pet Trimmer
4. Manager

Job descriptions for these positions are in Appendix B. The full-service pet grooming salon operating six to seven days a week will have seven staff positions. Except for the manager and bathing department supervisor duplicate the other positions as mandated by expansion. You will only have one manager and bathing department supervisor, but you might have two or more telemarketers.

With the seven positions filled and working as a team you have a staff with the best potential for maximizing profits.

The Telemarketer

Hire a person dedicated to telemarketing at the start of Step Three. Consult Chapter Eight for hiring procedures. Assign the telemarketing responsibilities to one person or divide them between two or more based upon the availability of personnel. In Step Three one position handles

ACTION PLAN
STEP THREE OF THE BUSINESS PLAN

MANUAL   FORMS

PREPARATION
Before beginning to accomplish the actions you must answer *yes* to every question on the Evaluation Checklist For Step Two. Post a copy of the Objectives for Step Three of the Business Plan (illustration 5-1) and this action plan at your desk.   4

5

ACTION 1.
Complete *Action 1. Actions for hiring the telemarketer, bathing department supervisor, and master pet trimmer.*   5

Read *Creating a Successful Support Staff.*   7

Complete the instructions in *The Support Staff at Step Three.*   5

Prepare job descriptions, employee handbooks, personnel files, employment agreements (from your attorney), and the training program for the telemarketer, bathing department supervisor, and master pet trimmer.   7   B

Include the telemarketer, bathing department supervisor, master pet trimmer, and manager in the supervisory system.   9

Include the telemarketer, bathing department supervisor, master pet trimmer, and manager in the safety program.   10

ACTION 2.
Complete *Action 2. Actions for increasing appointments.*   5

Fully-implement the Madson People and Pet Marketing Program.   12

Make every customer a loyal client with the client relations program and encourage them to join the Preferred Client Program.   11

Add "swing-shift" pet care services (if not already in operation).   12

ACTION 3.
Complete *Action 3. Actions to hire a manager.*   5

Prepare a job description, employee handbook, personnel file, employment agreement (from your attorney), and the training program for the manager.   7   B

Have the manager read *The Pet Grooming Salon Manager* and discuss its content with you.   6

Set reasonable client base expansion and financial goals for the manager as discussed in *The Pet Salon Manager at Step Three.*   5

Track the manager's progress to achieve the client base expansion goal following the instructions in *Using the Client Base to Measure Achievement.*   12

ACTION 4.
Complete *Action 4. Actions to prepare a budget for Step Three.*   5

Prepare monthly financial statements and track profit and loss operating ratios.   14

Review the salon's financial statements and Annual Profit and Loss Projection with the manager at a monthly management meeting.   14

Prior to each monthly management meeting evaluate the contributions of the manager's job performance to achieve the salon's financial goals. Discuss the results with the manager at the meeting.

Follow the supportive procedures for daily bookkeeping and record keeping.   13

ADDITIONAL ACTIONS
Read *The Pet Grooming Salon Manager* at least once each week.   6

Complete an Effective Management Checklist each day. Also, have the manager complete one for each shift worked.   6

Spend at least two hours each week planning for the future.   15

telemarketing. That is the main difference with the first two steps where other personnel divide the responsibility between them.

The salary for the telemarketer is insignificant when compared to the increased revenue created by telemarketing. The experienced telemarketer will average twelve appointments for each three-hour shift during the week. On Saturday a telemarketer working a six-hour shift will average twenty appointments. Therefore, a telemarketer's financial contribution to the salon will be $1,496.00 when working Tuesday through Saturday and the average booking is $22.00. Even at a generous salary of $6.00 an hour the weekly salary will be no more than $108.00. After deducting the telemarketer's salary, the adjusted gross revenue is $1,388.00 each week. An effective telemarketer will bring in at least ten times their salary. It is not only cost-effective to have a dedicated telemarketer, it is essential. Telemarketing is invaluable in helping you achieve the financial growth you desire.

The receptionist, previously trained in telemarketing during Step Two, can assist you with training the newly hired telemarketer under your supervision. The two should work together until the telemarketer is competent to handle the job without supervision. At that point free the receptionist from telemarketing to concentrate efforts on client relations service promotions.

The Bathing Department Supervisor

The bathing department supervisor is responsible for promoting safety and orderliness in the bathing department. They act as safety engineer for the bathing department. This is the department which most often lacks consistent supervision by the owner. The bathing department supervisor is accountable for cleanliness, efficiency, supplies, and quality control.

The bathing department supervisor also assists the owner by supervising and training newly hired pet bathers. Direct supervision and the potential for promotion reduces pet bather employee turnover.

The job description for the bathing department supervisor lists the position's duties. If a current pet bather has the skills and supervisory abilities promote them to the position. After training, give them full responsibility for the pet bathing department.

Impress upon the bathing department supervisor the importance of their position. Announce the promotion to the staff. Explain the importance of having a bathing department supervisor in the increasingly busy bathing department.

The Master Pet Trimmer

The People and Pet Marketing Program will create a demand for services. Even with an assistant pet trimmer there is a point where demand will exceed supply. This is the point to hire the master pet trimmer. The most likely candidate for this position is the current assistant pet trimmer. An assistant is hired in Step Two. By Step Three they will have become an experienced trimmer. To warrant the promotion the assistant must be able to complete ten to twelve trims per day. His experience must include several breeds including Poodles, Cockers, Terriers and similar long-hair mixes. The assistant is a good candidate if they have these abilities. If not, you will need to find a master pet trimmer who has the necessary skills.

It is always advisable to promote from within if at all possible. The promotion of the assistant pet trimmer has definite advantages. Train them to duplicate the owner's trimming style. As an artist's signature on a painting, the owner's trimming style bonds clients to the business. Don't

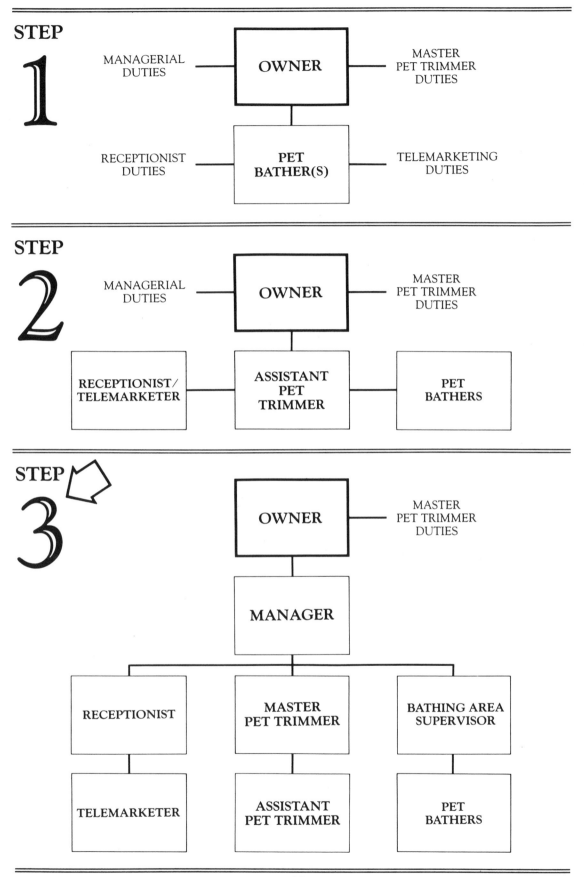

risk the loss of your clients' loyalty by hiring pet trimmers who can't, or won't duplicate your distinctive style. It can be difficult to get new pet trimmers to learn your unique style. They must be willing to accept change and adapt quickly.

THE PET SALON MANAGER AT STEP THREE

Review the job description for manager in Appendix B. Managers have an extensive list of duties. They are the most significant component of a support staff poised to produce greater growth and profits. Hire the manager when the client base has reached approximately 1,500 clients. Since some rural areas may never get 1,200 clients they can hire a part-time manager when their client base reaches approximately 750.

Select the manager primarily on their knowledge of business management rather than their ability at grooming. They must know, or be able to learn many things. They must understand bookkeeping, client relations, salon policy and procedure, financial planning, data analysis, marketing, and dozens of other tasks. One possibility is to hire a master pet trimmer and have the owner quit trimming and devote full-time to managing. This is not recommended at this time. It would require the addition of another master pet trimmer to replace the owner's trimming contributions. It will take on-the-job training to develop a competent manager so promote from within the salon when possible. This is good for employee morale, and the employee usually needs less training than an outside job applicant.

Develop a candidate for manager from your present support staff. Assign management tasks occasionally to the most likely person and privately evaluate their performance. A candidate may evolve from this procedure. If they do, promote them to manager-trainee. This gives them time to study and learn the operation and procedures of a successful salon. The manager-trainee undergoes training for at least six months. The trainee assists with management tasks while the owner continues to trim. Upon completion of training promote them to manager. Manager-trainees "pay their way" by working to increase the client base and the number of appointments. They also "pay their way" by sharing management tasks. This allows the owner to devote more time to trimming. That keeps costs at a minimum and quality at a maximum.

One option which may then be desirable is to have the new manager serve as both receptionist and manager. This combination of positions reduces overhead until a full-time receptionist is warranted. Consider moving the receptionist displaced by this practice to the position of second telemarketer.

The manager has the responsibility for salon operations and the growth of the client base. However, their first responsibility is to increase revenue. Apply a portion of the replenished cash reserve to pay the newly hired manager. This should only be necessary during the first several weeks of training. Careful screening of applicants will help avoid the costly and inefficient process of termination. If after a ninety-day introductory period the manager is not fulfilling the job agreement terminate them.

Along with the owner, the manager is responsible to achieve the salon's financial goals. The Annual Profit and Loss Projection (Chapter Fourteen) sets these goals. At the end of each month, quarter, and year, review the financial statements. Determine whether the goals for the number of pet's groomed, gross revenue, and costs are being achieved. Also, determine the increase in the client base since the last review and encourage the manager to further its expansion. The manager should always be working to achieve a reasonable client base expansion goal under the direction of the owner. When goals are unmet the manager and owner must devise a plan to correct problem areas.

Owners who also serve as trimmer and manager are too busy to spend qualitative time on making the business grow. A manager keeps the salon operating safely and efficiently supervising employees more effectively than an owner occupied with trimming. A manager with time to develop a professional liaison with clientele enhances the image of your salon.

An argument owners may use to avoid hiring a manager is that the salon cannot afford the salary. This is not true. Hiring a manager provides an exceptional opportunity to expand the business and revenue at a reasonable cost. The annual salary of a manager, about $12,000.00 to $18,000.00, can be recouped. Opening the salon a seventh day each week creates new revenue to pay the manager's salary. This is possible while still allowing both manager and owner to have two days off a week.

Owners of businesses are sometimes fearful of hiring their first management staff because they fear losing control. This fear is not useful, and unjustified, when the manager follows the job description given by the management system. The manager is your ally and not your competitor. Work with the manager from the perspective of a team member and you will mutually succeed.

THE PET GROOMING SALON MANAGER

CHAPTER 6

This chapter contains information to develop management excellence in a pet grooming salon manager. It provides a clear perspective of the role and responsibility of a manager when implementing the Madson Management System. Anyone managing a pet grooming salon should commit its principles to memory.

The term manager refers to either a managing owner or a manager hired by the owner. Regardless of who wears the hat of manager, it is the most responsible position in the pet grooming salon. The manager must study the Madson Management System manual and consult its resources for information when questions arise. He should consult daily with the owner when making important business decisions and keep him informed of the salon's progress.

MANAGEMENT RESPONSIBILITIES

The owner's responsibility is organizational and financial planning, and supervision of the manager. The manager's responsibility is operating the salon. This responsibility includes personnel management, material and supplies control, records management, health and safety, quality control, client relations, and marketing. Most salon owners also function as salon managers. Because of this, they have the responsibility of both positions.

The manager is at the core of salon operations and the proverbial buck always stops at his desk. He is responsible to safely and profitably guide the business and achieve the goals of the business plan. Successful managers are not afraid of responsibilities, they invite them. They are

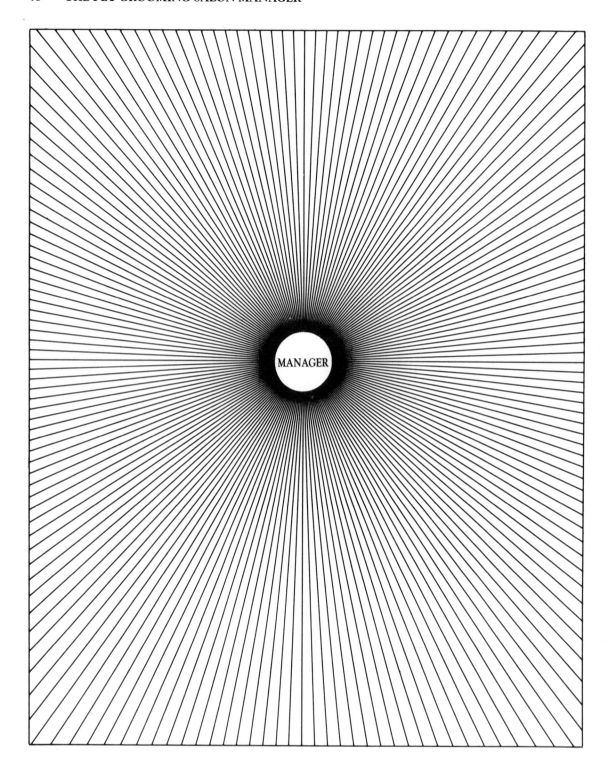

MANAGER

The heart of the
Madson Management System

MANAGEMENT RESPONSIBILITIES

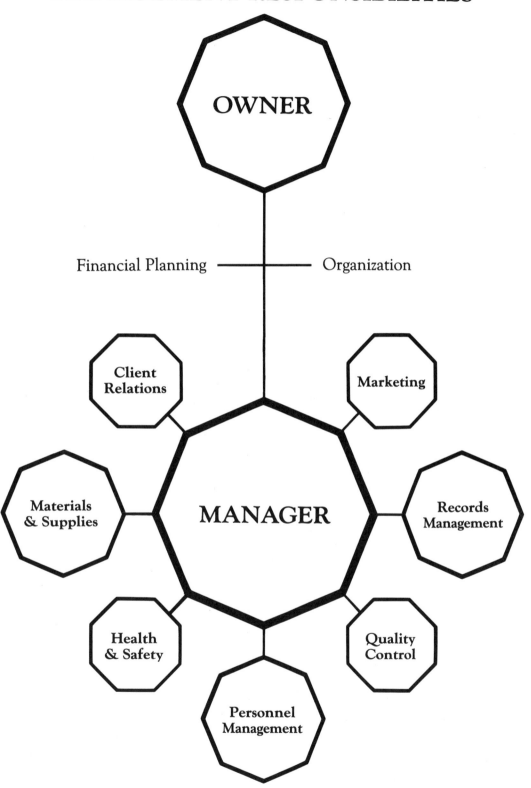

Financial Planning ———— Organization

alert to every incident involving their responsibility. Dogs whining in the back cage. Conversations at the front counter. A bather having a long, personal conversation on the telephone. The car pulling in the parking lot. The client heading to the front door. The safety and comfort of the pets in their cages. Keeping the salon's operation on schedule. A vast assortment of information is constantly available to decipher and act upon. Alert salon managers use this information to react responsibly to those aspects of the operation that need correction or adjustment. Some of this information is noted for discussion at staff meetings. Of course, always take immediate action when safety is in question.

If you were not a manager, and simply a pet bather, your scope of responsibility would narrow. You could then concentrate on bathing and fluffing techniques and become quite skilled. As a manager, responsible for operating the salon, you cannot focus on one duty to the neglect of other duties. Therefore, try to improve a little at everything, each day. Eventually each small achievement will add up significantly.

Many pet grooming salons concentrate on only one area of responsibility. For example, one salon I observed was skilled at trimming, but clients had to endure a messy, smelly, and rude reception area. In addition, there was no area for clients to potty-walk their pets. Management had focused on pet trimming services but forgotten the client who brought the pet.

CHARACTERISTICS OF A SUCCESSFUL MANAGER

The manager must have the ability to reason and make sound judgments if he is to fulfill the obligations of the position.

He must have "people skills," such as a diplomatic touch with clients. He must have the ability to effectively communicate, as in getting ideas across to the staff. The manager serves as a role model for the employees and must be punctual and considerate of others. His attire and personal grooming should reflect the image of a professional grooming salon. He must be clean and dressed appropriately. The manager must maintain loyalty to the owner and hold in confidence financial, legal, and personal matters.

The manager must become, and stay informed in the principles of effective management. This reasoning prompts corporations to train management personnel in management skills and to refresh skills previously learned.

THE SUCCESSFUL MANAGER'S ATTITUDES

The manager's attitudes either assist the salon's movement toward success, or create a barrier to reaching that success. Examining your attitudes can create a dramatic opportunity for improvement. Client satisfaction and quality of workmanship are two principle concerns of a successful manager.

Attitudes Toward Client Satisfaction

The client is the true employer of management and staff. It is the client who pays the salaries. Realizing this makes it easier to have the proper attitude toward the client's satisfaction.

EFFECTIVE MANAGEMENT CHECKLIST

These attributes will help you become a more effective manager. Every step leads to increased effectiveness. It will soon come naturally to you.

☐ I worked on achieving the objectives of the business plan.

☐ I improved my supervision of the pet salon today by making several "tours" keeping my eyes and ears open.

☐ I gave up at least one ineffective behavior.

☐ I worked on improving many things by a small amount.

☐ I instructed at least one employee in a new skill.

☐ I asked at least three clients today for their evaluation, whether favorable or unfavorable.

☐ I only made promises that I can, and will fulfill.

☐ I improved my working relationship with every employee by giving them constructive feedback.

☐ I looked at long-term goals that I have written and evaluated my progress.

☐ I have planned and prepared myself for tomorrow's achievements.

☐ I double-checked for proper grooming and ensured every pet was given respect and provided humane pet care services.

1. Make copies of this checklist and complete one at the end of each day.
2. Check off the attributes that characterized your performance.
3. Keep completed checklists in order by date and review your progress weekly.

PROMINENT ACHIEVERS

PROFILE OF SUCCESSFUL MEN AND WOMEN

The way you approach life and success predicts the outcome. You can learn and follow the traits of prominent achievers. Practice them until they become natural to you and you will be richly rewarded.

GOAL DRIVEN

Achievers put their goals in writing and refer to them often. They set a time frame in which to achieve their goals. They include rewards for the achievement of their goals, such as a vacation. They know where they want to be in one year, five years, and beyond.

PROFESSIONAL ADVANCEMENT

They concentrate on improving their business management skills as well as their professional skills. They are working members of professional organizations.

ACTIVE LIFESTYLE

They get involved with the business community. They keep informed about their local government. They join in with family activities. They are active members of their religion. They love their work and it shows.

IMPROVE HEALTH AND SPIRITUALITY

They maintain good health through exercise, weight-control, and nutrition. They emphasize positive thinking and nurture their self-esteem. They enjoy relationships with family, friends, and business associates.

EXECUTE PLANS

They study and make plans before they act. This allows them more freedom to effectively execute their plans.

FINANCES IN ORDER

They have personal and business financial limits which they do not exceed. They consistently save a portion of their earnings. They make long-term financial plans including life, accident, and health insurance, retirement income, and succession plans for their business.

ATTITUDES
of the successful pet grooming salon
MANAGER

QUALITY

* I emphasize quality in all salon services.
* I am wholly responsible for my operation.
* I try each day to be a little better at everything.
* I am available to the staff for their questions.
* I ensure that pets receive respect and humane pet care services.

CLIENT SATISFACTION

* I provide superior services equally to all clients.
* I listen to my clients for their feedback.
* I never guess what my clients are thinking.
* I benefit from working relationships with my clients.
* I keep my promises and acknowledge my mistakes.
* I accept my clients for who they are.

STAFF

* My objective is to hire, train, and maintain a successful support staff.
* I am not in competition with my staff.
* My success is judged by how well my staff performs.
* I give job performance evaluations not to punish but to provide opportunity for improvement.

6-5

The time-honored admonition "the customer is always right" reflects this understanding. You may remember a situation in which the customer was wrong — but that is missing the point. A cavalier attitude toward client satisfaction is unlikely to bring them back or increase the client base through referral. Operating the salon may occupy you so much you fail to evaluate it objectively. To correct this, adopt the attitude that you will listen to everything the client says. Use their feedback as an evaluation of the services you offer. The client may not offer criticism as you would like to hear it. However, their negative feedback could be a favor in disguise if you value making a profit.

Some clients only want their pet trimmed to your standards. While appreciating simple courtesies, they require little if any special attention. Other pet owners are quite gregarious and want to know everyone on your team. That's fine. Give them the special attention they require and enjoy. Sometimes a crabby client arrives at your door. They may not really be dissatisfied with you or your service but have a problem in their personal life. Nonetheless, listen to them thoughtfully and with empathy before you go on about the business of earning your fee. Even a grouch is important.

Your attitude must be flexible enough to accommodate many types of people. Remember, by using the Madson Management System you will soon be increasing your client base. A much larger cross-section of society is going to be coming through your doors. If one client seems a little strange to you, find it in yourself to accept them. Accept everyone who comes through your door for what they are — a potential employer. With this attitude, you might add another regular client and increase your gross profits for both now and the future. Besides, every client deserves the same superior service.

Clients never deserve criticism in return for their patronage. Every client deserves an equal and gracious "thank you." Their pets also deserve humane treatment, whether they are playful and happy, or a problem pet. Clients are very close to their pets and judge your salon by the way you handle them.

To have the privilege of being recognized as a professional requires accepting the responsibilities of a professional. Your relationship legally with the client is a "fiduciary relationship." This means that the client places their "faith and trust" in you as one accepting the responsibility for the health, safety, and welfare of their pet. This continues as long as they are in your care and services. For instance, they have the right to be informed of any procedures used in grooming their pet. They have the right to make an "informed decision" regarding any grooming service entailing potential hazards of which they might not reasonably be aware. This obligates you to inform them of the consequences to their pet's health, safety, and welfare, of any services you perform. You must inform them of anything that might affect their decision regarding acceptance of that service. You are not required to be a veterinarian. Yet, you must inform the client of any health concerns you discover while grooming their pet, of which you might reasonably be aware.

Every manager at some time will make a mistake or break a promise. Even though this may occur rarely handle it wisely — this means full disclosure. Hidden mistakes all too often come back to haunt you, so a manager must always acknowledge them. If a trimmer slightly nicks a pet, give it first-aid immediately. When the client arrives inform them of the accident and the treatment administered to the pet. Fortunately, these situations are very rare and avoidable when safety procedures are responsibly practiced. The more important issue is your integrity as a manager.

Most mistakes in the pet grooming salon are not so serious as to involve injuries. It is still required that you inform the client, however. This is not a legal obligation but out of concern for client satisfaction. For instance, delays may make a scheduled morning pick-up unlikely. Call the client as soon as you are aware of this. Save them an unnecessary trip. This courtesy, and a simple apology, should keep them satisfied with your services. You might even offer to personally deliver the pet after closing. Having a client's business today is one concern, but a successful manager is also concerned about keeping it.

Attitudes About Quality

Successful managers are proud of the quality of their service. Managers should demand quality from their operation and staff. If they don't, who will? The answer is — the client. That alternative is not desirable. You want the client to come to your salon because it provides quality, not having to demand quality. Every customer has the potential to become a regular client and to recommend you to others. However, they must receive quality service and feel valued.

Attitudes About Staff

"No man is an island." And neither is a manager. Successful managers know they must develop a professional staff to accomplish their numerous responsibilities. Managers promote success by encouraging, improving, and rewarding the contributions of the team and each team member.

WORKING RELATIONSHIPS

The term "working relationships" is important to your salon. It means those interactions with employees, clients, vendors, and professional advisors which have a direct impact on business. Effective handling of these relationships can make a dramatic impact on the success of your pet grooming salon. Unfortunately, many owners neglect forming and nurturing good working relationships. Carrying a heavy workload trimming and managing deprives them of the benefits that can be derived from good working relationships. The Madson Management System provides methods of dealing more productively with working relationships so as not to lose this benefit.

Working relationships fall into two categories. They are, external and internal relationships. External relationships are those with clients, vendors, and professional advisors. Internal relationships refer to those with staff.

Internal

The Owner and Manager.   Owner and manager must develop a good relationship with each other. There is no room for competition between the two. Even the old concept of friendly competition is inappropriate. The joint achievement of business goals followed by shared rewards is the relationship to emphasize.

The Owner and Staff.   An owner with a full-time manager has less involvement with the staff than the manager. His primary responsibility is not to undermine the manager's authority with the staff. The owner must delegate all concerns regarding the staff to the manager.

He must not permit the staff to bypass the manager by bringing issues directly to him. The owner's job is to manage the manager and the manager's job is to manage the staff. Allowing the staff to go over the manager's head creates a "lame-duck" manager. Depriving the manager of authority in this manner is economic irresponsibility. When you hire someone for a position, not letting them perform the functions of that position is a waste of money. If you as owner do not have confidence in your manager hire someone you do have confidence in! A staff with two managers is a two-headed monster that cannot survive.

The Manager and Staff.   The relationship between management and staff is of such importance an entire chapter is devoted to it. Chapter Seven discusses how to create a successful support staff in more detail.

External

Management and Vendors.   Developing a good relationship with vendors is important for three reasons. First, vendors are a valuable source of information about your competition. Because of visits to other salons the pet industry vendor is usually well-informed on the state of their business. Ask them how your business compares to others and what the latest news is in your field. If a vendor tells you of a successful salon, further exploration may reveal a technique that is useful for your salon. Secondly, since the vendor is providing you with information about other salons, you can assume he is providing information about you to other members of the pet industry. Knowing this gives you the advantage of only giving him information that you want others to know. This is an indirect method of advertising and creating a positive image of your salon. Finally, a good relationship with vendors can sometimes result in special deals on products and speedier delivery.

Management and Professional Relationships.   These include relationships with your banker, accountant, attorney, insurance broker, management consultant, financial advisor, and veterinarians (see illustration 6-7).

Veterinarians.   Successful relationships with veterinarians can bring many client referrals to your salon. Increasing your client base through gratis referrals from local veterinarians is a bonus you can't afford to ignore. Here are some tips.

1. Invite your local veterinarian, and his staff, to visit your salon. Let them see first-hand the expertise, efficiency, and hygiene of your service. Ask for comments and pay attention to his need for professional recognition. Inquire about his services and request the method of referral to him he most prefers. The implication of referring to him will implant the idea of reciprocation. To further solidify this idea ask him directly of any way you could make him more comfortable about referring clients to your salon. When he leaves provide him with a package consisting of your brochure, business card, and price list.

2. As a community service request a veterinarian to conduct a training session. The training can be on various health issues related to pets. Have your staff attend and invite your clients. His motivation is the prospect of gaining new clients for his own practice. Conduct these regularly, such as once a month using various local veterinarians, or periodically through the year.

YOUR WORKING   RELATIONSHIPS

INTERNAL

- ■ OWNER AND MANAGER
- ■ OWNER AND STAFF
- ■ MANAGER AND STAFF

EXTERNAL

- ■ MANAGEMENT AND CLIENT
- ■ MANAGEMENT AND VENDORS
- ■ MANAGEMENT AND PROFESSIONALS

Insurance Broker.   An insurance broker is different from an insurance agent. An agent works for one company while a broker can select from a wide range of insurance companies. This allows you to select fullest coverage for the lowest cost. Insurance companies are just beginning to understand the coverage needs of pet grooming salons. It is unlikely that an insurance agent can provide you with adequate coverage from one company. Get to know a competent broker in your area. Acquaint him with your business so he can design a policy unique to your needs. For years, insurance companies have been reluctant to provide coverage for pet grooming salons. The reason is that salons did not have professional standards, adequate staff training, or good hygiene. Following the Madson Management System will correct these deficiencies.

Banker.   Form a relationship with a banker not a bank. Interview bankers until you find one who shows an interest in understanding your business. The better a banker knows and understands your business the better the potential for receiving the financial assistance you need.

Management Consultant.   A management consultant who understands your business can provide invaluable assistance in those business procedures which contribute to increased profits and growth. The Madson Management System manual is one source of management consultancy. The Madson Management Systems division of The Madson Group provides additional pet grooming management assistance. This is in the form of newsletters, seminars, videotape training, advertising, pet grooming salon design and space planning, computer and software automation, and on-site evaluation and assistance.

Financial Advisor.   A financial advisor sets up investment and retirement portfolios. Be wary of insurance agents masquerading as financial advisors. They will use the disguise as an opportunity to sell their products. What they wish to sell may not necessarily be what you need to buy. A bonafide financial advisor does not work for a company whose products he is expected to sell. He is a financial expert who works for you. He makes financial decisions which reflect your best interest, not his.

Accountant.   When choosing an accountant, choose one qualified as a Certified Public Accountant (CPA). He provides the preferred level of training and experience. Assistance in setting up your books and completing your tax returns are just two of the contributions an accountant can make. He can assist you in preparing loan papers for your bank. He can explain and prepare other financial aids, such as income statements and financial projections as well.

Attorney.   An attorney who understands tax planning and business affairs can save you tax dollars and protect your investment through legal safeguards. Furthermore, an appropriately qualified attorney can serve in several advisor capacities. He can provide legal counsel, financial planning advice, and tax consultancy and tax return preparation.

The importance of a good working relationship with an attorney and accountant is impossible to stress too much. Don't wait for an unfortunate situation to occur before finding an attorney or accountant. If such an incident occurs, and it will, you will appreciate having established a previous relationship with these advisors. In time they will save you money and provide a resource for promoting greater success. Also, there is peace of mind in knowing professional help is a phone call away.

Management and Client.   Devoting another entire chapter to this subject stresses its importance. Chapter Eleven discusses client relations principles.

PROFESSIONAL (WORKING) RELATIONSHIPS

Veterinarian

Accountant

Attorney

Insurance Broker

Management Consultant

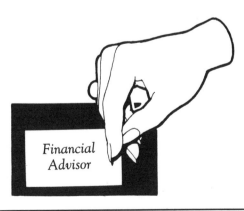

Financial Advisor

Banker

6-7

One function of management is to collect and analyze business data. Evaluate the flow of information from your working relationships for relevancy and use it in making business decisions.

MAKING DECISIONS AND GETTING RESULTS

Studying this management system means you have made a decision. You have decided you want greater success.

You are responsible to make any decisions that affect your business. How you handle the decision-making process is as important as the actual decision. Procrastinating about making business decisions can be dangerous and making an average decision is frequently better than making no decision at all. Assuming that you have adequate training and preparation make the majority of your decisions quickly. Making decisions quickly does not mean making them impulsively. Impulsive decisions are quick but without benefit of mental preparation. When you have digested business information let your mind respond to business decisions spontaneously. This will provide better results than anxiously deliberating over various possibilities. Unmade decisions create concern and waste your time.

Every time you face a decision pass it through a screen in your mind. Start the screening process by asking yourself if you need to make the decision right now. When the answer is yes, then ask yourself if more facts are necessary to make the decision. You usually won't need more facts if you are up-to-date on the state of affairs of your operation. The key to effective decision making is to have a clear picture of all the business data relative to your salon.

When you develop quick decision-making, others will notice. This skill will impress clients, vendors, and employees. It is also quite likely they will show confidence in your judgment and simply accept it without hesitation.

As important as decision-making is, the manager must also be able to "make things happen" at the salon. Implementing the Madson Management System is a way to make things happen. It requires a manager driven to accomplish the goals targeted by the management system and to follow up on projects. Attend to details of the salon operation but never lose sight of the big picture.

Pay attention to your salon's competition. Nearly every competitor will be doing a few things right that can be useful in your salon. For instance, if they are benefiting by advertising in a new magazine, place your own more attractive ad in the next edition. You will not gain a unique identity by copying their methods so enhance their methods by adding your own style.

Making things happen requires you to vary your accustomed methods and institute new procedures. Many people fear potential risks when trying something new. They prefer old, comfortable ways even if they lead to mediocrity. However, following a proven program such as the Madson Management System, minimizes the risk and increases the rewards.

REWARDS OF THE MANAGEMENT SYSTEM

With the Madson Management System, you can experience training that offers more rewards than you have come to expect in pet grooming. Increasing your earnings by 100 to 200 percent is certainly rewarding. Yet the most valuable reward is the increased self-esteem that accompanies the development of a successful business.

The scope of the operation defined in this manual, and the demands it places on the manager may sound technical and complex. However, it is better to convert to a system proven to be profitable than to continue with a haphazard, unprofitable operation. Studying and implementing this system will yield profits both personally and financially.

Remember that you make the rules so you can change them if it means enhancing your operation. If some of the goals of this management system seem impractical, reconsider. They are tested and proven. When the information is reliable, risks minimal, and rewards splendid, it is prudent to make a change in your business operation. Successful businesspeople are flexible enough to change old, ineffective methods for new, successful methods.

CREATING A SUCCESSFUL SUPPORT STAFF

CHAPTER 7

I t is unfortunate that some groomers believe that only a minimal income is possible in pet grooming. That is not the case when using modern management and marketing techniques. You can convert a mediocre job into a rewarding profession by developing a well-trained support staff.

A successful support staff has a dual purpose; to increase the demand for pet care services and to satisfy that demand. It requires extensive training and supervision of each member of the support staff. This will not only achieve the owner's goals, but their own as well. Their goals include stable employment, recognition of competence through raises and promotions, and the satisfaction of being a member of a successful team. Management assists in the form of job titles, employment agreements, fair salaries, merit awards, and competent supervision.

A stable and skilled support staff with minimal employee turnover is essential to having a successful salon. Pet salon employees aren't laborers or pieceworkers. They are supporting members of a business team. A recent grooming survey by Groom and Board magazine was enlightening. It reported personnel problems were the number one business concern of pet grooming salon owners. Use the principles of this chapter and personnel will not be your primary business problem. The first principle is to develop job descriptions for all positions.

JOB DESCRIPTIONS

Large corporations consider job descriptions a critical feature of personnel management. Small companies like pet salons can also benefit from the use of job descriptions to manage employees and protect their interests. Job descriptions can be crucial in the unfortunate case of litigation. When acknowledged by an employee, they serve as proof that they were aware of their responsibilities.

To be effective the job description must be written by someone with first-hand experience. If not, it is of no use to anyone. If the description is poor to start with, it becomes worse over the years.

The job descriptions in the Madson Management System were written by a highly qualified pet salon manager and groomer. They establish professional standards. They are fully-detailed but easy to read and understand.

The job descriptions state the duties and performance standards expected of each position. You may add to the duties if it eases the implementation of the management system. They are flexible enough for any pet grooming salon. Both a novice as well as an experienced salon owner can use them.

Seven job descriptions, one for each position on the Madson Management System support staff, are in Appendix B. The job descriptions are:

1. Manager

2. Master Pet Trimmer

3. Assistant Pet Trimmer

4. Bathing Department Supervisor

5. Pet Bather

6. Receptionist

7. Telemarketer

There are two basic objectives for a job description. The first objective is to define the responsibilities of the position and the working relationships with management, staff, and clientele. The second objective is to set performance standards for the position.

The manager should be completely familiar with each description in order to rate the performance of every employee. A good method for gaining command of the descriptions is to lay them out on a table. Then mix and match them to form different, but workable, staff structures. No matter how large your business grows the Madson job descriptions can meet your needs.

Job applicants review the job description to compare their strengths and weaknesses with that position. Applicants, after reviewing the job description, can recognize if they have any of the requirements for the position. The job description provides a clear picture of what the applicant can expect working for the salon. It also shows them where they fit on the staff-team. This clarification of their position helps prevent future misunderstandings.

The job description is in four sections.

SECTION 1
The Job Title.

This section describes the position being offered and emphasizes the standards of the company.

SECTION 2
Eligibility Requirements.

The second section provides the general eligibility requirements for the position. Some job descriptions specify a preference for experience, but do not require it. When required, type the

JOB DESCRIPTIONS

There are seven Madson Management System job descriptions written by, and for, pet grooming professionals to establish professional pet grooming employee standards. Copies of the job descriptions are in Appendix B.

MANAGER

MASTER PET TRIMMER

ASST. PET TRIMMER

BATHING DEPT. SUPERVISOR

PET BATHER

RECEPTIONIST

TELEMARKETER

previous experience requirements on the appropriate job description(s) before distributing them to job applicants. Consider the following guidelines for determining when to require experience.

You can train entry-level pet bathers, but full-charge pet bathers need previous experience. Promote bathing department supervisors from within your bathing department when possible. If you hire the supervisor from outside the salon require some bathing and supervisory experience. Assistant pet trimmers should have bathing skills or some experience handling pets. You can train them to trim. The master pet trimmer must have previous experience, either in a pet grooming salon or reputable grooming school.

It is acceptable to give on-the-job training to the receptionist and telemarketer. Applicants for these positions with previous experience in pet grooming are rare. So it is impractical to require pet salon experience. However, you may choose to require some previous customer service experience in another field.

The manager job description requires more extensive experience including client relations or grooming experience in a pet salon. The manager must possess the ability to develop bookkeeping, organizational, and supervisory skills.

SECTION 3
Position Duties.

Job duties and responsibilities are in three parts. First, there are job duties and responsibilities specific to each position. Second, there are general duties and responsibilities expected of every position such as those documented in the Madson Employee Handbook. Third, the applicant is told he may be needed to cover duties from other positions on an as needed basis. You can supplement or modify any of the duties in the job description to reflect your method of operation more accurately.

Do not permit the employees to decide what duties they do or do not perform. Only management can define or modify the job descriptions.

SECTION 4
General Information.

The job applicant is notified every employee is expected to comply with the policies and procedures of the salon's employee handbook. Also, the applicant is given a schedule for job performance evaluations. Add the hours and days of the week the employee can expect to work. Note that employees may be requested to work on Saturdays, Sundays, and holidays if the salon is open.

Fill in the blanks for salary on the job description. If you choose not to follow the recommendation to pay by salary, describe the payment method in this section. Include a list of employee benefits you provide such as group health or life insurance. Complete this section with the time benefits, such as paid sick days or vacation.

Prepare job descriptions with your pay schedule before distributing them to applicants. Update them as necessary.

PERSONNEL FILES

The Madson Management System has several personnel forms to assist with the creation and maintenance of a successful support staff. In effect, they establish a personnel department with complete employment documentation.

ORGANIZING A PERSONNEL FILE

EMPLOYEE DATA SHEET

- Employee name and job title
- Home address
- Telephone
- Emergency contacts
- Social Security number
- Date of hire

Update Records As Needed

—also includes—

✳ Copy of Form I-9

✳ Copy of completed W-4 and updates

✳ Other federal, state, and local employment regulatory agency forms

✳ Copy of signed Job Applicant Practical Exam

✳ Copy of signed Probationary Agreement

✳ Copy of signed Job Agreement

✳ Requests for time off

✳ Attendance records

✳ Application for employment and resumé

✳ Employment Questionnaire

✳ Copy of signed Employee Confidentiality Agreement

✳ Job Performance Evaluations

✳ Vacation schedule

✳ Benefits information

✳ Manager comments and miscellaneous notes

✳ Other

Create a file for each employee. Keep all employment documentation and any other personnel forms in their file. This includes the job application, employment questionnaire, practical exam agreement, introductory period agreement, employee confidentiality agreement, job agreement, performance review, attendance records, benefits data, and miscellaneous notes. An important item for the files is the record of which employees have keys. This can be of valuable assistance to the police in the event of a burglary. Coincidentally, after terminating an employee, or when a key is lost, it is wise to change your locks. Even after an employee leaves your salon retain their personnel file in your permanent records.

Updated personnel files are an asset for both productivity and protection. When a manager needs information about an employee, such as a social security number or address, the file is a ready resource. Use the personnel files when planning employee work schedules. They contain valuable information about employee desires for vacation time, doctor appointments, personal leave, and other requests. With such information easily located there is no waste of time. This makes the manager more productive. In the event of employee disputes the personnel file becomes a valuable witness in the employer's behalf.

PERSONNEL POLICIES AND PROCEDURES - THE EMPLOYEE HANDBOOK

Not having written personnel policies and procedures to enforce is an unnecessary hazard. It risks revenue, and safety and health. The Madson policies and procedures are specifically for the pet grooming profession, tested and proven over many years. They are an essential productivity tool that also offer protection in the event of litigation.

The five parts constituting the Madson Employee Handbook for a pet grooming salon are:

1. Employment Policies
2. Personnel Policies and Benefits
3. Salon Cleanliness Standards
4. Client Courtesy
5. Safety

The Madson Employee Handbook is in Appendix B. Make a copy of every page and bind them together to form an Employee Handbook. Include your salon's additional employee policies and procedures as necessary. Always notify employees of any revisions and additions in writing.

You can also purchase attractive, more durable copies of the valuable Madson Employee Handbook at a nominal cost.

TRAINING GUIDELINES

Reading the Employee Handbook is important but it isn't a substitute for an effective training program. The essential goal of training is to maximize the potential performance of each employee. In this fashion, employees can become top-level performers regardless of their previous skills.

TEN ELEMENTS OF THE EMPLOYEE TRAINING PROGRAM

1 Job duties and responsibilities.

2 The Employee Handbook.

3 Client relations procedures.

4 The Preferred Client Program.

5 The Groom Alert System.

6 Instructions for using the:

A Pet Groomer's Report and Health Alert   **D** Client and Pet History filecards

B Daily Caging and Payment Register   **E** Information Center

C Weekly Employee Timekeeping Record   **F** Client promotion materials

7 Grooming and cleaning supply usage.

8 Equipment and grooming tools usage.

9 Cash register procedures (authorized employees only).

10 Emergency procedures.

The training program should include guidelines for physical appearance, client relations, effective communication, teamwork, pet care and safety, and professional poise. The Madson Employee Handbook contains descriptions of the desired behavior in each of these categories.

Proper training is the key to a job performance that contributes to the achievement of business goals. No one is exempt. Before training, the orientation procedure expresses the management's philosophy to provide quality client and pet care services. Employees need to know that everyone works together to provide pet care services. Training shows them their place in the team structure of the pet salon operation. Experienced employees need periodic training as a refresher for old skills and an opportunity to learn new skills.

Training improves safety by showing the proper uses of salon equipment, tools, and grooming supplies. Good training produces a staff that provides humane treatment for animals in a hygienic environment. It also creates a support staff that works together as a team to groom more pets and increase profits.

The training of pet grooming and client relations skills is concrete and measurable. Employees can memorize the salon's policies and procedures, but training is more complex than that. It is simpler to train work skills than teach an effective work attitude. The employee must be friendly, dependable, loyal, and willing to contribute to the pet salon's success. Attempting to teach a proper attitude is worthwhile. It sends a message to the new employee that their attitude is important to you.

Never assume that employees know what they are doing. It may appear they have skills but resist using them. It is more likely they simply do not know what to do, or how to do it. Develop a training program for your salon. Each employee needs to know what is expected, and how to do to do it.

Individual, on-the-job training by demonstration, is the training method of choice for the pet grooming salon. The manager is responsible for the training program. He directs the client relations and clerical training and selects and supervises the most qualified grooming trainer. This will usually be the master pet trimmer and the bathing department supervisor.

The trainer first describes the activity and then demonstrates its correct procedure. Then, reverse the role. Have the trainee describe and demonstrate the same activity under the trainer's supervision. The trainer then repeats the process describing and demonstrating any necessary corrections. This process continues until the trainee acquires minimum competency.

Plan demonstrations ahead of time to teach new pet care techniques and reinforce skills. For instance, a rare breed of dog coming to the salon is a good opportunity. Demonstrate how to trim the breed correctly. If a pet's nails are being clipped improperly, give a nail clipping demonstration. The subject of a demonstration may be for just one employee, but invite the others also. This will add to the staff's general knowledge and is effective time management.

Prepare written instructions to reinforce training. The Telemarketing Procedures Form (Appendix C) is a sample of instructions you can use to design your own instructions. Provide trainees with copies of instructions (Appendix A) to complete the Client and Pet History filecard, Daily Caging and Payment Register, and the Pet Groomer's Report and Health Alert.

Never assign the training of a new employee to a departing or non-supervisory employee. Typically, an employee who is leaving has no interest in training the new employee correctly. Non-supervisory employees lose time from their regular duties and usually lack the knowledge of how to train. Pet safety demands constant supervision of all training. Grooming is a joint project between trainer and student. It doesn't end until the trainee is competent and the safety of others and pets is certain.

Your own daily work performance is a form of training. It is useless to mandate employee policies and procedures and not demonstrate them in your own behavior. Follow the old saying "actions speak louder than words." If you follow your own rules you will strengthen the staff's confidence and respect in your leadership.

SUPPORTING TEAMWORK

A good manager understands teamwork. The manager as coach knows if the team doesn't do well, the coach didn't do well. Further, a coach understands that a team is interdependent. Encourage them to support one another. If a team member fails — the team fails. This failure is an opportunity for the manager to reinforce the need to support, encourage, and work closely with each other. When each player supports the other's efforts to achieve as a team they can achieve far beyond their individual capabilities.

The manager must remember that the team is the product of many personalities. They require individualized coaching to bring the team members to a common purpose. Winning a game or setting a new record for the number of pets groomed is the same. The team must remain aware of the importance of a common goal. Teach the team that in reaching their common goal they will also reach their individual goals. As the employees submerge their needs to achieve the team's goal — the objectives of the business plan — they will rediscover their own individuality.

SALARIES

The evolution of pet grooming to a professional status demands a change in the payment structure of its personnel. Stop using commission and piecework methods of payment. Start paying salaries. Salaries are desirable for two reasons. They promote the development of teamwork and they enhance the profitability of the salon. The number of beauty salons that have begun paying salaries is increasing annually for these very reasons.

The fears that many salon owners have about paying salaries are unfounded. The payment of salaries will not discourage pet groomers from seeking employment. Nor will it be an economic nightmare. Introducing the payment of salaries in a salon requires the education of the employees about the benefits they will derive. A steady reliable paycheck allows employees to budget and makes them more creditworthy. It eliminates the economic roller coaster caused by busy weeks and slow weeks, and provides the opportunity for advancement. The benefit for the owner is more than financial. The payment of salaries produces an employee who is less competitive, more team-oriented, and more attentive to quality. Salon owners will find that a professionally operated salon will attract good workers. This type of person will upgrade the stature and operation of their salon also.

Nearly all pet grooming salons paying by commission pay fifty to sixty percent of the service fee. After deducting the cost of taxes and overhead, the owner has as little as twenty per cent of the original fee left. Pet grooming is constricted by high operating costs worsened by inflation. To stay profitable you must continually seek ways to trim unwarranted expenses.

A trimmer paid by commission generates the same revenue as a salaried trimmer, but substantially reduces the salon's profit. A comparison of commission versus salary for an assistant pet trimmer will show you where that profit is going. A master pet trimmer with an assistant can do eight or more trims per day than a trimmer working alone.

If a salon has an average trim price of $22.00, and completes eight additional trims daily, revenue increases by $176.00 per day. The potential annualized increase to gross revenue is nearly $46,000.00. Even paying the assistant a generous salary of $250.00 a week there is a net increase of $33,000.00. By paying a fifty percent commission the net increase would be $23,000.00. That amounts to $10,000.00 removed directly from the owner's pocket. The additional expense incurred by paying a salary, the employer's contribution, still leaves most of the $10,000.00 in the owner's pocket. A steady paycheck, and the opportunity to advance is an excellent financial arrangement for both owner and employee.

There is no place for commission or piecework payments in a business desiring to be professional and profitable. The sooner you change to a salary structure, the sooner salon profits will increase. When you stop paying commissions you will soon wonder how it ever became so prominent. Costs are spiraling upward. If salon owners do not stop paying by these methods there will be no need for pet groomers. Salons won't be able to afford them.

Start paying salaries to every employee when you first implement the Madson Management System at Step One. Most owners at this stage will have only one or two pet bathers to transfer to a salary status. In the future, advise job applicants that your salon pays by salary.

DEVELOPING A REWARD SYSTEM

Employees will work more effectively when there is a defined and consistently applied reward system. It reinforces good work behavior and increases employee loyalty. The least expensive reward is verbal praise from management. Approval is important to everyone, it reinforces behavior and increases its frequency. Criticism may deter a poor performance but it can never teach a good one. Make a point of complimenting good work behavior at least three times a day. This will get you in the habit of looking for behavior to appreciate. As you look for it and compliment it, you will find it occurring more frequently.

There are other rewards important to employees also. Bonus pay, benefits, awards, and time-off can demonstrate the value you place on their contributions. Monetary incentives do not have to be large to be effective, $25.00 to $50.00 can be significant to a pet salon employee. However, money is not always the most effective, or desired reward. There are other effective incentives for performance excellence. A day off, theater or sports tickets, gift certificates, or a group dinner or picnic are examples.

The most satisfactory rewards are those that reward team effort. Individual rewards create competition, jealousy, and resentment. A support staff competing with each other is not nearly as successful as a support staff working as a team. This is why major corporations offer incentives to all members of a department when they achieve departmental objectives.

To be effective, goals should be specific and measurable. Assign specific goals to each of the three departments; client relations, bathing, and trimming. When a department reaches its goals, reward each member of the department. The annual bonus is gaining in popularity in the corporate world. A recent national survey of 1,598 firms by the American Compensation Association found that thirty percent issued annual bonuses. Of those firms, seventy percent had started the practice in the last five years. The annual bonus is contingent on the achievement of team objectives and is a percentage of increased profits. The staff should understand that if the business does well, they will do well.

An effective use of a reward system is to improve the performance of problem areas in your salon. Pick out the most troubled area of a department and establish a reward for a specific, measurable improvement. If the client relations department needs improvement, offer a reward for a specific number of increased appointments. Be sure the goal is reasonable. Asking the impossible invites feelings of futility and no improvement is likely. Set a reasonable goal, reward it, and set another. Let the employees know frequently how they are doing, verbally, graphically, or preferably both. A support staff who are all winners is a sterling indication of effective management.

A valuable reward for your support staff is the implementation of a group health insurance plan. By the time you reach Step Three of the Business Plan begin investigating employee health plans. The announcement to your staff that you are beginning a health plan will increase morale and bring the team closer together. If you cannot afford the full-cost of health insurance, you can offer to make a contribution toward each employee's premium. The cost to the employee will still be significantly less than they would pay individually.

HIRING THE SUPPORT STAFF

There are ten steps in the hiring process. Detailed instructions to complete each step are in this chapter. Follow the hiring process completely to hire the most qualified job applicant. The ten steps with chapter heading references are:

1. Prepare job description.
   (*Job Descriptions*)

2. Check sources for job candidates.
   (*Sources of Job Candidates*)

3. Review applications.
   (*Job Applications*)

4. Conduct interviews.
   (*The Hiring Interview*)

5. Check references.
   (*Selecting the Best Candidate*)

6. Conduct job evaluation testing.
   (*Practical Examinations for Applicants*)

7. Evaluate candidate.
   (*Selecting the Best Candidate*)

8. Employment offer.
   (*The Introductory Period Agreement*)

9. Provide orientation.
(Orientation)

10. Begin job training.
(Training Guidelines)

Choose applicants first for their ability to perform the duties of the open position. Secondly, choose them for their ability to perform the duties of other positions. Throughout the hiring process emphasize the skills specific to the open position. For instance, a receptionist doesn't have to know how to bathe or trim. She must understand how to judge the quality of a pet's grooming before returning it to the client.

SOURCES OF JOB CANDIDATES

Every time you hire a new employee keep the job applications of unhired, but eligible candidates in your files. This becomes a resource for future job openings.

Another good source are local high school and college job placement offices. Eager and bright students, especially those studying animal husbandry with an interest to be a veterinarian, make ideal employees.

Recommendations from your staff are another source of candidates. Use an incentive program to enlist the help of the staff to fill an open position. Provide a reward for staff members who recommend a candidate who is hired and completes a ninety-day introductory period. The reward may be a cash bonus, tickets to a ball game or theater, or a complimentary dinner for two. The cost of the incentive is much less than advertising, and is worth the security implied by an employee's recommendation. An additional bonus is that applicants recommended by your employees are often quickly accepted by the other staff.

Post a help-wanted sign in your reception area. Your clients are a potential source of referrals. List the position's requirements and offer an incentive, such as a complimentary pet grooming if a recommended applicant is hired. When clients respond be sure to thank them for their interest and tell them to invite their candidate to apply. Client recommendations may be unacceptable, so don't endanger their loyalty by making promises to hire their applicant. Tell them only that you will consider the person and decide in the interest of all concerned.

Pet industry vendors may know of a potential candidate. They travel through many other salons and often learn of available candidates.

Local veterinarians or 4-H clubs may have recommendations. If you belong to business groups, ask other members. Sometimes your local Chamber of Commerce has names of agencies that are a source of job candidates. Be certain these contacts understand you want applicants capable of working with animals and prefer some experience with pets.

If you have time to train an applicant, and there are no other qualified applicants, newspaper publications are a viable alternative. If you are seeking a candidate with experience always stress the requirement and the position's title in the ad. Begin your ad with "Pet." For instance, "Pet Bather wanted, experience preferred," or "Pet Trimmer wanted, experience required." You may have more success with pet trade magazines and newsletters. Check their "Job-Wanted" classified section. Typically, applicants in trade publications are career people.

If you are advertising a position, put a message on the answering machine. Ask applicants to leave their name, phone number and a brief description of experience. When you listen to the messages evaluate each person's verbal skills. This provides an indication of their ability to relate to your clients. Pleasant attitudes are needed for good client relations and are a real plus to a support staff. Respond to all messages and invite eligible applicants to complete an application for employment.

Most employment agencies have few if any applicants for positions in pet grooming so do not rely on them for applicants. Contact an employment agency counselor and discuss your requirements. They may be able to evaluate their applicants and find appropriate candidates. They are more likely to find a candidate needing training than one with experience.

The Madson Management System simplifies the search for employees needing experience. The master pet trimmer, assistant pet trimmer, and bathing department supervisor are examples. By conforming to the staff organization defined in the business plan, you are preparing experienced staff members the salon will eventually need. For example, you can promote part-time pet bathers to full-time. Promote a pet bather to assistant pet trimmer or bathing department supervisor. You can promote an assistant pet trimmer to a master pet trimmer.

JOB APPLICATIONS

The Madson Management System provides an employment questionnaire designed specifically for pet grooming. Make copies of illustration 8-1 and have job applicants complete one. The applicant should also complete a standard job application form available from office supply stores. The completed employment questionnaire gives you more specific information about an applicant's prior pet grooming experience than the standard job application.

Allow applicants to review the job description before they complete an application. By doing so you will take fewer applications from applicants with none of the required qualifications. Consider applicants with no previous experience in pet grooming, but otherwise qualified, for entry-level trainee positions.

Be sure the applicant has filled in all the requested information including a phone number and thank them for their interest. Tell them you will inform them of your decision within twenty-four hours when you are actively seeking an employee, and when you are not, that you will keep it on file. Keep completed applications in the salon's file cabinet, separated into stacks organized by job title. Paperclip each stack together and file them. When an opening arises you can quickly review the job applications suitable to the open position.

Accept applications for employment even if no positions are open. Emergency employment needs can occur without notice. Temporary and permanent vacancies arise from conflicts, relocation, allergies, illness, or pregnancy. By investing your time in accepting applications before an opening occurs you will have a hiring resource. It can eliminate the expense of a help-wanted ad, or overtime resulting from the missing staff member.

When reviewing applications, consider experience as well as education. The lack of a high school diploma could mean the applicant lacks the discipline necessary for a successful support staff member. Pertinent education or skill training is necessary for positions involving clerical or accounting duties such as the receptionist, telemarketer, and manager. Evaluate applicants for grooming positions on past grooming experience and their ability to learn your style of grooming, rather than educational background. All applicants should display good communication skills and the aptitude and willingness to learn the duties of their position.

THE HIRING INTERVIEW

Conduct a hiring interview with every applicant. A successful interview benefits both the applicant and the business. The interview is your opportunity to assess the personality of the applicant and their level of vocational and verbal skills. The impression received from an applicant's job application may be quite inaccurate compared to the information from an effective interview.

The key word for the interview process is opportunity. You have the opportunity to avoid hiring a poor employee if you're willing to conduct the interview properly. Ask the right questions and listen carefully to the answers.

Guidelines

Construct a list of questions from the categories and samples listed below. They will help you gain an accurate picture of the applicant's grooming skills and knowledge. Keep a neutral attitude during the interview and do not display a negative reaction to the replies to your questions. Applicants will perceive your attitude and either fake the answers, or withhold important information. An applicant at ease with both you and your questions will provide the most complete feedback.

EXPERIENCE

1. Can you tell me what your experience in pet grooming has been?
2. What is your experience in other lines of work?
3. Do you have any achievements in your employment history of which you are most proud?
4. What did you like most about your last job? What did you like least?
5. What were your duties like in your last job?
6. Have you worked in physically strenuous jobs before?
7. May I call your previous employer for a reference?
8. When can you begin work?
9. Do you have any goals that you are working toward?
10. How long will you be able to stay at this job?

INTERPERSONAL SKILLS

1. How well do you get along with others?
2. Have you ever worked as part of a team?
3. What kind of problems with supervisors have you had in the past?

ANIMAL CARE

1. Do you have experience handling animals?
2. What kind of pets have you owned?

EMPLOYMENT QUESTIONNAIRE

Applicant's Name_____   Date_____

Please answer the following questions:

1. Describe your past experience with animals and pet grooming.

2. Do you fear animals?

3. Do you have any pet-related allergies?

4. What is the date of your last tetanus booster injection?

5. Do you have arthritis or similar conditions? Do you have back, elbow, or wrist problems?

6. Are you a member of pet-related organizations? If so, which?

7. What did you like about your last job?

8. What did you dislike about your last job?

9. What are your hobbies?

10. What are your goals one year from now? Five years?

8-1

3. How well do you like animals?

4. Are you involved in any pet organizations, shows, or other aspects of the pet industry?

TRAINING

1. We use a system (The Madson Management System) requiring intensive training. Are you willing to undertake this training?

2. Are you able to accept correction?

3. Do you want to earn promotion?

CONDITIONS OF EMPLOYMENT

1. Are the salon's employee policies and procedures acceptable to you?

2. Do you understand and accept the introductory period agreement?

3. If you satisfactorily complete the introductory period do you have any objections to signing a job agreement?

4. What hours and days are you available to work?

5. Do you find the pay satisfactory?

6. Will you sign an Employee Confidentiality Agreement form if hired?

TESTING

1. Do you agree to the practical examination?

2. When are you available for the examination?

HEALTH

1. Is there any reason that you cannot stand all day while working if necessary?

2. Do you suffer from any allergies that might prevent you from working here?

3. Do you have any illnesses or disabilities that might prevent you from doing your job?

MOTIVATION

1. Why would you like to work for this salon?

Make photocopies of your list of questions. Have one copy with the applicant's name on it, the application and resume' for each interview. Record the applicant's answers on the copy.

To set up interviews, first review the applications to find those most qualified for the position. For instance, applicants for pet groomer who have never trimmed a pet are obviously not qualified for the position. Select the most eligible candidates and set up interviews with them.

When arranging the appointment with the applicant, use the term discussion instead of interview. This term is less threatening and will create a more relaxed atmosphere. Inform the applicants that references and an on-the-job examination are mandatory. If they resist the testing or reference requirements it may signal they have exaggerated the level of their skills or falsified their references. This announcement may forestall interviews with candidates who have provided inaccurate or misleading information on their application.

Open the interview with a statement about your business objectives and what the position involves. To attract a promising candidate be sure to show respect for their potential contribution to the business. Don't have the attitude "I'm doing you a favor if I give you a job." You may lose an ideal candidate who decides to work for someone with an appreciative attitude. Show enthusiasm for your business and the desire for applicants to share that enthusiasm.

Don't rush the interview, yet don't allow the applicant to ramble on with empty answers. Set aside about 30 minutes for the interview and adhere to that limit. If you aren't certain about a potential employee, schedule a second interview.

Grooming positions require special knowledge and skills. When screening applicants for grooming positions, give their present grooming skills and ability first priority. They must be adaptable to learn the pet care services characteristic of your salon. Though you can train an inexperienced groomer, an applicant with prior experience is more likely to make an immediate contribution.

Ideally, job applicants should have the potential for promotion to more skilled positions. They need the willingness to take on new tasks and learn new skills. A growing business needs employees who can grow with it and the Madson Management System will ensure growth. Project the goals for the business and the potential available to them in those projections. Look for applicants who react favorably to your enthusiasm for the business.

When posing questions to candidates, consider body language as well as verbal responses. Allow for normal anxiety to the interview process but in general consider these principles. An upright posture, eye contact, and responses made without hesitation or uncertainty are preferable. These are usually indicators of self-confidence and social poise both of which are desirable in an employee. Restless movement, the avoidance of eye contact, and uncertain or frequent changing of answers are indications of undesirable characteristics. These may reflect a lack of personal security and confidence, or worse, evasiveness and deceit.

Attitudes

The attitude an applicant has toward their previous employers and employment is the most accurate predictor of their future attitude toward you. Notice if the applicant holds a grudge against past employers, or speaks disparagingly of fellow employees. They are providing warning of potential employment problems.

All job applicants considered for employment must have sincere feelings of affection and respect for animals. Do not waste valuable time with applicants who are unwilling to learn proper pet handling techniques. You do not want an employee who expresses hostility toward people by abusing pets. It is not enough to love pets, they must have the willingness to respect animals. They must continually learn more about animal grooming and behavior. Your staff should understand that the client judges the salon by the way they respect and care for pets.

It is hard to imagine bathing the wild animals of centuries past. It would not be practical. Yet the animals of the past are ancestors of the pets brought for grooming. They still have some of their ancestors natural fear of man. They have an acute sense of smell. They notice that humans smell different and are larger in size. This strangeness and difference in appearance and size arouses an instinct of caution in pets.

Each pet reacts differently to a visit to the salon. Some will react by trembling and restless movement. Many will bark or whine, and some will bite because of innate fear and distrust. A few will issue a warning by snarling and exposing their teeth to whoever approaches. Some will salivate or vomit while others appear docile and happy. Your employees must be considerate and respectful of pets to properly and safely care for them.

Regulations

There are many new anti-discrimination laws in effect of which the owner should be aware. In general, you may not ask applicants any question unless it has a direct bearing on the job. This is to avoid answers which could discriminate against them.

- You may not ask applicants about their age, race or color, marital status, creed, religion, husband or wife's occupation, war service, or the age of their children.
- You may not ask how any of these subjects would affect them if they were an attribute of another employee.
- You may not ask about the national origin of their last name, parents, or spouse.
- You may not ask about their ability to speak a second language unless required by their job.
- You may not exclude handicapped persons from a job unless it will measurably and directly affect their job performance.
- You may not ask any question about their size or weight.
- You may not ask them if they have ever been arrested.

* * * * *

- You may ask if there is anything that would prevent them from working certain hours and days, or fulfilling the requirements of their position.
- You may ask if they have ever been convicted of a felony.
- You may ask about the status of their citizenship.
- You may ask about the legal status of their residency in the United States if they are not a citizen.

If a candidate volunteers information about an issue legally forbidden, ignore. Treat it as having no bearing on your decision and avoid discussing it further.

The owner is responsible to be current on federal, state and local Fair Employment Practices, and to comply with the regulations. Fair employment regulations are available at federal, state and local employment offices. Some of them require public postings in the place of business. Anyone involved in "hiring and firing" must be aware of these regulations.

The Immigration and Naturalization Service now requires employers to use a new employment form, the Federal Immigration Form I-9. Complete it and keep it on file at the salon. The I-9 form, and a photocopy of the new employee's birth certificate, or state driver's license, or U.S. passport belongs in the employee's personnel file. You must complete this process within three days from the first date of employment. The I.N.S. can inspect your I-9 forms after giving you three days notice. Failure to produce the completed forms can result in penalties. This could be a fine of from $250.00 to $10,000.00 per illegal alien, and six months in jail for repeat offenders. The immigration officials give special scrutiny to companies with a thousand or more employees. Nonetheless, it is wise to be in one hundred percent conformity with the immigration law even if your business is small.

After the interview, thank the candidate and listen to their response. A polite thank you, a request for you to contact them with your decision, and eagerness to follow-up on the interview suggest a favorable response to the interview. After the interview record any last minute thoughts or follow-up instructions for yourself. Keep all interview materials in a specially marked file. Even if you do not hire the applicant then, the file may be useful for future reference.

When you discover someone likely to contribute to the support staff, the next step is to check their references. Guidelines for reference checking are in illustration 8-2.

If the response to your reference checks is acceptable, arrange a practical examination. If you have more than one candidate, arrange a test for each at different times.

PRACTICAL EXAMINATIONS FOR APPLICANTS

The purpose of the practical exam is to determine the level of an applicant's skills. The results will either confirm or disprove the skills you believed the applicant to have. You can also determine how much training is necessary to bring the applicant to the expected level of performance. Do not use personality or vocational tests. They may conflict with Equal Employment Opportunity Commission regulations and are not very useful in selecting pet grooming employees anyway.

A practical examination can last up to four hours. Pay the applicants an hourly wage based on prior experience and skill. Do not pay them less than the legal minimum wage set by the state in which your salon does business. The purpose is to only pay applicants for their time. It is not a salary and does not reflect the salary they can expect to receive if hired.

A sample of The Job Applicant Practical Exam Agreement is in illustration 8-3. Have your attorney leave a blank space for the rate of hourly pay. Each time you use the form fill in the blank with the appropriate rate of pay. Every candidate must sign the form before the examination. Two copies of the form must be signed. The original copy remains with the owner and the applicant receives the duplicate. Keep the signed forms with the salon's permanent records.

You can end the exam anytime during the four hours. Applicants can also end the exam at any time if they no longer desire employment. Pay them for the time spent up to that point.

Health problems such as arthritis or allergies to pets can prevent them from doing the work properly. If you have reason to question the health of an applicant, ask for a doctor's release before testing.

Once the employee signs the Job Applicant Practical Exam, the exam begins. It is mandatory that any applicant taking the grooming exam be supervised. The quality of grooming must be compatible with the salon's normal pet care services and the pet must be safe.

Examine the master pet trimmer in three phases. They should be able to bathe a pet, perform a satisfactory pre-clip (Chapter Four), and finish trim. Have them do as many pets as necessary to make your determination as to their level of skill.

Examine the assistant pet trimmer in two phases. They should be able to bathe a pet and perform a satisfactory pre-clip. Once again, have them do as many pets as necessary to determine their level of skill.

Have the bather prospect bathe and blow-dry a pet. Let an experienced pet bather work with the applicant on another pet, perhaps another breed. Repeat the exam until determining the skill level.

REFERENCE CHECKING GUIDELINES

Selecting the wrong person for a position can be costly both in terms of time and money. Aside from the time and expense in terminating a poor choice and hiring a replacement, there are new concerns. In the past few years, employers have been dealt two severe legal blows with respect to checking references. These two potential legal vulnerabilities are itemized below along with suggested safeguards.

Legal Danger #1.

1. When asked to give a reference for a former employee you may be sued for defamation of character based on statements made to a potential employer.

Safeguard #1.

You can reduce your vulnerability to lawsuits based on defamation claims. If you can document information given during a reference check as truthful, there is no basis for a defamation lawsuit. Documentation means having your claims in writing. Therefore, keep accurate, written performance evaluations and document supporting facts. Do not discuss personal issues concerning the ex-employee with a prospective employer, only work-related ones. If possible, obtain a written release from the employee allowing information to be given to prospective employers and releasing you from all claims that might arise the reference-giving procedure. As with all legal agreements, the employee must fully understand the meaning of the signed agreement. Finally, references should only be given by the owner, or the manager with the owner's approval.

Legal Danger #2.

If you forgo checking an applicant's background and references you may be sued by a third party for negligence in hiring the employee.

A charge of negligent hiring can occur if an owner fails to check references. If an employee has a prior history of work misconduct which was not thoroughly investigated by checking references, and that employee is involved in a harm-causing incident, a third party such as a client or employee may sue for injuries sustained based upon negligent hiring practices.

Safeguard #2.

To ensure making a more informed hiring decision and reduce liability check as many references as possible before hiring the applicant. Keep records of all responses and even those that did not respond. When in doubt, consider a second interview to check for the consistency of the applicant's information. Have the applicant account for any gaps in employment. You may ask if the applicant has been *convicted* of a crime—you may not ask if they have been arrested. Ask the applicant if you may contact their previous employers and what response you can expect. Encourage the applicant to sign a form drawn up by your attorney releasing information from previous employers.

By carefully following these guidelines for both giving and checking references you can minimize the risk of liability from defamation or negligent hiring.

JOB APPLICANT PRACTICAL EXAM AGREEMENT

Dear Job Applicant:

Before being considered for a position at _____(salon)_____ you must take a practical exam to test your skills, your ability to work with the staff and the animals, and your ability to follow instructions.

The practical exam will take up to four hours. The exam may be terminated if it takes less than four hours to determine your qualifications. In addition, you may terminate the practical exam at any time if you no longer want to be considered for employment. You will not be considered for employment until the practical exam is completed.

You will receive a $_____ allowance for each hour, or part of an hour, of your test. This is to compensate you for your time. It is not a salary nor does it reflect the salary you will be receiving if you are offered a position.

Thank you,

SAMPLE
CONSULT YOUR ATTORNEY

(salon)

_____
I have read, and understand the above.

8-3

Aside from observing technical skills, note the attitude of the applicant toward pets. Is the applicant kind, gentle, and patient? An attitude of respect toward animals is as important as technical skill.

Give a practical exam to the manager, receptionist, and telemarketer positions also. Have them sign the exam form and pay them in the same manner as the groomer applicants. Examine them for clerical and client relations skills. Have them make telemarketing and appointment confirmation calls. Have them greet clients and assist the front counter person accepting pets in the morning and returning them in the evening. The manager-applicant participates in this part of the examination. In order to supervise effectively he must understand how to perform the tasks. The telemarketer, not usually working at the front counter, still performs that portion of the examination. It may be necessary for them to fill in during emergencies.

Have the manager applicant assume some management tasks during the test period. Pick two or three tasks from the job description. For all applicants, observe their relationship to staff and clients for friendliness, courtesy, and business acumen.

At the end of the four-hour test, pay the applicant and tell them you will call when you decide. Write a summary of the applicant's test results and attach it to their job application.

Do not ignore the practical exam job testing method as a part of the hiring process. The examination is especially important for assessing groomers because interviews are an inaccurate indicator of grooming skills. Some groomer applicants may interview poorly but have excellent grooming skills. You cannot assess a groomer's competence verbally, it requires an examination. It is expensive to hire an applicant on their assurance of pet grooming skills and find otherwise when they begin employment. It pays to invest time in practical examinations.

SELECTING THE BEST APPLICANT

Employment decisions have financial consequences for the future. Do not make them by hunches or "gut feelings." Also do not base them solely on an applicant's pleasant personality. A pleasant personality does not substitute for an applicant's skills. A highly-skilled employee with an average personality is more valuable than a socially skilled employee with few job-related skills. The importance of the hiring process demands the adoption of a formal, structured, selection procedure. Use each applicant's application, resumé, interview, references, and practical exam results to select the most qualified candidate. This information supplies measurable evidence of necessary skills and potential.

Overall physical health and adequate physical strength are basics. In addition, there are six other areas to consider in selecting the most qualified candidate.

1. *Grooming Skills.*
   This means bathing and trimming competence.

2. *Communication Skills.*
   This is defined as the ability to express oneself accurately and to hear and understand the expressions of others. It also includes using these abilities to defuse potential conflicts and create a positive image for the salon.

3. *Clerical Skills.*
   This is competence in organizing records, bookkeeping, and written correspondence.

4. *Attitude.*
   The willingness to learn and cooperate with others in a team effort, along with an affection and respect for animals are the desired attitudes for an employee.

5. *Dependability.*
   A sense of responsibility toward one's position expressed in punctuality, work attendance, and consistent work effort are examples of dependability.

6. *Business Acumen.*
   This means the employee understands that the success of the business depends on his work efforts. It is expressed in behavior and appearance.

All employees must have at least some of the work characteristics described. However, each position requires a different emphasis. Illustration 8-4 shows the degree of emphasis placed on each work characteristic for the seven support staff positions. For example, the receptionist has greater need for communication and clerical skills and less need for grooming skills. Review these guidelines when faced with an employment decision.

The applicant that rates very high in most categories could conceivably still not be hired. Supplementary information from reference checks and staff feedback may preclude hiring an otherwise acceptable applicant.

The opinion of your staff toward a new employee is critical and if their reaction is negative you must determine why. Resentment toward a new employee may occur when the position was coveted for themselves or for a friend. Not promoting an employee who wants the position, can cause that employee to feel anger and dislike toward any applicant. Another common problem is resistance to being supervised by a new, untested supervisor. In these situations the staff can neglect their goal to work as a team and achieve the objectives of the business plan. The manager needs to work with such a staff to realign their working relationships and revive team spirit.

An applicant is not hired at times in spite of exceptional credentials. The owner may feel threatened by the applicant's superior ability and shortsightedly rejects a valuable contributor to the salon. Only if such a candidate is self-centered, uncooperative, and cannot work with a team, is it correct not to hire them.

When you have selected a qualified candidate schedule an appointment to make a job offer. At the meeting, clarify any last questions you may have, and then present the job offer. Applicants should realize that the owner will help them if they help him. He will provide opportunities for growth and advancement if they agree to become a team member and achieve the owner's business goals. Applicants must understand this is the fundamental reason for their employment.

Remind the new employee of the ninety-day introductory period. It includes orientation and training and the requirement to sign a job agreement after its satisfactory completion. With the acceptance of these requirements new employees are ready to begin their first day.

NEW EMPLOYEE FIRST DAY PROCEDURES

The Introductory Period Agreement

Standard procedure for any sound business is to place new employees on probation for the first ninety days. This is an opportunity to assess the new employee. It demonstrates whether he fits into the team structure of the salon and conforms to the salon's policies and procedures. The Madson Management System calls this period an introductory period because it includes indoctrination and training.

Sample introductory period agreements are in this chapter. There are two types. Use the Manager Introductory Agreement only for manager candidates, and the Introductory Period Agreement for all other employees. These agreements provide the new employee with written notice of the ninety-day introductory period and other employment specifications.

As in the sample introductory period agreements, you should have your company attorney provide blank spaces for the information listed below.

1. Name of your pet grooming salon

2. Position title.

3. Monthly salary during the introductory period.

4. Monthly salary after the introductory period.

5. Benefits such as sick-leave and vacation days after one-year of employment.

6. Number of confirmed appointments to achieve each month (manager only).

7. Signature of new temporary employee.

8. Date signed.

9. Other expectations specified by the salon owner.

The new temporary employee signs the introductory period agreement in duplicate. Keep the original in the employee's personnel file and provide a copy to the employee.

The ninety-day introductory period begins the day the employee signs the agreement. Note the start and finish dates of an employee's introductory period on your business calendar, and in their personnel file. Keep accurate track of the ninety-day period and follow the terms in the introductory period agreement.

Within the introductory period you may terminate employees at any time. There is no liability to unlawful termination charges during the introductory period. Terminations after the introductory period must adhere to strict legal guidelines and therefore are not as easy to do. If an employee is not performing satisfactorily after ninety days, ninety percent of those will still be performing unsatisfactorily after twelve months. Don't waste valuable time, and subject yourself to a potential legal headache by continuing with a temporary employee who is not performing adequately. Terminate any employee who is not performing satisfactorily by the end of the introductory period.

Don't promise an employee a position for a specific time period such as six or twelve months. This is a verbal contract making you vulnerable to litigation if you terminate the employee during that time period. Use the protection provided by the introductory period to safeguard your business interests.

The first weeks of the introductory period expose the new employee to the duties of the position, salon operations, and its owner and staff. After a period of familiarization, place the

SELECTING THE BEST CANDIDATE

	Receptionist	Tele-marketer	Pet Bather	Bathing Dept. Supervisor	Asst. Pet Trimmer	Master Pet Trimmer	Manager
GROOMING SKILLS	LOW	LOW	MED.	HIGH	MED.	HIGH	LOW
COMMUNICATION SKILLS	MED.	MED.	MED.	HIGH	MED.	HIGH	HIGH
CLERICAL SKILLS	MED.	MED.	LOW	MED.	LOW	MED.	HIGH
ATTITUDE	MED.	MED.	MED.	MED.	MED.	MED.	HIGH
DEPENDABILITY	HIGH	HIGH	HIGH	HIGH	HIGH	HIGH	HIGH
BUSINESS ACUMEN	MED.	MED.	MED.	HIGH	MED.	HIGH	HIGH

LOW: Candidate has fair knowledge and skill level

MED.: Candidate has good knowledge and skill level

HIGH: Candidate has excellent knowledge and skill level and can teach others

INTRODUCTORY PERIOD AGREEMENT

This letter outlines your employment agreement with _____ Salon in which you are asked to accept certain conditions of employment in exchange for a position as _____ together with a compensation arrangement that we think you will find reasonable and satisfying. The individual points of the agreement are listed below. Your introductory period is ninety days from date of hire. Satisfactory completion of this introductory period will determine your becoming a regular staff member.

1. During the ninety day introductory period, you will be paid $_____ monthly salary.

2. At the completion of the introductory period, an evaluation of your performance will be conducted and if employment continues you will be paid $_____ monthly salary.

3. During the introductory period paid sick-leave is not available, however, if employment continues after the introductory period you are given _____ paid sick-leave days on a yearly basis (non-accruable). After one year's employment, you will be given — working days vacation.

4. During the introductory period a Receptionist or Telemarketer is expected to complete _____ confirmed appointments a month. During the introductory period a Master Pet Trimmer, Assistant Pet Trimmer, or Pet Bather is expected to complete _____ pets a week. The amount of this figure represents the minimum for satisfactory performance. A review of your progress will take place every thirty days during the introductory period. Thereafter, regular job performance evaluations are given twice annually.

5. You agree that in the event of intentional or willful disregard by you of any projects or employee policies and procedures of _____ Salon, the owner shall have the right to take disciplinary action up to and including termination based upon the circumstances of the individual event.

6. The manager will be responsible for your training during the introductory period. The manager will be available for any questions concerning the conditions of your employment and work performance. You may request an interview in writing with the owner.

7. In the event your job performance is not acceptable (below minimum satisfactory levels) employment will not continue.

8. This agreement may be terminated at any time by yourself or the salon owner during the introductory period. When the introductory period is satisfactorily completed you will become a regular staff member. You will be required to sign a job agreement at the end of the introductory period when employment continues.

SAMPLE
CONSULT YOUR ATTORNEY

Please indicate your acceptance of the above agreement by signing and dating it below. A signed copy of this agreement remains with the salon owner and a copy is provided for you.

_____   _____
Signature   Date

MANAGER INTRODUCTORY PERIOD AGREEMENT

This letter outlines your Manager Agreement with _____ Salon in which you are asked to accept certain conditions of employment in exchange for a position as Manager of Client Services and Personnel together with a compensation arrangement that we think you will find reasonable and satisfying. The individual points of the agreement are listed below. Your introductory period is ninety days from date of hire. Satisfactory completion of this introductory period will determine your becoming a regular staff member.

1. During the ninety day introductory period, you will be paid $_____ monthly salary.

2. At the completion of the introductory period, an evaluation of your performance will be conducted and if employment continues you will be paid $_____ monthly salary.

3. During the introductory period paid sick-leave is not available, however, if employment continues after the introductory period you are given _____ paid sick-leave days on a yearly basis (non-accruable). After one year's employment, you will be given _____ working days vacation.

4. During the introductory period you are expected to complete _____ confirmed appointments a month. The amount of this figure represents the minimum for satisfactory performance. A review of your progress will take place every thirty days during the introductory period. Thereafter, regular job performance evaluations are given twice annually.

5. You agree that in the event of intentional or willful disregard by you of any projects or employee policies and procedures of _____ Salon, the owner shall have the right to take disciplinary action up to and including termination based upon the circumstances of the individual event.

6. The owner will be responsible for your training during the introductory period. The owner will be available for any questions concerning the conditions of your employment and work performance. You may request an interview in writing with the owner.

7. In the event your job performance is not acceptable (below minimum satisfactory levels) employment will not continue.

8. This agreement may be terminated at any time by yourself or the salon owner during the introductory period. When the introductory period is satisfactorily completed you will become a regular staff member. You will be required to sign a job agreement at the end of the introductory period when employment continues.

SAMPLE
CONSULT YOUR ATTORNEY

Please indicate your acceptance of the above agreement by signing and dating it below. A signed copy of this agreement remains with the salon owner and a copy is provided for you.

_____   _____
Signature   Date

8-6

emphasis on assessing the employee's ability to conform to the position's quotas and standards. For example, a pet bather expected to complete eleven baths daily is only able to complete eight after the first two months. Devote the last month of the introductory period to increasing their output. If they are unable to correct their performance, let them go.

Schedule a weekly job review with the new employee during the introductory period. Use the job performance evaluation forms discussed in Chapter Nine for all performance reviews. Keep all performance evaluations in the employee's personnel file. At the end of the introductory period use them to make your decision to employ or terminate them.

Employee Confidentiality Agreement

At the same time the employee signs a introductory period agreement, they also sign an Employee Confidentiality Agreement. By signing the agreement the employee agrees to hold in strict confidence any proprietary or confidential information obtained while in your employ. The agreement also requires the return of any keys, documents, tools and equipment, which are property of the salon.

Review the agreement with the new employee and have them sign two witnessed copies. Keep the original in the employee's personnel file and provide the second copy to the employee. Continue preparations for the orientation procedure including both employment documentation and the organization of the new employee's workplace, tools, and training program.

Open a personnel file for the new employee and place all employment documentation in it. This includes a copy of the W-4 federal employment form, I-9 immigration form, and any other required forms. Also, complete any benefit forms such as life and health insurance.

Orientation

Give the Employee Handbook to the new employee and review its contents with them until they clearly understand it. Advise them to read the book carefully at home and bring any questions to the manager. The new employee is now ready for staff introductions and a tour of the salon facilities. Introduce the employee to the staff by each one's name and position. The manager should personally make the introductions to show support of the new employee.

Show the bathing, trimming, and other areas of the salon such as the place to keep personal belongings. Point out emergency posted procedures, fire extinguishers, and emergency exits. Finally, show them the work area and tools for their position.

Getting the new employee ready to make contributions to the business is dependent on the helpful attitude of the support staff. Encourage them to ask as many questions as desired and remind the staff to give assistance while they learn the job.

Maintain close contact while they adjust to the salon. Ask them how they are feeling, how they like their duties, and what it is like working with the other staff. Remind new employees they can come to you at any time. Be sure to include the new employee at all staff meetings even during the introductory period.

EMPLOYEE CONFIDENTIALITY AGREEMENT

In consideration of my admission to and employment on the premises of _____ SALON, hereinafter referred to as the "shop," which I acknowledge is for my benefit, I agree to hold in strict confidence, any proprietary or confidential information which is disclosed or otherwise made available to me, or to which I otherwise gain access, or of which I otherwise obtain knowledge, during or in connection with any visit by me or employment of me on the premises of the shop.

I further agree that I will, during the course of my visit and or employment, whether before, on or after the date hereof:

(a) preserve the privacy of the oral, taped, diagrammed or written information, instructions and or discussions of the shop, its employees, managers, owners, patrons, and vendors.

(b) protect the confidential information used in the shop.

(c) limit disclosure of information to persons outside the shop in relation to known information, techniques, formulas, processes, procedures, plans, designs, statistics, or other data.

(d) refrain from soliciting or disrupting shop employees, managers, owners, patrons, or vendors.

I further agree that I have no present intention to use shop procedures, information, materials or equipment for my personal benefit, during or after shop hours, other than that of furthering or implementing the business relationship between the parties to this agreement.

I further agree that I will not remove from the shop premises, nor will I copy or reproduce, any document, material, equipment, data or other information of any kind, regardless of form, without the specific permission of the owner or manager of _____ Salon.

I further agree that upon termination of my employment, I will return to the shop any and all keys, equipment, documents, materials of any kind including copies, replicas, reproductions and samples.

SAMPLE
CONSULT YOUR ATTORNEY

Dated this _____ day of _____, 19_____ at the address of _____ _____ in the city of _____, state of California.

Signature _____

Address _____

_____

Witnessed by:

Signature _____

Title _____

JOB AGREEMENTS

After satisfactory completion of the introductory period, welcome the new employee to the support staff. The signing of the job agreement completes the hiring process. Job agreements are a vital tool to protect the interest of the owner in employment litigation.

The job agreement states the minimal standards expected of an employee's performance. This may include the number of pets a groomer must groom daily, or the results expected from the receptionist and telemarketer. The manager's job agreement includes the increase in the client base expected each year by the owner. It is apparent that all expectations in the job agreements must be fair and reasonable. The purpose of the agreement is not to test or challenge the employee. It is to define the minimal standards expected of their performance. Achievements above the minimal standards determine raises and promotions.

The job agreement includes holidays, vacation time, and sick leave policy. The employee who signs the contract agrees to complete all job duties and follow employee policies and procedures.

JOB AGREEMENT - CLIENT RELATIONS DEPARTMENT

This letter outlines your employment agreement as a regular staff member with
_____(salon name)_____ in which you are asked to accept certain conditions of employment
in exchange for a position as _____(job title)_____ together with a compensation arrangement.

1. You are expected to properly schedule and/or confirm _____(#)_____ appointments weekly,
_____(#)_____ appointments monthly. The amounts of these figures represent the minimum for
satisfactory performance. Regular job performance evaluations are conducted twice annually.

2. Salary _____(monthly amount and interval of payment)_____ .

3. Group health insurance is provided effective _____(date)_____ .

4. You are provided _____(#)_____ paid sick days per calendar year (non-accruable).

5. After one year's employment you are given _____(#)_____ days paid vacation. You will be
given _____(#)_____ days paid vacation after the second and following year's employment.

6. The salon manager is available for questions concerning the conditions of your employment and
work performance. You may request an interview in writing with the owner.

7. You agree that in the event of intentional or willful disregard by you of any projects or employee
policies and procedures of _____(salon's name)_____, the owner shall have the right to take disciplinary action up to and including termination based upon the circumstances of the individual
event.

SAMPLE
CONSULT YOUR ATTORNEY

Please indicate your acceptance of the above agreement by signing and dating it below. A
signed copy of this agreement remains with the salon owner and a copy is provided for you.

_____   _____
Signature   Date

JOB AGREEMENT – TRIMMING & BATHING DEPARTMENTS

This letter outlines your employment agreement as a regular staff member with _____(salon name)_____ in which you are asked to accept certain conditions of employment in exchange for a position as ____(job title)____ together with a compensation arrangement.

1. You are expected to properly complete assigned grooming duties for ____(#)____ to ____(#)____ pets daily, ____(#)____ to ____(#)____ weekly. The amounts of these figures represent the minimum for satisfactory performance. Regular job performance evaluations are conducted twice annually.

2. Salary _____(monthly amount and interval of payment)_____ .

3. Group health insurance is provided effective _____(date)_____ .

4. You are provided ____(#)____ paid sick days per calendar year (non-accruable).

5. After one year's employment you are given ____(#)____ days paid vacation. You will be given ____(#)____ days paid vacation after the second and following year's employment.

6. The salon manager is available for questions concerning the conditions of your employment and work performance. You may request an interview in writing with the owner.

7. You agree that in the event of intentional or willful disregard by you of any projects or employee policies and procedures of ____(salon's name)____ , the owner shall have the right to take disciplinary action up to and including termination based upon the circumstances of the individual event.

SAMPLE
CONSULT YOUR ATTORNEY

Please indicate your acceptance of the above agreement by signing and dating it below. A signed copy of this agreement remains with the salon owner and a copy is provided for you.

_____   _____
Signature   Date

JOB AGREEMENT-MANAGER

This letter outlines your employment agreement with ___(salon name)___ in which you are asked to accept certain conditions of employment in exchange for a position as Manager together with a compensation arrangement.

1. Under your supervision, the Client Relations Department staff is expected to properly schedule and/or confirm _____(#)_____ appointments weekly, _____(#)_____ appointments monthly. The amounts of these figures represent the minimum for satisfactory performance.

2. Your management performance of ___(salon's name)___ personnel, client and pet care services, safety program, marketing program, records, payroll, employee training, cash receipts, professional working relationships, maintenance, and the achievement of financial and service goals will be formally evaluated twice annually.

3. Salary _____ (monthly amount and interval of payment) _____ .

4. Group health insurance is provided effective _____(date)_____ .

5. You are provided _____(#)_____ paid sick days per calendar year (non-accruable).

4. After one year's employment you are given _____(#)_____ days paid vacation. You will be given _____(#)_____ days paid vacation after the second and following year's employment.

7. The owner is available for questions concerning the conditions of your employment and work performance.

8. You agree that in the event of intentional or willful disregard by you of any projects or employee policies and procedures of ___(salon's name)___, the owner shall have the right to take disciplinary action up to and including termination based upon the circumstances of the individual event.

SAMPLE
CONSULT YOUR ATTORNEY

Please indicate your acceptance of the above agreement by signing and dating it below. A signed copy of this agreement remains with the salon owner and a copy is provided for you.

_____   _____
Signature   Date

AN EFFECTIVE SUPERVISORY SYSTEM FOR THE SUPPORT STAFF

CHAPTER
9

The purpose of this chapter is to sharpen supervisory skills. The manager is responsible for the work of the support staff. An effective supervisory relationship with the employees will enhance pet care and client relations. This will cause the salon to grow. Do not underestimate the role of a supervisor. Improving supervisory skills is an effective way to promote the growth and profitability of the salon.

Historically, the importance of supervision in the pet grooming salon has been largely underrated. This must change because supervision benefits both morale and productivity. Its primary goal is to accomplish business objectives through the efforts of the support staff.

In the pet grooming salon, not only is the supervisor responsible for employees, but also many pets. Every pet care service involves a potential risk. A pet is far more valuable than most products in the service industry because it cannot replaced. It is beloved by its owner and the affection and memories of a pet owner for his pet are irreplaceable. Litigation arising from the neglectful handling of even one client's pet can result in the owner being forced out of business. The owner and manager of the pet grooming salon must become effective supervisors to protect the interests of the business.

Your supervision must be consistent. The support staff needs to know what to expect from you if they are to join with you. They expect you to deal with difficult situations and are more secure when you are confident. Be as quick to stand up for them as you are to correct them.

While the principles of supervision are consistent, your style of supervision is individual. The characteristics of your personality, character, biases, habits, and respect for pets all influence your style. Be aware of how others see you. Your staff may not see you the way you see yourself. Be willing to learn how to be a better people manager. You can demand the respect of the support staff but it is more of a tribute if you earn it. Teammates need to have confidence in the coach in order to be successful. Gain their confidence through your competence, fairness, and respect for them. Build a team spirit where employees cooperate to meet the business' objectives.

In summary, the manager's role as a supervisor centers on getting the employees to participate in the achievement of business goals. This is easier when the employees feel valued for their contribution to the business. Always be available to them, and ready to learn new ways to improve your supervision.

EFFECTIVE COMMUNICATION WITH THE SUPPORT STAFF

Good management requires more than knowledge and the willingness to work hard. It requires the ability to communicate effectively with the support staff. Feeling overwhelmed by demands of salon operations you may not take time to explain the management system to the staff. It is essential to take the time. Take the time to talk, to listen, and to respond to the employees. It is crucial to talk to each employee. Explain to them their duties, relations with others on the staff, the system of rewards, and the goals of the pet grooming salon. The larger the staff grows the more the need to effectively communicate increases. Maintain your awareness by developing a flow of communication between you and the employees.

There are three departments in every salon which need channels of communication between them. The three areas are the client reception department, the bathing department, and the trimming department (see illustration 3-7). When you implement the management system at Step One define the communication channels to the present employees. Then explain the network as part of the orientation procedure for new employees. You want each employee on the staff to be able to say, "I'm responsible for 'this' and they are responsible 'that.' " Each employee must understand not only the contributions he makes to the operation, but those made by other staff members.

Establishing channels of communication means, "Talk to each other about what you do, let the right hand know what the left hand is doing."

The goal of communication with the staff is to communicate in a way they can understand and act upon. There are four methods of accomplishing this.

1. Verbal Communication.
2. Written Communication.
3. Listening Techniques.
4. Demonstrations.

Verbal

Before you communicate verbally to the salon's employees organize what you want to say. Remind yourself to be aware of non-verbal communication such as body language, eye contact, tone of voice, facial expressions, and posture. Your non-verbal communication should reflect concern and respect for the employee. It should not be threatening or intimidating. Do not be condescending in either language or tone. Use words the employee can understand and easily related to examples. Speak clearly and not so softly that the message is lost. Get to the point quickly, and relate only the pertinent information. Be specific, if the message is too general it is not effective.

The timing of communication is very important. Pet bathers and trimmers are typically on tight schedules requiring intense concentration. If you don't need to communicate the information immediately wait until the employee has time to be receptive to considering and replying. The groomers must give full attention to the pets to protect their safety.

Verbal communication results in an immediate response and permits you to see the reaction of the respondent when they reply. It is preferred when you desire those characteristics.

Written

There are times when communication with employees should be in writing. One example is to communicate policies and procedures that don't change frequently. An example is the Madson Employee Handbook. By distributing it to every employee you communicate the policies and procedures you expect the support staff to follow. Written communication is best for salon rules, practices, policies, and procedures. These are formal issues which protect the interests of the business. Documenting them proves that employees were informed. You can never prove that an employee heard your verbal communication, but you can if it is in writing.

Use written communication when updating employee policies and procedures or when adding new ones. Type a notice of the changes and distribute a copy to each employee. Be sure to update the original Employee Handbook with the notices so all employees are aware of your expectations. It is a good idea to discuss written communications at staff meetings. Ask the employees if they have any questions regarding contents. Demonstrate your intent to keep them informed.

Written communications also make various issues part of the pet grooming salon's official record for future protection. The introductory period and job agreements, and disciplinary letters are examples of matters to record. A rule of thumb is, if you think you may ever need to prove you said something, put it in writing now.

Instructions are another example of communication that needs to be in writing. This allows the trainee to repeatedly study the material until they have committed it to memory. If an employee doesn't use a procedure and forgets the instructions, having written instructions to refer to becomes important.

Memos requesting a reply are not a good communication technique. Questions issued by memo to the support staff imply that you have no time to deal with them. Memos can be effective as reminders for such things as staff meetings. Otherwise, they have no place in the pet grooming salon.

Listening

Effective communication involves more than talking and writing. Information offered and not received is not communication. It must be offered and received in order to be communication. This requires listening skills. You can get a staff to listen to what you have to say, by listening to what they have to say. If you only spend time sending out messages, you're closing the door on your responsibility to receive messages. You don't learn much by talking. The most valuable lessons about how to improve your business will come when you are listening, not when you are talking.

Listening is a mental discipline improved only by practice. Become a better listener by never interrupting the speaker except to ask for clarification and to express understanding. When the speaker finishes do not give your response until you have confirmed you heard correctly. Use statements like, "It sounds like you are saying...", and then supply the essence of what you believe you heard. When you have received confirmation that you heard correctly you may give your comments. It will take patience, especially if you don't agree with what you are hearing or if you have heard it before. Nonetheless, stay with the formula of listening, and responding only to ask for clarification and express understanding. Then ask for confirmation before commenting. It will surprise you to find out how often the old saying is true, "What you thought you were hearing is not necessarily what they were saying."

The support staff in the pet salon may not be articulate speakers. They may communicate slowly when the message involves personal matters. If you act impatiently or show disagreement through postural or facial expressions, you may cut short and lose the message. Keep any personal bias to yourself. Concentrate on what they are saying instead of whether you agree with it. Listen to understand, not to evaluate. Accept what the speaker feels even if you disagree with how they express it. While you may not share their feelings, show respect for them. All communication is important to you. You never know when you will hear something that has a profound impact on your business. To discount a message because of the way it's delivered, or because of the person who gives it to you, may cause you to ignore something valuable.

You can benefit from listening to an employee's honest opinions even if they are negative. For example, Sally, a salon manager, noticed that the quality of the bathing department's work had deteriorated. Without requesting the bathing staff's opinion of the problem she admonished them to improve. Yet nothing changed and the quality remained poor. If she had said, "Could you help me understand why your performance has not been up to its usual high standards?" She may have learned that the new brand of shampoo she selected did not rinse well. The bathers had been afraid to tell her anticipating, from experience that she would respond angrily and defensively. So the salon's standard of quality for pet care services declined.

An important part of a manager's role is to find and solve problems. Listening only for supportive opinions denies a manager the opportunity to learn about problems that need his attention. It is much easier to listen to praise than it is to listen to criticism. Still, listening only to praise limits the opportunity to improve. Be prepared to hear unfavorable comments. It is far better for management to seek awareness of problems than to let them multiply unattended.

When your staff learns that you are a good listener they may make valuable contributions to your business. They know if the new shampoo is working well or if there are areas that need your attention. Encourage them to pass on to you the client's comments. Request their input and listen to their solutions when problems arise. Traditionally, in corporations, government, and the military those in command ask for the opinions of their staff before making decisions. Though you have a much smaller operation, obtaining the opinions of your staff is equally important. If you ask the right questions, and listen to the answers, your management will be more effective.

Demonstration

Demonstration uses visual presentation methods to communicate skills followed by the student's attempt to duplicate the procedures. Demonstrations are invaluable to communicate your salon's grooming styles, safety procedures, and client relations procedures.

IMPROVING AND MAINTAINING EMPLOYEE MORALE

The finest morale is when employees enjoy what they are doing, do it well, and feel valued for doing it. Producing that atmosphere is the direct responsibility of management. Management's role is selecting the right candidate, providing training that develops competence, and then recognizing and rewarding that competence. This is the most crucial aspect of building morale. Poor morale spreads swiftly throughout the pet salon requiring swift correction. If your salon has been characterized by poor morale, you can improve it. If morale has been adequate, you can make it better.

Observe, and listen, to the employees. Employees who work slowly or carelessly may be reflecting poor morale. Employees with poor morale complain about work conditions and remuneration. This infection of poor morale spreads to the other support staff members during the day. This destroys the team spirit so essential to an effective and profitable business.

Examine the ingredients of good morale to see if they are missing in your salon. Do the employees enjoy what they do? Sometimes the problem is simply that you have selected the wrong person for the job. Unfortunately, some individuals have deep-seated problems and will never enjoy anything they do. If you are sure this is the case, hire a more suitable one. Fortunately, there is almost always something else you can do to correct the situation.

Creating a sense of identity with the salon is one of the most important ways to build morale in your employees. The Madson Management System uses methods that cause employees to feel that they are an important part of a winning team. A professional job title and job description, and management that inspires confidence is also crucial. It gives the sense that they are a valued contributor to an organization that is achieving its goals. This encourages identification with the salon.

Remind each employee of the contribution they make to the success of the salon. When speaking of the business include them, by saying "we" and "our." If employees identify with the goals of the business it is an indication of good morale. Employees who are proud of their position on the staff and think of the salon as "our salon" are valuable contributors. It is only natural that people work harder for what they consider theirs than for what they consider yours. If the salon employees are lacking this attitude, the morale needs improvement. Strengthen your employee's indentification with the salon and its goals and the need for a team effort to achieve those goals.

Pet grooming is hard work. Fatigue from the physical work of grooming and attending to pets can affect the performance of the workers. Minimize the use of overtime. Part-time, or on-call workers can fill the need and you can avoid paying an inflated wage. Boredom also diminishes an employee's performance. It is reduced by varying work assignments whenever possible. If eligible, let the employee practice new skills under your supervision. This can reawaken lagging interest and also be a source for future expansion. The better paying positions on the support staff should be filled by present employees who have learned advanced skills under your supervision. Keep your business growing to create interest and the opportunity for promotion.

Display trust in their work by not monitoring it excessively. Don't abandon them, however. Except trainees, the team needs to know that the coach is checking on them, but not "standing over" them. Frequently discuss each employee's work with them. Learn their individual capabilities and put them to use. When problems arise, let the employees know you are there to help them and they can count on receiving a thoughtful answer. With the assembly line method of operation the manager is the last to see the pet. This provides an opportunity to evaluate the grooming performed up to that point, affirm the strengths, and correct the weaknesses. Keep in mind that you and the employees have an agreement to work together to achieve the goals of the business plan.

Protect the integrity and authority of each position on the staff. If you have a concern about the bathing department, talk to the pet bathers. Don't address your concerns about the bathing department to the receptionist or trimmer. The bathing department supervisor is responsible for the bathing department. Reinforce his authority and responsibility by taking your question to him directly.

Make each employee feel significant. Let them know their work is important to you. Pay as much attention to their successes as you do to their failures. Communicate the attitude that their growth and development is important to you. Respect their achievements by praising them when they make a valuable contribution to the operation. Acknowledge that they help bring the goals of the business closer to fruition. When they need improvement tell them how to improve their performance. If an employee isn't doing well and isn't given instruction, the eventual reprimand comes as quite a shock.

Good morale doesn't just happen in a pet grooming salon, it is created. The manager exercises control in a manner that gains the trust and commitment of the team. A high wage contributes to good morale, but is not enough to maintain it. Feeling appreciated, respected, and part of a proud team pursuing mutual goals is far more important.

BENEFITS OF SUPPORT STAFF MEETINGS

Staff meetings are characteristic of pet grooming salons following the Madson Management System. The most common purposes for a staff meeting are to gather ideas, update information, announce decisions, provide a demonstration, dispel rumors, and provide new information.

You can exercise your own judgment as to when to schedule staff meetings to discuss issues. Schedule them when the noisy environment of a pet salon cannot distract the process. Hold them in an open, comfortable, and well-lit area conducive to seating the employees together.

Schedule staff meetings into the appointment book at regular intervals. You may choose to book one or two fewer appointments on the day of the meeting. This will allow the workers to finish their duties earlier and invest the time in a productive staff meeting. During the meeting the receptionist can cover the phone and front counter as necessary. Alternatively, the employees can stay for one hour after the salon closes for a staff meeting. A nice touch is to provide a light snack for the employees. If you plan to serve a snack at the meeting, save it for afterwards. A full stomach inhibits an employee's participation.

General staff meetings include all employees of the pet salon with an agenda applicable to every member of the staff. Hold departmental staff meetings when the agenda is specific to that department. A staff meeting for trimmers, for example, would only cover topics for trimmers. Before the meeting inform the staff of the agenda so they will have time to consider issues they wish to discuss.

The general format of a staff meeting is; announce the agenda, present the agenda, ask for comments about the agenda, summarize the meeting and its conclusions, and adjourn. Plan and organize the meeting ahead of time. Remain in control of the meeting by keeping all comments material to the agenda. Keep the attention of the employees by encouraging their participation.

The effective manager has a number of questions for which answers must come from others. Staff meetings can be an opportunity to form a "think tank" among the participants relative to a specific issue. Pose questions and open the floor to response. Listen for replies no matter how diverse. While comments will start from different points of view, strive to find common agreements. The conclusion should reflect this diversity of opinion.

Staff meetings have not been in common use in most pet grooming salons and many employees have never attended one. At the first staff meeting explain the format and purpose of staff meetings. The relatively small number of employees in a pet salon, usually two to five, will contribute to the flow of information. Unlike employees of large businesses, pet salon employees have the opportunity to develop close relationships. They are usually less shy with each other and more inclined to speak up at staff meetings. Express your desire to hear from them by saying things such as, "I would like to know what your thoughts are." Staff meetings, to be effective, must be more than pronouncements by the manager. They must be forums for the views of all employees.

If two employees conflict with each other at a staff meeting, do not permit it to become disruptive to the purpose of the meeting. Invite comments from others about a solution to the disagreement. If they have no comments, then you must advise and get things back on track. If you are unable to do so, ask the involved employees to meet with you privately to attempt a resolution of the conflict. The principle is that a few must not allowed to disrupt the agenda of the many.

If one employee "takes over," interrupt and say, "let's get another opinion" to transfer control of the floor to another participant. If someone interrupts a speaker, move the conversation back to the one interrupted. Say, "Did you finish making your point?", or "Did you have anything more to add?"

When an employee disagrees don't become defensive. If the question draws an emotional response, find out why. Listen carefully to the speaker with a calm expression and never interrupt the objector. When they have finished, consider what they said, be certain you understand their point, then respond. If the objector seems hostile, seek the opinion of others and thereby ease the display of hostility. Ask others for suggestions. If you don't remain calm and in control, the hostile person gains strength. Hostility seems to spread when it meets with more hostility, however, it loses impetus when you remain relaxed. The hostility then becomes an annoyance to the group and they will resist it. Face the group, and in a composed manner say, "He is upset because of...are there any comments?" This involves the group in the discussion and helps the hostile individual feel understood. Sometimes a participant won't drop a personal subject. Say in front of the group, "I would be glad to discuss that with you privately, why don't we talk after the staff meeting."

A fun exercise to induce camaraderie at staff meetings is to have each employee admit one mistake made since the last meeting. When one employee starts admitting mistakes, the others in the group will usually remember their own. The managers good natured acceptance of these mistakes will encourage openness. Employees respect a manager who allows room for honest mistakes. Employees who feel free to acknowledge errors will make fewer mistakes.

A good practice to follow before adjournment is to open the floor to suggested topics for future meetings. A number of matters can arise and if you can resolve an issue quickly, do so. If it isn't important to have an issue resolved at the meeting, make a note and follow-up faithfully on any commitments. An exception is when an important matter arises such as safety. Don't wait until the next meeting. Take the time to get the facts, discuss it with the staff, and plan corrective action. If there are no further comments from the staff, close the meeting by thanking them for their participation. Remind them you are always available to answer their questions. At the next staff meeting, review all the matters brought up at the previous meeting and the action taken on each.

If the meeting runs too long, set a time limit for the next one and stick to it. This restriction usually keeps the meeting on track without sacrificing employee feedback.

The pet salon employees have a natural concern about changes in the salon's operation caused by implementing the management system. General staff meetings keep them updated on the progress toward the achievement of the business plan. The employee's concern is a positive sign of their involvement in the business. Yet, if you don't explain new goals, fear for their job can arise and discourage future contributions. The Madson Management System presents the pet grooming salon with short-range goals to accomplish in the early stages, and long-range goals for the future. Employees stay involved when they are aware of their contribution and potential for advancement in both the short-term and long-term.

Effective staff meetings benefit the salon operation and the support staff. Manage work time better by delivering information to the whole staff. You can obtain immediate reactions and clarification to avoid misunderstandings can be promptly requested and given. Problems with the content of the previous meeting can also be reviewed and corrected. Perhaps more importantly, the staff meeting promotes camaraderie, and a sense of contributing to the objectives of the business.

COMMON PERFORMANCE PROBLEMS

Where there are employees there are job performance problems to resolve. Some of the most common problems are conflicts, tardiness, absenteeism, substance abuse, lack of motivation, and rumors. The sooner you resolve a problem the better for the employee, the support staff, and the achievement of objectives. Some performance problems affect the safety of the staff and pets and corrective action must be immediate.

Correction is difficult to accept for anyone but especially for groomers with an artistic temperament. It can open personal wounds, lower morale, produce resentment, and reduce productivity rather than resolve a performance problem. Properly handled, it can also do exactly the reverse and benefit the working relationship. Before you attempt correction get all the facts in order and secure evidence, particularly when it involves hearsay.

Administer the correction as promptly as possible and in private, never in front of the other employees. Show your awareness of the positive contributions they have made, and ask their help in correcting a problem. Approach the problem seriously, with concern, and the determination to find a remedy. Remain patiently focused on the purpose of the counselling. Don't become sidetracked if the employee becomes angry or defensive. The purpose of counselling is to secure an agreement that the behavior will not recur.

Conflicts

Conflicts among the workers can arise in any pet grooming salon. Resolve conflicts without being drawn into the hostility. Encourage them to bring the conflict into the open rather than hiding it where it will only worsen, and erupt again. The source of the conflict is usually from a personality clash, old grievance, or jealousy. Sometimes one employee will be clearly in the wrong. However, most of the time there are gray areas and the conflict requires mediation by you.

When mediating a conflict between two employees, never take sides. Unless the employees resolve the issue between them it will remain unchanged. You cannot impose solutions from the outside. Employees will look for indications that you favor one or the other, and feel resentful toward you if you show favoritism. Don't shake your head in agreement or dissent and hold your comments until you have allowed both sides to speak. When you reply, emphasize that your perspective is work-related. If you must make a judgment it will be in the interest of the business. Encourage them to resolve the conflict between them. Do not allow it to continue affecting the work of the support staff and the goals of the business.

Tardiness

Employees who have a habit of tardiness are a frustration. If you are indifferent to tardiness it will continue disrupting your schedule and harming morale. It discourages employees who make an effort to be punctual. Allow for occasional, unavoidable incidents, such as traffic jams, late public transportation, or medical emergencies. However, frequent tardiness is different. It's causes lie in their personality and attitude toward their job. Make a note of every incident in the employee's personnel file. Tell the employee you observed the time they arrived, and then ask what held them up. Remind them that the Madson Employee Handbook informed them of the necessity of reporting on time. If they are repeatedly tardy, let them know they risk receiving a poor job performance evaluation.

If the habitually late, but otherwise good employee has a reason that merits consideration, consider arranging a more flexible schedule. Commend timely employees at the salon's staff meetings but do not rebuke late ones, do that privately.

Absenteeism

Pet grooming salons have relatively small staffs which suffer from absenteeism. Members of a pet salon's staff cannot be replaced by calling temporary employment agencies. Absenteeism is costly in a pet grooming salon. Sometimes it forces the owner to cancel appointments if a replacement worker cannot cover the scheduled pet care services. When absenteeism is caused by illness it is unavoidable. Try to develop contacts with groomers who are willing to work on demand. When absenteeism is not caused by illness you must discover and correct the cause.

The reasons for absenteeism are many. It may indicate a poor work attitude, boredom, family problems, or vindictive behavior aimed toward the manager. Whatever the cause, keep it to a minimum. When an employee is absent record the occurrence in their personnel file. Be sure they know you keep records of absenteeism and other job performance issues. Let them know their absence was difficult for the entire staff and find out why they were absent. If the absence was unavoidable, forgive it; if it was correctable, require them to correct it. If absenteeism is habitual, make sure your staff knows it is cause for termination.

Excessive absenteeism drains the salon's profitability. If an employee's absenteeism is excessive, and there is no acceptable explanation, document the missed days in a warning letter. Give one copy to the employee and place the second copy in the employee's personnel file. The letter warns of the consequences of suspension, probation, and termination unless the employee improves their attendance record to the satisfaction of the manager. The support staff functions by teamwork and the habitually missing employee has turned their back on the team.

Review the attendance records at the same time as the twice yearly job performance evaluations. Institute a reward system for employees with perfect, or near perfect, attendance records. Offer small gifts or complimentary tickets to events. If an employee is absent because of long periods of overtime use part-time and on-call assistance instead.

Substance Abuse

Substance abuse has become endemic in the business world. It is possibly the most difficult performance problem to correct. Dependency on alcohol or drugs is destructive resulting in the loss of a job, family, and savings. Employees with the problem will hide it. You need to be able to tell if substance abuse is the source of performance problems. Substance abusers often call in sick, and are accident prone. Temperaments may change from day to day or even several times during the same work day. Productivity will suffer, and the safety of pets and staff will be jeopardized along with failing performance standards.

Slurred speech, bloodshot eyes, a chronic cold, lack of coordination, frequent use of the bathroom (to use the substance), and a fixed stare with dilated pupils can be physical indications of substance abuse. If enough indicators exist, intervention is required.

The employee must be confronted. However, have intervention programs such as local substance abuse programs ready. If the employee's behavior places the safety of the pets at risk, do not allow them to continue grooming. They must be terminated. If they demonstrate a sincere desire to correct their problem, agree to an intervention program. If the risk to pets is manageable, a probationary period may be appropriate. Document the agreement and have the employee sign it. As with all agreements and other personnel communications, keep a copy in the employee's personnel file.

At the end of the probationary period you have three options; return to normal employment status, suspension, or termination. Return them to normal status if the employee has shown substantial improvement. If the employee is making improvement but continued employment is risky, suspend them. If the condition deteriorates, or there is no change, terminate them. Substance abuse problems require constant monitoring even when there is improvement. Relapse is the rule, not the exception.

Lack of Motivation

Employees may lack motivation for several reasons, but the more common reasons are the ones that apply to business. They may be lazy, feel bored, unappreciated, or without chance for achievement. Suspect a lack of motivation when an employee's work effort is inconsistent with their ability.

Schedule a personal meeting with the employee and accurately describe the deficiency in their performance. Ask them why the deficiency is occurring and what they intend to do about it. Express understanding and concern and be sympathetic to their reasons, but never let sympathy absolve them of their responsibility.

If a problem in the salon is causing the behavior, take corrective action. If the problem is in the employee's personal life avoid probing or permitting excessive disclosure. If they begin revealing too much, be sympathetic but do not let the revelation continue. Do not take the role of a counselor. You cannot be their employer and their counselor at the same time. Encourage them to get professional counselling. Be supportive of the employee but do not take responsibility for their personal life nor exempt them of responsibility for their behavior.

Boredom.   A lack of motivation is often caused by boredom. The repetitious grooming of pets can be boring and risk their safety. The cure for boredom is variety and there are many ways to vary the work effort in a pet grooming salon. Give the groomers opportunity to groom various breeds and challenge them to learn more about them. Enrich each position by adding tasks that demand more cognitive involvement with the job. The more they have to think about what they are doing the less bored they will be by it. Provide opportunities to learn new job-related skills. Assign tasks that let them become more involved in the business and give them extra pay. For example, you can assign telemarketing duties, or have them order the salon's materials and supplies. They can distribute client brochures to a neighborhood area, run errands, or learn the responsibilities and skills of another position.

The more each employee understands the duties and responsibilities of the other members the greater benefit they will be to the salon. This creates a sense of involvement and expedites communication between team members. It also provides a resource when sudden, unexpected vacancies occur.

Lack of Recognition. An employee can lack motivation because they feel unappreciated. Remember to acknowledge an employee's performance even if it is expected. The surest way to increase a behavior is to recognize it. Don't wait until the performance is exceptional before you show appreciation for it. People need recognition for even normal, routine work behaviors. Letting the staff hear the praise will enhance its effectiveness on the receiver.

In almost every case where employees lack motivation it is because they feel insignificant. Make them feel important for their contributions. Periodically ask employees how they are doing and show an interest in them as people. Ask their opinion about decisions you must make. Employees will appreciate your interest in their contribution. Some people need more attention than others and as you discover who these employees are give them the attention they need. The research on work motivation is clear. Recognition and praise are more effective in improving work performance than a raise in pay — and a lot cheaper.

Encourage a team spirit and the attainment of team goals. Remind them of the salon's reward system and be sure to issue rewards due at performance evaluations. If the employee is passed over for promotion, offer training and advice that will increase their chance of obtaining promotion.

If the lack of motivation relates to a desire for higher pay, don't hurriedly say a raise is out of the question. Listen to and confirm the facts supporting their position. The Annual Profit and Loss Projection (Chapter Fourteen) assists you in preparing a budget that provides for raises at performance evaluations. If the facts support it, offer the employee an opportunity for a raise at the next review. In the meantime try to find other ways to compensate the employee, such as a day off with pay. If a raise is the only cause for the lack of motivation, and they are valuable, consider a small raise until the next performance evaluation.

Remind an employee whose poor performance is caused by deficient work habits or indifference that there are consequences. A poor performance evaluation reduces or precludes raises, opportunities for promotion, bonuses, or special favors. Sometimes a firm reminder is enough to stimulate an employee's participation and team spirit.

Rumors

Rumors can occur in any business and as they spread they become more distorted destroying morale. They are a common and disruptive occurrence when communication from management is poor. Rumors arise to fill the vacuum caused by ignorance. You can dispel rumors by providing the facts, using clear statements that cannot be misinterpreted. They also arise from apprehension and uncertainty. Employees often resort to rumors when they are insecure about their employment or frustrated with their job. If you are a good listener you can stop a rumor before it infects the employees.

Frequently, you can anticipate rumors. Unexplained changes in the business open the door to rumor. Provide the staff with explanations of why changes are being made before making them. Good supervisory communication with the staff reduces the prevalence of rumors.

Recurring and hostile rumors require immediate attention. If rumors originate from the same person, take corrective action directly with that individual. Hostile rumors are usually a retaliation against a supervisor or co-worker. Be willing to explore and correct the cause of the hostility but demand a halt to the rumors.

HOW TO CONDUCT A JOB PERFORMANCE EVALUATION

A performance evaluation is very rare in pet grooming salons. While nearly every business has a formal review method, the pet grooming field has neglected to adopt this valuable tool. Formally evaluate each employee twice a year. The prime months for performance evaluations are March and September. This gives you time to improve the poor performance of an employee before the busy summer and holiday seasons.

The evaluation of an employee's performance is the manager's responsibility. When there is both an owner and a manager the owner evaluates the manager and the manager evaluates the other employees. A performance evaluation compares the expectations established by the management system with the employee's actual performance. It is the formal method of reviewing the employee's performance and the basis for promotion or termination.

The primary purpose of a review system is to reinforce good performance and to improve poor performance. Both of which increase productivity. When an employee's performance is poor, achieve agreement on the need for improvement and establish a specific plan to achieve it. For instance, if a receptionist has inadequate people skills, design a remedial program of reading, demonstration, and application. When the Madson performance evaluation is completed it shows the employee where they did well and where they can improve. The evaluation process will give the manager a firmer grasp on salon operations. It will also impart greater recognition of the support staff and the extent of their contribution.

The Madson Management System minimizes paperwork. This training manual includes four sample performance evaluation forms. There is a form for the trimming department, the bathing department, the client relations department, and the manager. These forms document the evaluation process. If, upon termination, an employee denies poor performance and threatens litigation, the proof of discipline is in their personnel file.

The Madson performance evaluation forms are easily understood and filled out. Use the performance notes placed in their personnel file during the last six months to complete the performance evaluation form. Be sure to consider the entire six months prior to the review when rating the employee's performance. Don't let the performance of one month, whether exceptionally good or bad, overshadow the other five months.

The performance evaluation lists several expectations regarding work attitude and job performance. Rate the employee's proficiency with each by circling a value from one to ten. A rating of one to two is POOR. A rating of three to five is SATISFACTORY. A rating of six through eight is GOOD, ratings of nine or ten mean EXCELLENT.

Post a notice of which week in March or September will be performance evaluation week. Prepare the evaluation forms the week before the evaluation week. Schedule a private meeting with each employee of thirty minutes to one hour maximum.

Start the evaluation by making the employee comfortable with a beverage and light introductory conversation. Employees will view the twice-a-year evaluations with either apprehension or confidence, depending on how they view their performance. Therefore, a good technique to begin the evaluation is to ask the employee what they believe are their strengths and weaknesses. You then have a clue of their response when the ratings are unexpectedly low. Acknowledge your appreciation for the employee's progress since the last evaluation and encourage further development. Discuss the employee's job and make notice of the contributions they make to the objectives of the salon.

When making your comments, especially disapproval, don't damage the employee's confidence by being critical. The purpose of the evaluation is to correct performance, not criticize it. Focus your comments on specific work behavior and avoid making comments about personality characteristics. If an employee is often late, discuss the need to correct their frequent tardiness. Do not criticize their lack of responsibility. Use precise examples so the employee clearly understands the incident, or incidents, to which you are referring.

Don't wait for the performance evaluation to comment on the need for improvement, make suggestions in the period between reviews as needed. If you do this the employee will not be shocked at the evaluation when you discuss their shortcomings. If you fear hurting a sensitive employee's feelings by avoiding their weaknesses both they and the salon cannot improve. Also, they may think you don't care about their weak points if you do not discuss them at the evaluation.

When finished, allow the employee to state their reaction to what you said. After taking the employee's comments into account, seek agreement on a plan to improve the employee's weak points. By analysis of the performance evaluations you can verify the merit of a raise or promotion. You may also find an employee has capabilities or talents of which you were not aware. At the evaluation, employees can discuss their future, problems with the job, and any other job-related matters on their mind.

The practice of evaluating every employee's performance shows the intention of management to develop a professional support staff. The evaluation is a difficult process at times, but it's one of your most effective tools to meet the objectives of the business. When handled properly it creates good working relationships and a positive work environment. The completed performance evaluation becomes a permanent part of the employee's personnel file.

The Madson job performance evaluation forms are in Appendix B. Make several copies of each and keep a supply available in the salon's files.

PROCEDURES FOR EMPLOYEE TERMINATION

Termination is a word reserved for describing the departure of an employee from a company for disciplinary reasons. Terminating an employee is a last resort after failure to correct performance problems. An employer is vulnerable in this litigious society to unlawful termination lawsuits. They can literally destroy a business. By carefully following proper procedures when terminating an employee this need not be a concern.

The employee's personnel file should document every occasion when an employee has been admonished about performance problems. The file should describe the specific instances of deficient performance clearly showing why it was substandard and intolerable. The documentation must include written evidence that the employee had an opportunity to improve. This written evidence is in the form of a written warning.

A written warning is the next step following failure of verbal admonishments. It details the problem behavior and the correction that management requires. It also confirms that a failure to correct the problem behavior will result in probation. Offer assistance to the employee to help them correct their performance. Present the warning letter to the employee in private and clearly explain its impact. The meeting should occur after hours to avoid disrupting the work of the day. At the end of the discussion have the employee sign a copy of the letter. Explain to them that their signature does not signify that they agree, only that they have read and understand the warning. Give one copy to the employee and file the original in the employee's personnel file.

If there is no improvement within the time agreed upon, place them on probation. Allow a reasonable period to correct the behavior using specific beginning and ending dates. Don't abandon them during probation, continue affirming that you want to achieve a solution to the problem. If the employee does not take the opportunity to improve, it is grounds for termination.

Once you've made the decision to terminate act quickly, considerately, and unemotionally. Inform the employee in writing of the decision to end their employment. Include a request to return any property of the salon still in their possession. Present the final paycheck immediately, or, no later than twenty-four hours. Choose a time for this procedure when possible emotional flare-ups cannot affect the normal course of business. Minimize the trauma of termination for the employee and the other members of the support staff. By properly handling a termination a supervisor will develop and keep the respect of the remaining employees.

Since this procedure subjects the employer to potential wrongful termination charges it could result in substantial financial penalties. Therefore, it must follow strict guidelines which protect an employee's legal rights. Every employer should take responsibility for learning their own state and local guidelines but here are some general rules to follow. The rules cover all aspects of employment potentially exposing the employer to litigation and include summaries of information already discussed.

1. Print the following above the applicant's signature on the employment application: "If employed by the company, I agree to abide by its rules and regulations. I understand that my employment is not guaranteed for a specific time period."

2. When interviewing a candidate avoid any references that might construed as promises of permanent employment. Avoid all terms implying employer commitment, such as "permanent employment," "lifetime employment," and "career position."

3. Review employee handbooks and personnel manuals. Be sure they do not contain guarantees that an employee will not be discharged except for just cause. Eliminate words like permanent or career.

4. List in the handbook the reasons for termination. Include a general provisions clause permitting termination for any reason the salon deems sufficient.

5. In non-union situations, replace the term "probationary period" with introductory or orientation period. The term probation implies that once the employee has successfully completed this period, his or her employment is permanent. The words in The Madson Employee Handbook are chosen carefully to avoid improper insinuations.

6. Document every instance when an employee is verbally admonished to improve their performance. The documentation should include time, place, individuals, specific instances of the infraction, and admonishment. E.g. "On September 3, 1988 at the ABC Salon, I (manager's name), told (name of employee), that his frequent tardiness was unacceptable and must be corrected. He has been tardy six times in two weeks."

7. Following failure of verbal admonishments give the disciplined employee a written description of the behavior needing correction. Include a time-limit, and a warning that he will be placed on probation if the behavior is not corrected. Have the employee sign the letter confirming he has received and understands it.

8. If the problem continues place the employee on probation (not less than a week or more than thirty days). Give him a written warning that if the problem persists he will be terminated following probation. As before, have the employee sign the warning.

9. Document every proposed termination thoroughly. Review it to make certain a valid business purpose exists and that the termination does not violate any statute, policy, or specific employment agreement.

10. Termination can be immediate if a crime has been committed or when there exists an immediate danger to health and safety. In those circumstances where immediate action is necessary, suspend the employee in question pending investigation of the facts. If an investigation confirms the facts, send the employee a letter of termination. The letter must only inform them of the termination. Do not accuse them of wrongdoing.

Consult an attorney when doubt arises about how to proceed with any disciplinary procedure.

PROCEDURES FOR VOLUNTARY DEPARTURES

When an employee voluntarily leaves your employ it is a good business practice to have an exit interview. Schedule the exit interview for the employee's last workday and have their final paycheck ready. Information from the departing employee can be quite valuable to you. Ask them if they have any recommendations that they feel might improve the salon's operation. Assure them there will be no hard feelings regarding any information they might provide.

Ask questions and listen for answers that might suggest potential problems that could trouble the business. Determine if problems exist in the salon that led the employee to quit. Ask the employee if they would consider applying for work again at the salon in the future. If not, why? Always be alert for answers that propose ways to improve the operation.

Have the employee's personnel file available and confirm that the records are correct and complete. Ask them where they want the W-2 tax form sent. Collect any of the salon's possessions the employee may have, such as keys. When you complete your questions, wish the employee good fortune in the future and present the final paycheck. Be sure to provide a letter of recommendation for a deserving employee if they request one.

Take precautionary measures if the departure of an employee prompts any suspicion of potential vulnerability. Ask the employee to write a short statement explaining why they are leaving; then have the employee sign and date the statement. The typical reasons for a voluntary departure are pregnancy, illness, emergencies, retirement, or relocation. These are not volatile issues so it is probable they will agree to do this.

Whether by the employee's choice, or a management decision, the personnel file should contain a concise picture of the reason for departure.

DEVELOPING A SAFETY PROGRAM

CHAPTER
10

A safety program is an essential component of a professionally managed pet grooming salon. Pet grooming involves safety concerns for humans as well as the additional safety measures required for pets. Train the support staff in the proper handling of all sizes and breeds of pets. Train them also in the safe use of the salon's equipment, tools, grooming supplies, and emergency procedures. As an added precaution, require employees to have a tetanus booster before beginning employment.

The pet grooming salon safety program is the responsibility of the manager. He must make the employees aware of their responsibility to protect the safety of every person and pet. He must train the employees in safety policies and procedures, and continually enforce them. Aside from health and welfare concerns a safety violation resulting in the injury or death of a client or pet could result in litigation and bankruptcy.

The manager is a safety engineer of sorts caring for the personnel, clients, and pets. Two other positions have supervisory responsibility for safety. These positions are the master pet trimmer and the bathing department supervisor. The master pet trimmer ensures that the trimming department follows proper safety measures. The bathing department supervisor acts similarly. He makes sure pets are treated kindly, shampoos and flea dips are mixed properly, towels are sanitized, and that pets are not left sitting alone.

A safety program includes initial training in preventive measures, regular sessions of reinforcement training, and practice drills in preparation for an emergency. The Madson Employee Handbook contains the most crucial safety procedures.

Train new employees in the salon's safety policies and procedures as part of their initial job training program. The safety procedures in the handbook serve as a reinforcement for this training. They remind the employee of his responsibility to care for the safety of the staff, pets, and clients. The creation of a safe environment requires the cooperation of all members of management and staff.

Pet Handling Safety. Pet care services entail the handling of pets by every employee. A pet safety program should train each employee in proper pet handling procedures. The issues covered should include avoiding problems by checking on caged pets, and proper ways to hold, lift, carry, and restrain pets. Pet salons use different types of pet restraints, such as nooses, which can be potentially lethal to a unattended pet. Make a standing rule in your salon never to leave pets unattended unless they are in their cages. Dogfights can occur spontaneously. Train employees how to avoid them, and how to separate fighting dogs when unavoidable.

If you are not using the Madson Employee Handbook, describe all of the handling methods practiced in your pet salon and include it with the employee handbook.

Bathing Safety. The tub is a dangerous area in a pet salon for both people and pets. Apply a non-slip surface to the bottom of the bathing tub to protect the pet. Place one on the floor around the tub to protect employees. Place vinyl boards with small holes in them on the floor of the tub. The water runs through the holes keeping the pet's feet out of soapy water and protecting it from slipping. Line the floor of the cages with the vinyl boards also. Urine from the pet flows through the boards to the bottom of the cage. This keeps the pet out of it and saves the time spent rewashing the pet. There are non-slip vinyl boards also for employees to stand on where the floor gets wet. Use these at the base of the tub where the pet bather stands, and consider their use at grooming stations.

Equipment Safety. A pet grooming salon safety program should include information about the use, maintenance, and repair of equipment. The correct use of your salon's heavy equipment and specialized tools should be in writing for easy reference.

Set up a regular service cycle for all equipment and mark the dates for periodic service checkups on the manager's calendar. Check heavily used equipment such as air conditioners and blowdryers weekly.

The heavy use of electricity in pet salons requires suitable wiring. Be sure your salon's electrical system can safely handle the demands of the salon's heavy equipment. Employees should check electrical cords for wear before they begin work and inform management if they detect burning smells. Establish a working relationship with a good electrician who is available on short notice. Have the electrical system checked periodically for signs of problems.

If an employee finds a loose nut or screw on the floor he should take it to the manager for repair. Repair broken furniture and equipment quickly or put a warning label on it until fixed.

Blow-dryers mounted on wheels rapidly accumulate hairballs which freezes the wheel movement. This causes them to tip over easily when moved. Have employees regularly check the wheels and clean them as required.

Sharp blades and scissors require protective storage and mounting. Mount them with sharp edges covered.

Sweep up pet hair after each grooming task and wipe up any liquid spills immediately.

Have employees inform you of any equipment problems to prevent accidents and further equipment damage. If you care for the equipment properly, it will last longer, perform better, and be safer to operate.

Fire Safety. Fire is the most catastrophic event that could affect a pet grooming salon. Whether or not local fire codes require it get a water sprinkler system. Sprinklers can dramatically reduce the danger to people and pets from a fire. Install smoke detectors and consider a no-smoking rule for your salon.

With or without sprinklers, management has the responsibility to have an adequate number of properly maintained fire extinguishers. Instruct employees in the location of every fire extinguisher in the pet salon. Many fire extinguishers include warnings about using them on certain types of burning materials. Read all of the warning and instruction labels and train the employees in their proper use.

A fire safety program should include fire drills. Stage a practice fire drill occasionally and evaluate the performance of the employees. Post the location of all emergency exits. Assign an employee whose first responsibility is to call the fire department. The fire drill includes the assignment of one employee per extinguisher. It should cover evacuation procedures for people and pets. While exiting, employees can attempt to save pets by releasing locks on cages. The main principle of evacuation however, to save human life first. Save pets as safety allows. Designate a specific location for the staff to gather themselves and pets outside the building. By practicing fire drills the management and support staff may save many lives, and the business.

Fire and water damage can destroy your records. Your client and pet history filecards and business files should be regularly duplicated and kept in safe storage outside of the salon. By doing this you could be back in business within a few days, with your records intact. The protection afforded by fireproof file cabinets is well worth the extra cost to protect vital records, and is a sensible alternative.

Instruct employees about the "danger spots" in your salon such as pilot flames, so they don't place flammable solutions near them.

Contact your local fire department and request assistance in formulating a fire safety program. Incorporate their instructions in safety policies to improve the safety conditions of the salon.

Chemical Safety. The manager is responsible for keeping a list of all toxic chemicals, such as flea dips, used in the salon. He is also responsible for giving employees instructions in their safe use, and emergency first-aid procedures. Store all toxic chemicals in a locked storage facility.

Emergency Procedures. In the event of an accident or emergency vital information should be readily available. Post emergency phone numbers at each telephone. Include the number for the salon's veterinarian and an alternative in case the first one is unavailable. Post the phone numbers for police and fire officials, and the name of the salon's physician and hospital or clinic.

The Emergency Report form (illustration 10-2) provides a systematic method to gather information about an emergency. Clients, lawyers, government officials, and insurance companies may require information about your emergency procedures. You can refer to the Emergency Report for information rather than having to rely on memory. There are federal, state, and local regulations governing accidents and injuries involving employees. You must be aware and in compliance with these.

THE GROOM ALERT SYSTEM

The Groom Alert system is an important feature of safe and humane pet care. It uses a Groom Alert symbol on the Client and Pet History filecard and a Groom Alert cage tag. These visual alerts inform the staff to check the filecard before grooming or handling a pet assigned a Groom Alert.

Every business day a few pets require special care. This can result from veterinary instructions, aged and ill health, or behavioral problems such as "biters." Special supervision of these pets is mandatory. Every employee must be aware of the special need and how to respond to it.

When a pet requires special attention the receptionist and manager assign the Groom Alert in two steps. First, the Groom Alert circle on the Client and Pet History filecard is marked according

WASTE DISPOSAL

- Waste storage area in safe location and regularly cleaned.
- Adequate container(s) to hold waste between collections.
- Pet hair waste placed in tightly-sealed disposable bags before the waste container.

PET CAGES

- Cages sanitized daily and after each pet elimination.
- Cage doors and locks regularly checked and maintained.
- Pet leashes, collars, and other possessions safely stored.

SUPPLIES STORAGE

- Flea-dip concentrate and other toxics stored separately in locked compartment.
- Flammables stored in safety cans.
- No flammables used near electrical or heating units.
- Inventory of hazardous materials.
- Smoking prohibited in storage area.

BATHING AND TRIMMING DEPARTMENTS

- Equipment maintenance program planned and implemented.
- Sharp pointed tools in safe storage when not in use.
- Regular use of grooming tool cleaners and antiseptics.
- Adequate ventilation for clipper boosters.
- Pet hair clippings placed in disposable bags and sealed when full.
- Cigarette butts or ashes never disposed with pet hair waste or other flammables.
- Entire trimming department adequately illuminated and additional spot lighting on each bather and trimmer station.
- Non-slip floor treatment at each bather and trimmer station.
- Well-stocked first aid kit available.
- Grooming table/counter surfaces replaced when worn, and sanitized regularly.
- Adjustable height work tables.
- Pets never left alone in tub or at groomer stations.
- Pet restraints used properly and regularly checked for repair or replacement.
- Towels properly sanitized between use and replaced when worn.
- Ventilation and air conditioning adequate to handle heat from blow-dryers.
- Pesticide/insecticide treatments as needed.
- Blow-dryer cords not allowed to run along floor or contact pets.
- No water near electrical sources.
- Ground fault interrupters used in areas near water.
- Area around water heater kept clear and water temperature controlled.
- Heating elements shielded.
- Pet stairways to grooming stations to minimize lifting of large pets.
- Adequate room between groomer stations to keep pets separated.
- No untended pets in departments.
- Protective gloves available for handling toxics.
- Pet and people safety guidelines posted for employees.

CLIENT RELATIONS DEPARTMENT

- Client reception area separated from operations area by wall, counter, and a gate opening toward the salon's interior.
- Client reception area well-lit, free from obstructions, and furnished with a large, uncluttered counter.
- No untended pets allowed in client reception area.
- Seating available and safe cigarette disposal.
- First aid kit available.
- Aerosol cans protected from heat.

ENTRYWAY AND PARKING

- Entryway clear of debris and pet urine or feces.
- Stairtreads, sidewalk, and handrails kept in good repair and free of ice, snow, or debris.
- Plant growth controlled and water hoses stored safely when not in use.
- Sanitary "potty-walking" area provided.
- Adequate day and night illumination.
- Electrical signs included in regular equipment maintenance program.

10-1

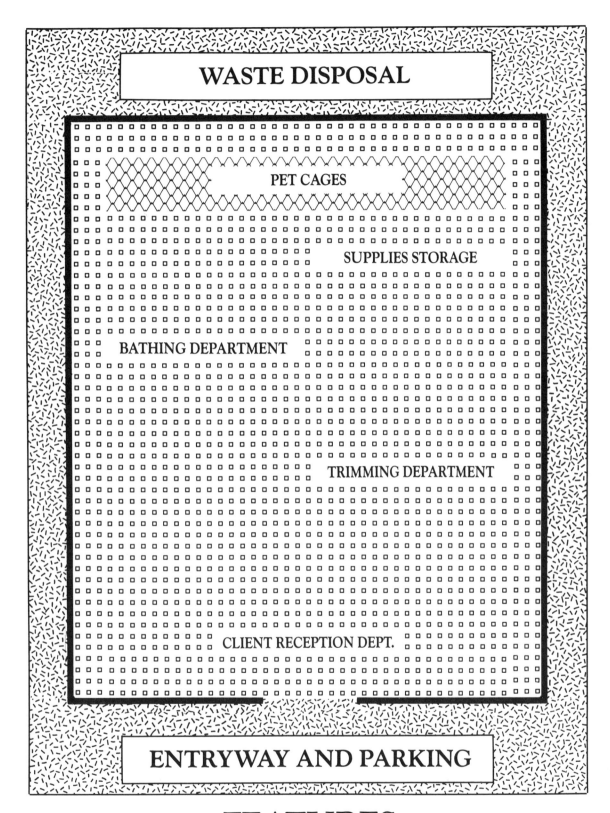

FEATURES
OF A
PET GROOMING SALON SAFETY PROGRAM

EMERGENCY REPORT

Date of emergency _____ Location _____

Description _____
_____
_____
_____
_____

Persons involved _____
(address and phone) _____
_____

Pets involved _____
(owner name) _____

Employees present _____
_____

Witnesses _____
(name, address & _____
phone) _____
_____
_____
_____

Emergency Transport _____
Physician/Hospital _____
Veterinarian _____
Police/Fire Officials _____
Treatment Required _____
_____
_____

Insurance Contact _____
(name/date/time) _____
_____

Attorney Contact _____
(name/date/time) _____
_____

Follow-up Action _____
_____

Manager Notes _____
_____
_____
_____

☐ Additional comments on reverse side of this report.

10-2

Groom Alert is a system of acquiring information necessary to provide consistently safe pet care services. Pets with conditions requiring special care are assigned a Groom Alert symbol. The symbol "alerts" the staff to read the description of a pet's condition, and before proceeding, discuss appropriate grooming procedures with the manager.

GROOM ALERT FILECARD INFORMATION

The Madson Client and Pet History filecard has been designed to display Groom Alert information for easy reference. Groom Alert symbols on the firecard alert the staff to the information. Instructions to complete Client and Pet History filecards are given in Appendix A.

GROOM ALERT CAGE TAGS

The Groom Alert tag enhances failsafe pet grooming. By attaching it to the pet's cage door, the staff is alerted to check the Groom Alert description and consult with the manager before handling the pet.

to the instructions in Appendix A. Include specific notes about the special condition on the client and pet history filecard. Attach any veterinary instructions to the filecard also. Second, place a groom alert symbol, such as the Madson Groom Alert Cage Tag, on the cage door. This will alert the staff to look at the filecard for special handling requirements.

Instruct employees to discuss the nature of the alert with you before they proceed with a pet. By following the groom alert system you will improve the salon's safety record and reputation for humane pet care services.

AVOIDING MISTAKES

Avoid an attitude of indifference to mistakes. Many mistakes are not inevitable. Proper training and supervision will prevent many mistakes. The worst mistake involves the neglect of a pet resulting in its injury or death. A pet care service business cannot afford mistakes.

Neglect is intolerable in a pet grooming salon. Clients intrust their pets to the salon's care and an ethical and legal responsibility exists to safeguard their welfare. A frequent cause of injury to pets is being left unattended by a staff member. The instinct of most animals is to jump off the grooming table, or out of the wash tub, resulting in an injury. Salons that use noose-style pet restraints know that if a pet jumps from a grooming table it can be strangled. This requires staff members to keep a constant watch on the pet. One injury or death can lead to a major lawsuit that closes a pet grooming salon.

Always be alert for safety violations and never hesitate to remind the support staff to be cautious when handling pets. Make them understand that their actions affect others. Remind them of their responsibility to follow the policies and procedures in the Employee Handbook.

Some mistakes are honest mistakes. The employee may be alert and doing their best yet a mistake happens because of inexperience, misinformation, or a lack of supervision. Never assign a task involving pet safety to an untrained and inexperienced employee. Don't take unnecessary risks.

Anticipate the effect of a mistake and ready yourself to handle the situation. Keep your anger in check and maintain control. You may be disappointed and upset but the first priority is to reduce the consequences of the mistake. When the situation has been corrected discuss the mistake with those involved. The correct response is, review the actions that led to its occurrence and train the offender in the proper procedure.

Tell employees how they handle a mistake is important to you and if they deny a mistake they make it worse. Encourage employees to come to you when they make mistakes. You can accomplish this by adopting the attitude that acknowledging a mistake provides an opportunity to learn. Many mistakes can be prevented if employees feel free to "bother you" with questions, so always be available. Bring up these mistakes in staff meetings for the benefit of the entire staff. However, two admonitions apply. Never address the problem in a manner which demeans the employee. Simply use the incident as an example of an error anyone can commit. Secondly, never let the emphasis on mistakes exceed the emphasis on proper conduct. In other words, don't put out more weed killer than you do fertilizer.

An employee who constantly makes mistakes needs firm correction and possible disciplinary action. All mistakes should be noted in the employee's personnel file for future reference. Reviewing the files to find similarities in past mistakes may help avoid repeating those mistakes. By taking this approach to mistakes the staff will know they can never overlook a mistake or say it was acceptable.

CLIENT RELATIONS THAT BRING THEM BACK AGAIN AND AGAIN

CHAPTER

11

The Madson Management System consists of policies, procedures, forms, records, and promotions enabling you to satisfy and expand the client base. The term client relations refers to the art of turning a customer into a client. You will notice that the word customer replaces the word client. A customer is someone who uses services on one occasion and may never return. A client is one who patronizes a salon and with whom the salon has a fiduciary relationship. Good client relations is the responsibility of the manager but requires participation by every employee. Financial success in pet grooming requires more than providing clients with the finest grooming. It requires developing a relationship with the customer that converts them to a satisfied and loyal client.

BONDING CLIENTS WITH EFFECTIVE CLIENT RELATIONS

Pet owners have many places to shop for pet grooming services. They will go elsewhere if they are dissatisfied with your salon's services. They are purchasing good grooming but they are also buying the way you treat them and their pet. Even if the pet is treated well a pet owner will not return unless they too are treated well. A satisfied clientele makes more appointments, and expands the client base by referring you to others.

When a client feels good about his decision to use your services it creates a bond of loyalty between client and salon.

121

Use these seven keys and
clients will return
again and again.

You do not need the lowest
price in town to increase client
loyalty. Few clients select a pet
grooming salon by the lowest
price. They desire the best value.
Your fees may be a little higher
than some competitors, but if
your quality is better you will
be known for offering the best
value and increase client loyalty.

Professional pet grooming
salons emphasize client services
as well as the finest styles of
grooming. Loyal clients enjoy
visiting the pet grooming salon
confident they will receive
courteous, dependable, informative, and personable service
from trained employees. Favorable impressions will stimulate
more client referrals and increase client loyalty.

Many pet owners try various
pet grooming salons looking for
quality. Quality pet care service
means not only the finest style
of grooming, but humane pet
handling procedures and showing concern for a pet's condition
by using a Pet Groomer's Report
and Health Alert. Quality
means you are serious in advancing your professional reputation and you believe your
client's pets deserve the best.

CONFIDENCE

When clients believe you are reliable, and stand behind the services you offer, they will have confidence in your pet grooming salon. Begin now to build client confidence by implementing effective management and you will increase client loyalty.

LOCATION

There is power in a convenient location, but it is not enough to increase client loyalty in a poorly managed salon. Pet owners are willing to travel further to a professional salon that properly cares for their beloved pets. It is a struggle to do business in a poor location, but until you can move to a better one, stress all of the other client loyalty keys.

INFORMATION

Encourage and answer client questions. Assist them in solving pet care problems and fully explain all service options available. Sharing the time with your clients increases client loyalty. Distribute informative materials to clients. If an employee can't answer a client's questions, have them tell the client they will get a supervisor to assist them.

PRESTIGE

Pet grooming salons can be prestigious. An attractive, well-maintained, hygienic environment creates a powerful image in the client's mind. Status conscious pet owners will identify with the professional image and tell others it is the only salon they patronize. Promote a prestigious image of your salon with advertising that emphasizes your salon's superior attributes.

Good client relations consists of satisfying the client at every level of expectation. A salon following the Madson Management System will condition clients to expect a full-service, professional pet grooming salon.

1. Expert grooming and humane pet care.
2. A hygienic and safe environment, both outside and inside.
3. Service by an attentive, courteous, and informative staff.
4. A clean, orderly reception area with detailed service records.
5. Informational forms explaining pet care services, fees, hours of operation, and appointment scheduling programs.
6. Extra assistance volunteered.
7. Quick resolution of complaints.

Every customer contact is an opportunity for manager and staff to bond a loyal client. Each telephone call, appointment, or drop-in visit, provides an average of three to five minutes to make a favorable impression. By consistently using the Madson Management System policies, procedures, and forms you can create valuable impressions in those few moments. You will build loyalty, increase referrals, and boost revenue.

CLIENT RELATIONS POLICIES AND PROCEDURES

The Madson Employee Handbook includes standards and procedures supporting effective client relations. Issues in the handbook directly related to client relations cover salon cleanliness, telephone and client courtesy, and personal appearance.

Actually, the contents of the entire handbook affect client relations. The sections on safety and the humane handling and grooming of pets all contribute to client satisfaction. Your service must go beyond grooming. Service which includes the health, safety, and comfort of people and pets is the mark of a successful pet grooming salon.

Don't assume new employees will understand and follow the client relations policies and procedures because they have read the Madson Employee Handbook. Follow through with instruction and enforcement during the orientation period.

CLIENT RELATIONS SKILLS

Effective client relations involves much more than a courteous greeting or friendly smile. It requires skills that promote the bond between clients and the salon.

Teach employees to make every client feel special and important. Help them to understand that the client is the actual employer. The words of an old song provide an important reminder, "little things mean a lot." Make sure the staff correctly spells and pronounces the name of every client and pet. At the beginning of every workday have them review the appointment schedule so they can use the proper names when clients arrive. Teach them to maintain direct eye contact with the client when accepting the pet for service. Tell them to ask for specific details on the pet care services desired. Never assume what a client desires. Even regular clients change their habits. This attention to detail makes a favorable impression on the client and lets them know you value their patronage.

Tell them to pay attention to the facial expressions, tone of voice, and body language of the client. These will give a clue to their attitude and desires. For example, if a client seems anxious to leave their pet and get to work, be thorough but hurry the process. If a client doesn't appear hurried, and wants to discuss pet care services, then take time to do so. Provide them with a Pet Care Services brochure and answer any questions.

Ask employees to take the lead in keeping the flow of information continuous between client and salon. Every client should have a thorough understanding of all of the services the salon offers. The staff should constantly provide informational materials explaining the salon's services, and encourage membership in one of the appointment scheduling programs. Rather than relying on verbal descriptions have employees display a photo album depicting the various trim styles offered.

CLIENT RELATIONS "SCRIPTS"

Effective dialogue between staff and client improves client relations. A common question such as, "Would you like an appointment next month?" is vague and non-productive. "Are you aware of our appointment scheduling programs?" piques the client's curiosity, offers information, and results in pre-scheduled and frequent appointments. Other examples of effective dialogue include, "Would you prefer a morning or afternoon appointment?", "Would you like a courtesy reminder phone call two or three days in advance?", or "Do you know we are open Sundays?" These examples make the client feel important, informed, and appreciated.

As part of the orientation and training give all new employees scripts of effective dialogue. Have them practice the lines until they learn to speak them naturally with a pleasant attitude.

THE PREFERRED CLIENT PROGRAM

Encourage every client to become a member of the Preferred Client Program. This program offers two appointment scheduling options which serve the purpose of increasing appointments. Option A is to become a standing appointment client by selecting appointment intervals of one to eight weeks. This is noted on their filecard and they receive the date of their next appointment when they pick-up their pet. As an additional courtesy, they receive a telephone reminder three days in advance of the appointment.

The second option, Option B, is to select the interval for appointment. They then receive a telephone call two weeks before the interval selected to schedule a confirmed appointment. For example, Mrs. Jones' interval between appointments is four weeks. Her last appointment was March 1. Four weeks later, March 29, her next appointment is due. Call her two weeks before March 29 to schedule the actual date and time. Instructions for the Option B scheduling program are in Telemarketing - The Revolution in Chapter Twelve.

Most important to members, the Preferred Client Program offers priority holiday appointments. This guarantees members an appointment during the peak holiday season. It is perhaps the biggest selling point of the program. If they must cancel a holiday appointment, offer them a priority position on a cancellation list.

CLIENT RELATIONS SCRIPTS

VAGUE: "Would you like an appointment next month?"

INFORMATIVE: "Have you been informed of our appointment scheduling programs yet?"

VAGUE: "Sorry, but we're booked," or "Sorry, we're busy today."

INFORMATIVE: "Our next available appointment is (date). We can make an appointment for you then, and place your name on the cancellation list for an earlier appointment. Is this arrangement acceptable to you?"

VAGUE: "We'll take good care of your pet."

INFORMATIVE: "Our staff are trained pet care professionals. (Pet's name) will receive a humane bath and constant supervision until you return."

VAGUE: "I dunno."

INFORMATIVE: "I cannot answer your question, however, the manager can assist you.

VAGUE: "Do you want the same trim again?"

INFORMATIVE: "I can show you photographs of alternative trims if you are interested in a new style for (pet's name)."

VAGUE: "Are you happy with our service?"

INFORMATIVE: "Your satisfaction is important to us. We welcome your comments about our service during your visits, and in-between." and "You can help us to serve you better by completing a Client Service Questionnaire and returning it to us at your convenience. Thank you."

PREFERRED CLIENT PROGRAM

OPTION A

Client receives

a standing appointment at a selected time interval and priority holiday scheduling. They also receive a reminder call three days in advance.

OPTION B

Client receives

an appointment scheduling call two weeks prior to a selected interval between appointments. They may then confirm the scheduling or reschedule. Priority holiday scheduling is included.

When starting a new appointment book in January, prepare the month of December for guaranteed holiday appointments. Reserve two or three weeks prior to Christmas for members only. In August, begin scheduling member's holiday appointments and inform them of the date. Non-members can schedule holiday appointments during the reserved period after November 1 once members have had first choice. Membership does have its privileges.

Every new client should have the Preferred Client Program explained to them on their first visit. They also receive the Pet Care Services brochure which explains the program. Members of the Preferred Client Program will make more appointments during the year than the average non-member. You will find your profits dramatically increased. Instruct the staff to encourage clients to become a member of this program.

APPOINTMENT CONFIRMATIONS

For Option A members, the receptionist makes an appointment confirmation call three days before each scheduled appointment. If not reached on the first attempt, call about every thirty minutes until you contact them. Any clients not reached receive calls the following day until contacted. A confirmation is not concluded until clients are reached directly or a message is left on their answering machine or with a responsible party.

When a client misses an appointment after several attempts to contact them by telephone, send a Client Response Postcard (illustration 11-11).

Daily Response Report (Receptionist)

The receptionist fills out a Daily Response Report (Receptionist) which tracks the results of appointment confirmation calls. Information about every call is noted on the report including confirmations, changes, or cancellations. There is space to record client comments about reasons for changes or cancellations.

The manager is to review the Daily Response Report when it is completed. There is a wealth of client service information in the report for use by the manager. If a client cancels because of a sick pet, express your concern by sending their pet a get well card. Make sure the receptionist follows-up. Respond to clients who have questions and special requests personally if the receptionist was unable to answer their need. This personal attention will demonstrate the importance they have with you and will increase client loyalty.

The Daily Response Report is also an excellent gauge of the receptionist's work performance. It confirms that every client was notified of their appointment three days in advance, and that detailed client comments were recorded. This provides evidence of the effectiveness of your receptionist. Underscore the significance of properly completing the report so the salon will have the information it needs. This helps the valuable Preferred Client Program members receive the excellence of service they deserve.

Make copies of the Daily Response Report (Receptionist) in illustration 11-4 and keep a supply ready for the receptionist. Instructions to complete the Daily Response Report are in Appendix A.

DAILY RESPONSE REPORT-RECEPTIONIST

Appointment Confirmation Calls

Date _____ Day of Week _____

Receptionist _____ Manager _____

CLIENT NAME	APPT. DATE	CONFIRMED? Y/N	CHANGED? Y/N	CANCELLED Y/N	COMMENTS

# of Pet Sympathy Cards	# of Get Well Cards	# of Client Response Postcards

TOTALS	APPTS. CONFIRMED	APPTS. CHANGED	APPTS. CANCELLED

11-4

MADSON CLIENT RELATIONS BUSINESS FORMS

These forms are designed to complement the management system. Properly used they enable your salon to provide client services superior to its competitors. They are tools, as important as the clippers and brushes necessary for grooming. The client forms promote your salon, organize client and pet service information, and create a professional image.

Client and Pet History Filecard

The filecard is the most important form in the pet grooming salon. It is a vital ingredient in the Madson Management System. No other filecard can replace it. It is strategically designed to accumulate the information necessary for keeping an accurate history of clients and pets. It also provides information for a sophisticated marketing program. Completing the filecard lets the client know you take a serious interest in providing professional pet care. The Madson Client and Pet History filecards are more than just a history of the pet and its owner. They are a key to higher profits.

Client Information.   List the name of the pet owner, spouse, and the address and telephone numbers, and the referral source. Note the client's rating and appointment frequency preference (Chapter Twelve), and to expedite check approval record the pet owner's driver license number. There is a "client since" space also.

Pet Information.   Record the name, gender, breed, size, color, and birthdate of each pet. Record the name and telephone number of the pet's veterinarian or clinic. The Groom Alert (Chapter Ten) area contains a checklist to identify arthritis, diabetes, epilepsy, and other medical concerns. In addition to the Groom Alert there is a Personality Profile checklist reflecting many groomer concerns about a pet's behavior. There is space to note problem conditions, such as very shy, urinating, and biting pets.

Service Information.   Enter the date of service, Groom Alert (Chapter Ten) if applicable, description of service, face-style, bather and trimmer initials, groomer comments, time promised for pick-up, total fees, total pet products purchased, and method of payment.

Client Contact History.   Enter the date, description, and type (telephone or mail) of every contact with a client.

The filecard is the lifeblood of a pet grooming salon providing information for both client service and marketing. It is crucial to keep copies of the filecards in a safe place. If you did not have safe copies, a fire could wipe out years of effort. With the copies you could be back in business in days. Instruct every employee, not just the receptionist, how to complete and interpret the filecard. They all use the filecards and must know how to do so correctly. Appendix A contains instructions on correctly completing a filecard. The filecard filing procedure in the Madson Management System is part of a unique marketing program (Chapter Twelve).

The filecard contains critical marketing information used by the receptionist and telemarketer. It allows measurement of the client base to track your success with the goals of the management system. It also permits the staff to provide those little service details that can mean so much to client satisfaction. For instance, the clients preference concerning placement of bows

© THE MADSON GROUP, INC. 1988

CIRCLE ONE **A B C D**
(Use Pencil)

APPOINTMENT FREQUENCY

WK   1   2   3   4   5   6   7   8 ____

Referred by: ____

CLIENT SINCE ____

CLIENT CONTACT HISTORY

DATE	DESCRIPTION	MAIL	PHONE

☐MR.
☐MRS.
☐MS.

OWNER LAST NAME ____   FIRST NAME ____

SPOUSE ____

STREET ____   APT. ____

CITY ____   STATE ____   ZIP ____

HOME PHONE ( ) ____   WORK PHONE ( ) ____

WORK PHONE SPOUSE ( ) ____   EMERG. PHONE ( ) ____

DRIVER NO. ____   EXPIRATION ____ / ____ / ____

VETERINARIAN ____   CLINIC ____

VET. PHONE ____   VACCINATION RECORD ____

PET NAME ____

BREED ____

COLOR ____   SIZE ____   ☐M ☐F

BIRTHDATE ____

GROOM ALERT

UNDER VETERINARY CARE ☐YES ☐NO

☐NO FLEA DIP   ☐SPECIAL SHAMPOO
☐DRY LOW HEAT   ☐BURNS EASY
☐BLIND   ☐DEAF
☐PREGNANT   ☐EPILEPTIC
☐DIABETIC   ☐ARTHRITIC
☐HEART COND.   ☐WARTS/MOLES
☐SKIN
☐OTHER ____

PERSONALITY ALERT

☐WETTER   ☐VERY SHY   ☐BITER
☐OTHER ____

PET NAME ____

BREED ____

COLOR ____   SIZE ____   ☐M ☐F

BIRTHDATE ____

GROOM ALERT

UNDER VETERINARY CARE ☐YES ☐NO

☐NO FLEA DIP   ☐SPECIAL SHAMPOO
☐DRY LOW HEAT   ☐BURNS EASY
☐BLIND   ☐DEAF
☐PREGNANT   ☐EPILEPTIC
☐DIABETIC   ☐ARTHRITIC
☐HEART COND.   ☐WARTS/MOLES
☐SKIN
☐OTHER ____

PERSONALITY ALERT

☐WETTER   ☐VERY SHY   ☐BITER
☐OTHER ____

SAMPLE — MADSON BUSINESS FORM

MADSON CLIENT AND PET HISTORY FILECARD — SIDE A

11-5

Actual Size: 5" x 8"

PET CARE SERVICE HISTORY

BOWS ☐YES ☐NO   PERFUME ☐YES ☐NO

DOES CLIENT HAVE A PREVIOUS FILECARD ☐YES ☐NO   IF YES, ENTER DETAILS OF LAST APPT. ON LINE 1 BELOW

DATE	GROOM ALERT See front	SERVICE DESCRIPTION	FACE STYLE	GROOM BY INITIALS	GROOMER COMMENTS	TIME OUT	TOTAL FEES	TOTAL PRODS.	CA, CK CH, M/V
1.	○ ☐BA ☐TR			BA TR					
2.	○ ☐BA ☐TR			BA TR					
3.	○ ☐BA ☐TR			BA TR					
4.	○ ☐BA ☐TR			BA TR					
5.	○ ☐BA ☐TR			BA TR					
6.	○ ☐BA ☐TR			BA TR					
7.	○ ☐BA ☐TR			BA TR					
8.	○ ☐BA ☐TR			BA TR					
9.	○ ☐BA ☐TR			BA TR					
10.	○ ☐BA ☐TR			BA TR					
11.	○ ☐BA ☐TR			BA TR					
12.	○ ☐BA ☐TR			BA TR					

SAMPLE MADSON BUSINESS FORM

© THE MADSON GROUP, INC. 1988

DO NOT DISCARD – KEEP WITH PERMANENT RECORDS

FORM 234-1

MADSON CLIENT AND PET HISTORY FILECARD — SIDE B

11-5

and perfume on their pet can be quickly and efficiently handled. Without the filecard information the staff must wait for the client to return resulting in unnecessary delays.

Pet Care Services Brochure/Mailer

The brochure describes all pet care services and health and safety standards. The Madson motto, "A Groomed Pet is a Happy Pet," is prominently displayed. It expresses concerns for pet safety, hygiene, and humane treatment. The brochure serves as a welcome to new clients. It makes the statement that you are attentive to the client's needs and proud of your salon's standard of service. The brochure enhances profits by enlisting clients as members in the Preferred Client Program. Follow the Madson Management System, provide quality grooming services, and you will keep the promise of client satisfaction presented in the brochure. There is a space for the salon name, address, telephone number and days and hours of operation. Include a copy of your fee schedule with each brochure.

The brochure is also a mailer for generating business. Of course, always present first-time customers with a copy of the brochure. Take the address of all telephone contacts and mail a copy of the brochure to them immediately. Veterinarians are a valuable resource for referrals. They will be favorably influenced by the standards presented in the brochure. They demonstrate your interest in operating a professional pet grooming salon. Send copies to community organizations such as the Humane Society and local pet stores. This brochure is an invaluable advertising tool.

Pet Groomer's Report and Health Alert

This form has received more positive response from clients than any other service. It is an important form of communication given to every client after each appointment. On the cover it informs the client of the date of their next appointment. Inside is vital health information about the pet. There is a description of the pet's eyes, coat, skin, legs, and overall appearance. It is a description, not a diagnosis, alerting the pet owner to a health condition that may need attention. They may take the completed form to their veterinarian for further evaluation. Filling out the form guides groomers in their efforts to provide complete service to pets. Because they sign the form it serves as a quality control monitor.

The form reminds the pet owner to advise the salon of any health conditions requiring special care. It also serves to protect the salon by advising clients to bring written instructions for the use of any prescribed medicated shampoos. Using this form will enhance your reputation with local pet professionals and create greater client loyalty for your humane and attentive services.

Instructions to complete a Pet Groomer's Report and Health Alert are in Appendix A.

Pet Sympathy Card

Occasionally you will learn that a client's pet has died. Send the grieving pet owner a pet sympathy card. The Madson Pet Sympathy Card expresses condolences on behalf of the management and staff of the pet grooming salon. This expression of concern will strengthen the bond between you and the client. Eventually, they will get another pet and remember your courtesy and concern.

The Get Well Card for Pets

When you hear of a client's ailing pet, send the Madson Get Well Card for pets. It expresses concern on behalf of management and staff. It is another way to strengthen the bond between you and the client. Long after the pet has recovered the client will remember your courtesy and sincere concern for their pet.

Pet Birthday Card

Pet birthdays are a happy occasion celebrated by many pet owners. Sending a Madson Pet Birthday Card will result in a big smile from your client and strengthen the salon-client rapport.

Client Response Postcard

Use the Madson Client Response Postcard to contact any client not reached by telephone. Send a postcard to any client who has not had an appointment in three to six months to express your concern. Find out the reason for their absence. If service problems kept the client away, resolve them. Clients will frequently respond to the postcard by scheduling an appointment. Experience proves that the postcard resolves misunderstandings which hinder the client's return. In fact, 70 percent returned to have their pets groomed.

Client Service Questionnaire

The Madson Client Service Questionnaire provides feedback of client satisfaction. Always keep a supply at the reception area. Ask each client to complete a questionnaire after their first appointment and then periodically. They can complete the form at the salon, return it by mail, or at the next appointment. Inform the client that you use the questionnaire to improve the quality of your service to them. Express your gratitude for their assistance. With this valuable input, you know what the salon is doing right, and what areas need improvement.

Pet Sitter's Information Record

A client planning a trip without their pet gives this completed form to a pet sitter or kennel. It provides information about the pet's care. Your clients will appreciate this form. You can sell it, give it in gratitude for a referral, or use it for a variety of marketing plans.

SAMPLE MADSON PET CARE SERVICES BROCHURE/MAILER — SIDE A

A Groomed Pet is a Happy Pet.

SERVICES

BATH & TRIM
The Humane Bath—Your pet is lovingly bathed by well-trained and supervised bathers. We use a special procedure called "The Humane Bath" which emphasizes your pet's safety and comfort.

The Trim—Your pet is trimmed by highly-trained and qualified pet trimmers. The Master Pet Trimmer will trim your pet to your request. If you prefer, we will select the most popular and fitting style for your pet from our wide range of options.

• Your pet is observed for any health problems and you will receive a report of these observations every time your pet is groomed.

• Your pet's ears are checked, cleaned, and deodorized.

• The anal gland is expelled.

• The Humane Bath protects eyes, ears, and sensitive body parts.

• A non-toxic flea dip is used as needed.

• Your pet is fluff-dried using strict safety standards (we do *not* use cage drying).

ILL, AGED, OR DISABLED PETS
Special services are available for ill, aged, or disabled pets. Just ask the receptionist.

For the safety of your pet prescribed shampoos must be accompanied by written instructions from your veterinarian.

FEES

An additional charge may apply to special conditions requiring unusual time and effort. These include: severely matted and knotted coats, and pets with behavior problems. You will be informed in advance if an additional charge is warranted.

STANDARDS

We subscribe to the highest pet industry standards in the care and grooming of your pet. Each of our staff undergoes special training before they begin their job. We have an ongoing concern for the humane treatment of all pets.

OUR EMPHASIS
• Your pet's health, safety, and comfort.
• A hygienic and esthetically pleasing environment.
• Products selected for safety and quality.
• Attention to detail.

PET GROOMERS REPORT & HEALTH ALERT
We provide a written report of observations made of your pet which concern its health. A recommendation for veterinary attention may be made. The report covers conditions which appear obvious to the groomer from experience handling pets. It is not intended to replace regular check-ups by your veterinarian nor is it a medical examination. It is a courtesy extended to the pet owner out of humane concern for the health of the pet.

PET RECORDS
Individual records are maintained about your pet.
• Owner's name, address, and telephone number.
• Emergency contact information.
• Pet's name, special needs, and health status.

pregnancy	lactation
inoculations	medications
heart conditions	epilepsy
skin conditions	allergies

• Veterinarian's name, address, and telephone number.

Please keep us informed of any changes in these records.

THE PREFERRED CLIENT PROGRAM

Have you ever wanted to have your pet groomed only to find there were no openings available when you needed them? That need never happen again when you take advantage of our **Preferred Client Program**. This special program insures that you will always have the appointment you need **when** you need it. The day and time is selected by you to conform to your busy schedule.

HOW DOES IT WORK?
Option A—The Standing Appointment Option
A specific appointment is pre-scheduled for your pet at intervals of one to eight weeks. This pre-selected interval is yours for as long as you wish.

You will receive a reminder call 2 or 3 days before your appointment to confirm it. At that time you may confirm, cancel, or schedule a more convenient time.

Option B—The Courtesy Call Option
As with Option A you select an interval between appointments of one to eight weeks. You will be called 2 weeks prior to the selected interval. Instead of the appointment being pre-scheduled subject to your confirmation, you schedule the appointment at the time of the call.

PRIORITY HOLIDAY SCHEDULING FOR PROGRAM MEMBERS
Never again will you have to scramble around trying to schedule a hard-to-get holiday appointment. As a member of the **Preferred Client Program** your appointment will be pre-booked and waiting for you.

ENROLLMENT
To start the program simply call the receptionist and say, "I want to start the Preferred Client Program," or ask to join on your next visit. It's as easy as that.

This is just one more way to say **THANK YOU** for trusting your pet with us.

© THE MADSON GROUP, INC. 1988

SAMPLE MADSON PET CARE SERVICES BROCHURE/MAILER — SIDE B

Welcome

(custom imprinting area)

Hours by Appointment

(custom imprinting area)

© THE MADSON GROUP, INC. 1988

YOUR BUSINESS NAME
ADDRESS

TO

STAMP

YOUR BUSINESS NAME
ADDRESS
PHONE

MADSON PET GROOMER'S REPORT AND HEALTH ALERT

COVER

INSIDE

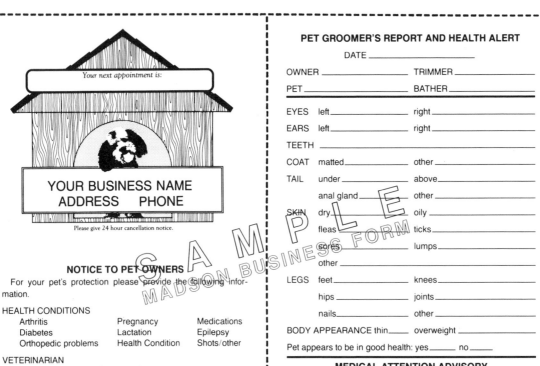

Your next appointment is:

YOUR BUSINESS NAME
ADDRESS   PHONE

Please give 24 hour cancellation notice.

NOTICE TO PET OWNERS

For your pet's protection please provide the following information.

HEALTH CONDITIONS

Arthritis	Pregnancy	Medications
Diabetes	Lactation	Epilepsy
Orthopedic problems	Health Condition	Shots/other

VETERINARIAN
Name, address, telephone number.

VETERINARIAN RECOMMENDATIONS
Please note that requests for veterinarian prescribed medicated shampoos must be accompanied by written instructions from the veterinarian.

THANK YOU FOR YOUR PATRONAGE

FORM 206-1   © THE MADSON GROUP, INC. 1988

PET GROOMER'S REPORT AND HEALTH ALERT

DATE _____

OWNER _____   TRIMMER _____
PET _____   BATHER _____

EYES   left _____   right _____
EARS   left _____   right _____
TEETH _____
COAT   matted _____   other _____
TAIL   under _____   above _____
          anal gland _____   other _____
SKIN   dry _____   oily _____
          fleas _____   ticks _____
          sores _____   lumps _____
          other _____
LEGS   feet _____   knees _____
          hips _____   joints _____
          nails _____   other _____
BODY APPEARANCE thin _____   overweight _____

Pet appears to be in good health: yes _____ no _____

MEDICAL ATTENTION ADVISORY

Your pet was observed to have the following conditions which may require medical attention by a veterinarian. This is not a medical opinion but an observation which from our experience may indicate the need for medical intervention. This is offered in concern for the protection of the health of your pet.

CONDITIONS _____

convulsions yes _____ no _____ MANAGER _____

Actual Size: 4" x 6", unfolded   11-7

SAMPLE MADSON PET SYMPATHY CARD

We're sorry....

©THE MADSON GROUP, INC. 1988

11-8

SAMPLE MADSON GET WELL CARD FOR PETS

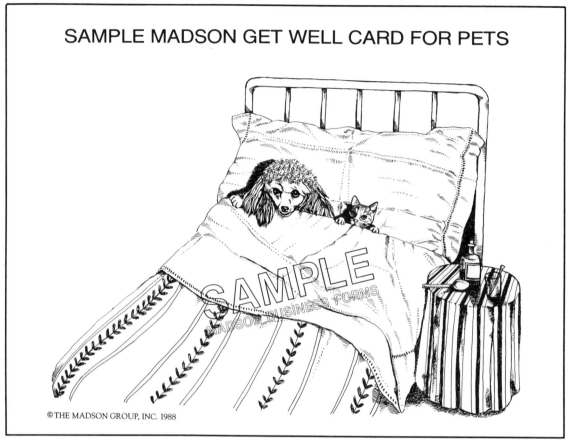

©THE MADSON GROUP, INC. 1988

11-9

SAMPLE MADSON PET BIRTHDAY CARD

Happy Birthday

11-10

SAMPLE MADSON CLIENT RESPONSE POSTCARD

Just a reminder. Regular grooming contributes to your pet's health and it's been awhile since we saw you. If there is anything we can do to serve you better please let us know.

It would be a pleasure to serve your pet care needs again. We enjoyed grooming your pet and we miss you.

YOUR BUSINESS NAME
ADDRESS
PHONE
HOURS AND DAYS OPEN

Actual Size: 3.5″ x 5.5″

11-11

CLIENT SERVICE QUESTIONNAIRE

We are committed to providing you with the finest pet care service. You can help us serve you better by letting us know how we are doing.

Please complete the information below and return the questionnaire at your convenience.

Thank you.

Please check the appropriate boxes.	VERY GOOD	GOOD	AVERAGE	POOR
Grooming quality	☐	☐	☐	☐
Courtesy and helpfulness	☐	☐	☐	☐
Service information	☐	☐	☐	☐
Salon's appearance	☐	☐	☐	☐
Timeliness	☐	☐	☐	☐

- FOLD HERE -

Please answer the following questions.

1. Are you aware of our Preferred Client Program and its advantages for members? _____

2. Are our times of operation convenient for you? If not, what other days and hours do you desire? _____
_____

3. What pet products would you like to be available for purchase at the salon? _____
_____

4. What are the things you like most about our salon? _____
_____

5. What are the things you like least about our salon? _____

6. Are there pet care services which you desire and we do not offer? _____
_____

7. Do you need special care appointments for an elderly, ill, or handicapped pet? _____
_____

Comment: _____

Actual Size: 7″ x 8″, unfolded

11-12

PET SITTER'S INFORMATION RECORD   Sitter's Name _____

PET OWNER INFORMATION

Pet Owner

Name _____   Home Phone _____

Street _____   Work Phone _____

City _____   Auto License # _____

State _____ Zip _____   Driver's License # _____

Departure _____   Return _____
                    (Date and Time)   (Date and Time)

While my pet is in your care, I can be reached at:

Date _____ Place _____   Telephone _____

Date _____ Place _____   Telephone _____

Date _____ Place _____   Telephone _____

MY PET'S INFORMATION

To assist you in caring for my pet(s), please review the following.

Pet Name 1. _____   Pet Name 2. _____

Breed _____ Color _____   Breed _____ Color _____

Weight _____ M/F _____   Weight _____ M/F _____

Birthdate _____ Age _____   Birthdate _____ Age _____

License # _____   License # _____

(Yes/No) #1 Spayed _____ Collar _____ Tag _____ Leash _____

         #2 Spayed _____ Collar _____ Tag _____ Leash _____

Veterinarian _____   Clinic _____

Street _____   Telephone _____

City _____   Emergency # _____

General Health – Pet 1. _____

                 Pet 2. _____

Please be aware of my pet(s) special medical needs described below.

_____

_____

In an emergency, please take my pet(s) to the nearest animal care facility or to: _____

The name of the person with financial responsibility for my pet during an emergency is:

Name _____   Relationship _____

Street _____   Telephone #1 _____

City _____ State _____ Zip _____   Telephone #2 _____

_____ has an appointment on _____
          Pet   Date

at _____
        Pet Grooming Salon   Address   Phone

SPECIAL INFO

Nutrition _____

Meal Hours _____

My pet likes _____

Doesn't like _____

Snacks okay _____

DO NOT FEED _____

© THE MADSON GROUP, INC. 1988   Signature _____   Date _____

Actual Size: 8.5" x 11"

11-13

CLIENT SERVICE PROCEDURES

The receptionist follows the client relations procedures for new and returning clients in illustration 11-14. Make copies of the illustration and provide one to the receptionist. Occasionally employees will need to assist the receptionist when several clients arrive at the same time. Therefore, post a copy of the procedures in the front counter area for reference by the staff. Also, include the client service procedures as part of the training program of every new employee.

THE PRICE SHEET

The price sheet consists of a list of all pet care services and prices. The receptionist gives it to clients. You can use the illustration as a model.

PET SALON PROMOTIONAL TOURS

Offering a tour of your pet salon can be an effective tool for public relations. Prepare an announcement of the tour and post it in the reception area. Send flyers to local community organizations; school and scouting groups have particular interest in this type of tour. Parents then learn of the salon's services through their children. Veterinarians who receive the announcement appreciate the professionalism and may make referrals to their clients.

Take reservations including a phone number, and maintain a sign-up list at the front counter. If the tour fills quickly, you can add another. Limit the size of the tour for safety reasons and be sure your liability insurance covers the visitors. Take the name, address, and telephone number of those you cannot accommodate and call them when you schedule the next tour. When the group includes children always have them supervised by adults. Don't allow tour participants to touch pets. Remember to keep all names and addresses for your mailing list.

PET GROOMING TUTORIAL

Another method to attract interest in your salon's services is to offer pet grooming training to the public. It may seem contradictory to offer pet grooming training which could potentially reduce sales. Very few of your clients will purchase the training, however, offering such complete and unique services will enhance the salon's image.

The recommended training program includes: eight hours of orientation, one hundred twenty hours of grooming patterns and one hundred seventy-two hours of finish trimming covering three breeds. Offer the total of three hundred hours training at a price reasonable for the area in which you do business. A charge of $2,500.00 for the training is typical for a large urban area.

Require the trainee to sign a tutorial agreement. A sample of an agreement form is in illustration 11-16. Show the sample agreement to your attorney and have one prepared or modified for use in your business.

CLIENT SERVICE PROCEDURES
for the new client

FIRST APPOINTMENT

Allow 10 to 15 minutes to introduce a new client to the salon's services and to complete the Client and Pet History filecard.

☐   Welcome the new client, introduce yourself, the staff, and the manager.

☐   Complete the client and pet history side of the Client and Pet History filecard.

☐   Exhibit the salon's photo album of trim styles. Briefly describe the services. Provide more complete explanations as the client requests.

☐   Be sure to stress that every pet receives a humane bath, and is given constant supervision.

☐   Check the condition of each pet to see if the client's service request is appropriate. When necessary, have the client sign a Release and Hold Harmless agreement.

☐   Complete the service history side of the Client and Pet History filecard with a description of the service order.

☐   Advise the client of when the pet will be ready for pick-up, the amount due when they return, and the salon check and credit card policy.

☐   Explain the advantages of The Preferred Client Program. Have them select Option A or B, and their appointment interval.

☐   Advise them of preferential appointments for pets that are aged, ill, or needing special care.

☐   Provide the client with a brochure, business card, pet sitter's information record, client service questionnaire, price sheet, and other promotional materials.

CLIENT SERVICE PROCEDURES
for the returning client

SUBSEQUENT APPOINTMENTS

- ☐ Greet clients and pets by name.

- ☐ Ask if they are pleased with the service at their last visit.

- ☐ Update the Client and Pet History filecard as necessary.

- ☐ Inquire if their pet(s) has been ill or under veterinary care. Assign a Groom Alert as needed.

- ☐ Show them the trim style photo album if they are considering an alternative style.

- ☐ Advise the client of when the pet will be ready for pick-up, and the amount due when they return.

- ☐ Provide them with recent releases of promotional materials.

CLIENTS RETURNING TO PICK-UP THEIR PETS

- ☐ Give each client their Pet Groomer's Report and Health Alert and explain any "Medical Advisories" issued by the manager.

- ☐ For Preferred Client's Option A, show them their next scheduled appointment on the front-side of the Pet Groomer's Report and Health Alert. Advise Option B members you will be calling to schedule their next appointment in "x" weeks.

- ☐ Give a friendly reminder of the advantages of the Preferred Client Program to non-members.

- ☐ Ask for the client's comments on the services and tell them you welcome their input at all times.

- ☐ When a pet is clean and attractive it is a good time for sales. Encourage sales by following techniques described in Chapter Twelve.

- ☐ Provide each client with a receipt for payment.

- ☐ Double-check that the pet's belongings have been returned.

- ☐ Ask them to keep you informed of the status of their pet's health.

Complete Trims

Poodles

TOYS & MINI'S

PUPS TO 3 MONTHS . . . .
PUPS 3 TO 5 MONTHS . . . .
ADULTS (OVER 5 MONTHS) . . . . .
PUPS IN ADULT PATTERN . . . . . .

CANICHES

PUPS TO 3 MONTHS . . . .
PUPS 3 TO 5 MONTHS . . . .
ADULTS (OVER 6 MONTHS) . . . . .

STANDARDS

PUPS TO 3 MONTHS . . . .
PUPS 3 TO 6 MONTHS . . . .
ADULTS (OVER 6 MONTHS) . . . . .

TOUCH UPS

TOYS & MINI'S . . . .
CANICHES . . . .
STANDARDS . . . .

Terriers

AIREDALE . . . .
CAIRN . . . .
KERRY BLUE . . . .
LAKELAND . . . .
SCOTTISH . . . .
WELSH . . . .
WIRE FOX . . . .
WEST HIGHLAND . . . .
SCHNAUZER MINIATURE . . . . . .
SCHNAUZER STANDARD . . . .

Cockers

AMERICAN . . . .
ENGLISH . . . .
SPRINGER SPANIELS . . . .

Long Haired Pets

SMALL . . . .
MEDIUM . . . .
LARGE . . . .

Note:

MATTED DOGS . . . .   PER ½ HOUR
VETERINARIAN APPROVED BATHS
Additional Service Charge,
Minimum Service Charge,

Nails

SMALL PETS . . . .
LARGE PETS . . . .

Baths Only

POODLES

TOYS & MINI'S . . . .
CANICHES . . . .
STANDARDS . . . .
PUPS TO 3 MONTHS . . . .

COCKERS . . . .

TERRIERS

AIREDALE . . . .
CAIRN . . . .
KERRY BLUE . . . .
LAKELAND . . . .
SCOTTISH . . . .
SMALL TERRIERS . . . .
WELSH . . . .
WIRE FOX . . . .
WESTIE . . . .
SCHNAUZERS MINIATURE . . . . .
SCHNAUZERS STANDARD . . . . . .

SHAGGY HAIR PETS

SMALL (TINY) . . . .
MEDIUM (REGULAR) . . . .
LARGE . . . .

Other Breeds

LARGE

SHEPHERDS . . . .
COLLIE . . . .
LABS . . . .
LARGE SHORT HAIR . . . .
AFGHAN . . . .
SMALL COLLIES . . . .
SMALL SHEPHERDS . . . .
ENGLISH SHEEPDOG . . . .
    TRIMMED . . . .
KEESHOUND . . . .
SAMOYED . . . .
SETTERS . . . .
SHELTIES . . . .
SPITZ . . . .
SPRINGERS . . . .

Cats

SHORT HAIR . . . .
LONG HAIR . . . .
PART PERSIAN . . . .
PERSIAN . . . .
TRIMMED . . . .
KITTENS (ALL BREEDS) . . . .

TUTORIAL AGREEMENT

The following agreement is by and between (owner), dba (salon) hereinafter referred to as (owner) and _____ _____, hereinafter referred to as "Trainee."

WHEREAS, (owner) is an experienced pet groomer; and,

WHEREAS, Trainee desires to receive on-the-job training in the art of pet grooming.

NOW THEREFORE, this agreement is entered into under the following terms and conditions:

1. Trainee agrees to employ (owner) and (owner) agrees to be employed by Trainee to teach Trainee pet grooming as specified below.

2. For and in consideration of this training, Trainee agrees to pay to (owner) the sum of _____ in advance, receipt of which is hereby acknowledged.

3. Trainee shall receive a total of 300 hours of instruction and on-the-job training. The 300 hours shall include:

        8 Hours—orientation to pet grooming

     120 Hours—grooming patterns, three breeds

     172 Hours—finish cuts, three breeds

     300 Hours—total

4. The instruction shall be on the day and at the hours shown on Exhibit "A." It is the responsibility of Trainee to be available on the dates and at the times of instruction unless prior arrangements have been made with (owner). Should Trainee fail to attend a scheduled training session, there will be no refund or repeat of said session.

5. (Owner) shall keep and maintain a training log as to the dates and hours of instruction received by Trainee. Said log shall be conclusive between the parties as to the hours of instruction.

6. (Owner) may delegate instructional duties to other personnel of (owner's) salon.

7. (Owner) may cancel this agreement at any time if in the opinion of (owner) Trainee has no real interest or aptitude for pet grooming or if the personality of Trainee is such that it is impossible for (owner) to continue instruction. In the event this agreement is cancelled by (owner), Trainee shall be entitled to a refund for the hours remaining on the agreement at the rate of $_____ per hour.

8. Trainee may cancel this agreement at any time for any reason on 10-days written notice to (owner). In the event Trainee cancels this agreement, Trainee shall be entitled to a refund for the hours remaining on the agreement, after the 10-day notice period, at the rate of $_____ per hour. Said refund shall be paid within 20 days of receipt of Trainee's written notice to terminate.

9. Training hours may be changed or rescheduled by (owner) from time to time on 24-hours notice to Trainee.

10. (Owner) shall make available to Trainee the necessary tools with which to train. Any specialized clothing, such as smocks and aprons, desired by Trainee shall be supplied by Trainee.

11. After Trainee has completed 30-hours of training, Trainee shall receive the sum of $_____ for each and every pet Trainee is required to bathe. Trainee shall receive instruction in at least three breeds of dogs.

12. Trainee acknowledges that (owner) and her course of instruction is not approved or accredited by the State Department of Education. Trainee further acknowledges that Trainee will not receive transferrable credit for this on-the-job training.

13. Trainee acknowledges that Trainee is not an employee of (salon) and is not entitled to wages, benefits, or other compensation other than specified in this agreement. Trainee further acknowledges that (owner) operates a pet grooming salon for profit which is open for business to the general public. Trainee agrees to dress and conduct himself in a manner consistent with dealing with the general public.

14. Trainee agrees that forms, systems and advertising material used in (salon) is the exclusive property of (owner) and is not included with this agreement. Trainee further agrees, for and in consideration of this agreement, that Trainee will not use the forms, systems or advertising material of (owner) and that Trainee will not solicit any client or customer of (owner) for a period of three (3) years after said training is terminated or completed.

15. Trainee agrees for and in consideration of this agreement that Trainee will not use or hold out to the public in any form or manner the name of (salon) or any association with (salon) without the express written consent of (owner).

16. Should any party to this agreement bring suit to enforce any provision of this agreement, now or at anytime in the future, the prevailing party shall be entitled to reasonable attorney's fees and costs.

17. Should any party to this agreement bring suit to enforce any provision of this agreement, the parties hereby agree and stipulate that venue for said suit shall be (county and state).

Executed on the date shown below in (county and state).

SAMPLE
CONSULT YOUR ATTORNEY

Dated: _____   _____
                                                           Trainee

_____
                                               Madeline A. Bright

The extra income is a welcome profit but don't allow the time spent training to detract from servicing your present business. Tutor clients on slow days or near the end of the day two or three times a week. Confirm liability coverage for the trainee with your insurance agent. The trainee must work under your constant supervision. The training gives you the opportunity to improve your skills. You may also discover a trainee with the talent to work for you.

PET CARE SERVICE LIABILITY ISSUES

A salon is liable for the pet care services it provides. A pet salon owner is subject to a law suit if those services injure the pet. Examine every pet before accepting it for grooming. Question the pet owner to see if the pet suffers any physical ailment or is under a veterinarian's care. If the pet is under veterinarian care for a condition which could be worsened by grooming, have the owner obtain a medical release from the veterinarian before grooming the pet. Express a sincere concern for the animal's health. Assure the client you will gladly provide proper care when you are certain the condition will not be worsened by your services.

When the client returns with the veterinarian authorization, and before you provide service, politely ask them to sign the Release and Hold Harmless Agreement (illustration 11-17). Explain the meaning and implication of the release and allow them time to read it over. If the pet owner refuses to sign, or obtain a medical release, express regret that you will be unable to offer service. This policy reflects a professional and humane concern for the welfare of the pet. It also alerts pet owners of the need to protect their pet. These procedures protect the interest of your livelihood, your business. You are performing a service for the client, the pet, your profession, and your business with such a conscientious policy.

A severely tangled coat ungroomed for many months or years is another dangerous risk. Under the matting the pet's skin is usually red, swollen, cracked, and dangerous to groom. Even a "kennel cut," clipping all the tangled coat away, may cause the pet's skin to break and bleed. Carefully demonstrate to the pet owner what pulling or clipping on the coat does to the pet's skin. Grooming can aggravate this condition. Don't assume the troubled pet will be okay. It is an unnecessary risk. You are responsible for the consequences if you accept such a pet without a veterinarian's approval and a signed release.

Pre-existing health conditions, matted coats, allergies, and aged pets are examples of potential liability risks. In fact, cases of skin ailments aggravated by grooming, and grooming products have risen dramatically in the last few years. Many ailments aren't immediately noticeable, as with a "trick knee," but a knotted coat is obvious. To protect your interest in such cases you must have the client sign a legally binding release authorization. Review the sample in illustration 11-17 and have your attorney prepare one for your salon. In severe cases combine this agreement with a medical release from a veterinarian. You must use your judgment to determine when one release is sufficient. The rule of thumb is; when in doubt require the veterinarian's release also.

Remember, in all cases of special care have the client sign a Release and Hold Harmless Agreement. In severe cases require a veterinarian's authorization also. Always retain the signed agreements in the salon's business files.

A further consideration in handling special care pets is scheduling with enough advance notice to make proper preparation for servicing the pet. One suggestion is to reserve the last appointments of the day for these pets. Request the client to be at the appointment, if at all possible, for the pet's psychological comfort.

It is advisable to post a sign, visible but not obtrusive, reserving your right to refuse service. Such a sign is usually available at your local stationery store.

RELEASE AND HOLD HARMLESS AGREEMENT

The undersigned for and in consideration of the grooming services of
SALON agrees to save and hold harmless   SALON
and its owners, operators, employees, officers and directors from any damage, loss or claims
arising from any pre-existing condition of the undersign's pet, either known or unknown to
SALON.

The terms special services or handling shall include, but not be limited to, veterinarian emergency services, boarding, caretaking and/or transportation.

In the event an emergency should occur with my pet, or in the event special services or
handling are required as deemed necessary by   SALON in the
care of my pet, I agree to pay all such costs.

Said damage, loss or claim shall include, but not be limited to, death, injury or shock. Said
pre-existing conditions shall include, but not be limited to, advanced age, extreme nervousness,
neurosis, illness, malformation or previous injury.

SAMPLE
CONSULT YOUR ATTORNEY

Dated: _____   _____
                                                                          Pet Owner

Description of Pet: _____
                                                                          Address

_____

_____   _____

_____   Phone: (_____)_____

11-17

MANAGEMENT'S RESPONSIBILITY FOR CLIENT RELATIONS

The manager's daily involvement begins when the salon opens and continues until the salon closes. His duties include instructing staff in policies and procedures, supervising their implementation, and building trust and goodwill with clients.

Effective client relations is dependent on the manager. He must develop a "quality control" attitude toward the salon. This attitude encompasses appearance, services, records, and the health and safety of people and pets. Maintaining a safe, humane, and hygienic environment creates a favorable impression with clients. The manager's neat and businesslike appearance, clear moderate voice, direct eye contact, and even temper also contribute to effective client relations. The concern of the manager must even include the exterior of the salon. For example, providing a sanitary "potty-walking" area for pets is part of a full-service attitude much appreciated by clients. Stop problems before they occur by continually observing, listening, and reacting constructively.

It is not enough for the manager to be sure pets are well-groomed and cared for properly. The manager must share his enjoyment of managing a pet grooming salon and make the clientele feel important. Having these two attitudes alone will bring pet owners back again and again to a pet grooming salon.

Effective client relations increases trust and goodwill between clients and salon management. Clients need to be able to trust that their pets receive humane and respectful treatment. Aside from humane considerations for a pet's welfare there are economic factors to consider as well. In a sense, the pets in a salon represent a valuable inventory similar to jewels, fine china, or precious metal. The lack of humane and respectful treatment may lead to litigation and courts may place a high value on a pet. Therefore, each workday the salon's pet inventory is potentially worth many thousands of dollars. These factors demand that a manager and his staff maintain a thoroughly professional attitude toward their responsibility.

The saying, "you get what you pay for" implies that high standards of service justify high fees. By providing clients with the highest quality of service you will rarely lose them when it becomes necessary to raise your fees. If they do leave when you raise your fees, they will usually return when other pet salons don't provide the same quality of service.

The manager must remain close to the clientele. It is detrimental for the manager to isolate himself from clients. Clients become emotionally involved with salons to which they entrust their pets. So, remember to show recognition and appreciation to your clients. It serves to strengthen their loyalty to you and the salon. Allow them the opportunity to say, "I know the owner." If you are a manager-trimmer situate your work area where clients can see and hear you from the reception area. Always express a warm greeting and an appreciation for their patronage.

Management must maintain an awareness of the quality of the competition and strive to offer better services. Even the most successful pet salon managers know they must continually improve all aspects of client relations to stay ahead in business.

EMPLOYEE RESPONSIBILITY FOR CLIENT RELATIONS

The performance of employees either impresses clients or runs the risk of offending them. Together, management and staff form a sales team that promotes the success of the business. Every member of the support staff must try to achieve total client satisfaction. To realize such a goal requires each employee to follow the policies and procedures of the Madson Management System for client relations.

Employees need to understand the benefits of having effective client relations. In the absence of client satisfaction the opportunity for advancement is unlikely.

The receptionist and telemarketer work in the client relations department under the supervision of the manager. They work closely with the public and are the salon's experts in client relations. However, employees working in the bathing and trimming departments also have occasion to serve clients. For example, during Step One of the Business Plan pet bathers assist with the receptionist and telemarketer duties. Even at Step Three of the Business Plan these employees may answer the phone or greet clients if the receptionist requests assistance.

When the client relations department performs its duties well it earns client satisfaction. They can create a pleasant ambience for clients. The reception area must be orderly, kept clean of pet hair, and supplied with informational materials and business cards. There must be no unpleasant odors in the reception area, just the light, fresh smell of cleaning products. The receptionist makes appointment reminder calls three days in advance. They must keep a sanitary entry area outside the building because client satisfaction begins before the client enters the salon. This treatment of clients makes them feel important and valued by the salon.

Make job applicants aware of the importance of good client relations from the time of their first interview. Astute applicants will observe the salon's commitment to client relations by the performance of the manager and support staff. Hire only those applicants who can provide a level of service that promotes the salon's reputation.

Effective client relations requires teamwork by employees. Any employee who sees a problem and does nothing about it needs reinforcement about the importance of their involvement. Discuss the employees contribution to client relations regularly at staff meetings. Ask questions about hypothetical situations and compare responses. For example, "What would you do if a client said...?" Have the staff describe and critique client relation situations occurring since the last staff meeting. Ask for the participation of every staff member in improving client relations.

Staff members serve as a liaison between management and clients. They speak to clients on behalf of management and to management on behalf of clients. Encourage them to keep the channel of information flowing between clients and yourself. You need to know what clients desire if you are to provide it. If a style of trim is losing popularity, you need to know so you can offer an alternative. The receptionist may learn that clients would appreciate the salon opening one hour earlier. Clients want to drop their pet off before driving the children to school, or going to work. Good communication between staff and clients increases client satisfaction and profits.

THE PEOPLE AND PET MARKETING PROGRAM

CHAPTER

12

The basic objective of a marketing program is to establish a professional image for your pet grooming salon. This creates and maintains a demand for your services.

There are over 115 million pet dogs and cats in the Unites States and about 15,000 pet grooming salons. That averages to over 7,666 pets for each salon and means that the average salon is not reaching thousands of pets. The profits are waiting for you if you employ an effective marketing program.

The manager of the pet salon is solely responsible for expanding the client base and obtaining higher volume of appointments. In sports, fans applaud the heroes for their determination and skill. Market your business with the same spirit.

Too many pet salon owners use lazy marketing methods. They rely on a sign, the yellow pages, and ineffective advertisements. The Madson People and Pet Marketing Program offers proven methods to expand the client base and generate more appointments.

The first marketing goal is to reach new people with pets and get them to schedule their first appointment. The second marketing goal is to improve the frequency of a client's appointments. When quality service and pet care bonds the new customer to your salon you will have a regular client. With every new client you move a step closer to the growth targeted in the Annual Profit and Loss Projection (Chapter Fourteen).

In addition to the Madson Management System, study reference books and articles in business magazines about marketing. Keep informed of newly evolved marketing methods available at reasonable expense. For instance, many video rental firms recently announced advertising space will be available soon on the protective cases used for rented videotapes.

The manager is responsible to execute the Madson People and Pet Marketing Program in a timely fashion. Marketing projects require planning well in advance of their presentation to the public. The Manager's Planning Schedule (illustration 12-1) alerts the manager to begin developing various marketing promotions three months or more in advance. For instance, Christmas planning should begin in July. By planning, you will have a more profitable, cost-effective holiday season. Promotions prepared at the last minute usually get poor results, are not cost-effective, and represent poor client service. You can control the financial destiny of your business with timely, well-executed marketing.

Begin the People and Pet Marketing Program by first defining your salon's market area. Then organize your client and pet history filecards, and measure the client base.

MAPPING THE MARKET AREA

The marketing area includes all residences and businesses within a forty-five minute driving distance of the pet grooming salon. Most pet owners are willing to drive this distance for professional pet care services. In one salon using the Madson Management System about twenty percent of the clients drove more than forty-five minutes one way. Nearly five percent drove over sixty minutes one way. Exceptional pet care services will create exceptionally loyal clients willing to travel above-average distances.

The market area is an arena in which you sell pet care services. Your success at winning the attention of new clients in the arena requires familiarity with the territory. You need to know the characteristics of your area's people and pets. Drive through and study the many neighborhoods in your market area to see what they are like. Find out which have the highest concentration of pet owners. Apartment dwellers own significantly more cats than dogs and single-family residences typically have both dogs and cats.

A wall map of the market area is an effective tool for marketing pet care services. The map allows you to plan marketing strategies and track client response. This process is "farming the area." You can purchase the following list of supplies at an office supply store to construct your map.

1. A current, fold-out style, street map of the entire community within a forty-five minute commute from your salon.

2. A cork bulletin board large enough to hold the unfolded map. (You can substitute an extra-heavy piece of cardboard at least 1/4 inch thick for the bulletin board.)

3. Straight pins with brightly-colored heads in at least seven assorted colors.

4. Pre-gummed, 1/8 inch dot stickers in at least seven assorted colors.

5. A yellow highlighter felt-tip marker.

6. A ruler.

Post the street map on the bulletin board, or heavy cardboard. Using the felt-tip marker and ruler, outline the salon's market area. Then place a colored dot sticker at the street location of every pet grooming salon, veterinarian, kennel, pet shop, breeder, pet sitter, and pet supply wholesaler. Assign a different color to each of the categories. For example, use blue stickers for veterinarians, red stickers for kennels, etc. Use the yellow pages to locate every pet-related business. Include the name, address, and telephone number of each business in the salon's address book or rolodex file.

Look for neighborhoods on the map that have few, or no pet grooming salons. These areas deserve top priority in your marketing plans. Your goal is to develop a working relationship with every pet-related business on your map. Pet-related businesses, other than pet grooming salons, may allow you to display promotional materials and be a referral source. Use the Pet Care Services brochure to promote your salon and keep them supplied with additional copies when they run low. Strengthen these relationships by thanking them, in writing, for every referral. Make referrals in kind if you know the business offers reputable services.

Use the map of the market area to plan strategies. For each marketing method, track the response on the map with the pins with colored heads. This allows you to analyze the success of your marketing efforts and can save thousands of dollars. Assign one color for each marketing method. Assign telemarketing, yellow page advertising, newspaper and magazine advertising, neighborhood canvassing, and referral customers a different color each. Accurate information about your marketing efforts allows you to spend your marketing dollars wisely.

MARKETING WITH THE CLIENT AND PET HISTORY FILECARDS

The Madson Management System uniquely organizes the client and pet history filecards. At first it may seem a little complicated compared to alphabetic organization. However, using the Madson Management System method will turn your salon's filecards into a profitable marketing tool.

Assign every client and pet history filecard one of four letter ratings based on the appointment scheduling habit of the client.

A. *Standing Appointment Client.*
   A member of the Preferred Client Program - Option A.

B. *Telemarketing Service Client.*
   A member of Preferred Client Program - Option B.

C. *Random Appointment Client.*
   Client prefers to call you for an appointment at his/her discretion.

D. *Inactive File.*
   No appointment for six months, and no positive response to inquiry by phone or Client Response Postcard.

The four ratings are pre-printed in the upper right-hand corner of the Madson Client and Pet History filecard. Simply circle, in pencil, the appropriate rating when first completing the filecard, and change it as the client's scheduling habits change.

Ratings "A" and "B" identify a client as part of the Preferred Client Program (Chapter Eleven). Offer clients membership in this program as a convenience. Clients who select Option A make standing appointments at the weekly intervals they prefer. Clients who pick Option B schedule the date of the appointment when called at a selected weekly interval.

"A" rating clients are the most profitable and the goal of management is to convert every client into an "A" client. "A" clients are more loyal to your salon, schedule more appointments per year, and deserve special attention. They are an effective form of advertising and most of your referrals will come from them.

MANAGER'S PLANNING SCHEDULE
for _____

JANUARY

- Complete year-end bookkeeping including 1099s, employee payroll records, and W-2s.
- Order Easter promotional materials and grooming supplies.
- Annual refurbishing of building and equipment.
- Regular monthly safety inspection and staff meeting.
- Monthly inventory of grooming supplies and retail pet goods.

- _____
- _____

APRIL

- April tax deadline.
- Regular monthly safety inspection and staff meeting.
- Monthly inventory of grooming supplies and retail pet goods.

- _____
- _____
- _____

FEBRUARY

- Provide accountant with bookkeeping records for tax preparation.
- Prepare job performance evaluations.
- Confirm Easter appointments for members of Preferred Client Program.
- Regular monthly safety inspection and staff meeting.
- Monthly inventory of grooming supplies and retail pet goods.

- _____
- _____

MAY

- Order extra flea-dip concentrate for summer season.
- Regular monthly safety inspection and staff meeting.
- Monthly inventory of grooming supplies and retail pet goods.

- _____
- _____
- _____

MARCH

- Conduct job performance evaluations.
- Place spring season advertising.
- Consult accountant for tax liabilities due April.
- Regular monthly safety inspection and staff meeting.
- Monthly inventory of grooming supplies and retail pet goods.

- _____
- _____
- _____

JUNE

- Place summer season advertising.
- Regular monthly safety inspection and staff meeting.
- Monthly inventory of grooming supplies and retail pet goods.

- _____
- _____
- _____
- _____

JULY

- Order Christmas promotional materials and grooming supplies.
- Regular monthly safety inspection and staff meeting.
- Monthly inventory of grooming supplies and retail pet goods.

- _____
- _____
- _____
- _____

OCTOBER

- Begin hiring process for additional holiday season employees.
- Prepare Christmas ribbons and promotional materials.
- Confirm adequate grooming supplies delivered for holiday season.
- Schedule Christmas appointments for members of Preferred Client Program.
- Regular monthly safety inspection and staff meeting.
- Monthly inventory of grooming supplies and retail pet goods.

AUGUST

- Prepare job performance evaluations.
- Confirm Christmas appointments for members of Preferred Client Program.
- Plan employment needs for holiday season.
- Regular monthly safety inspection and staff meeting.
- Monthly inventory of grooming supplies and retail pet goods.

- _____
- _____

NOVEMBER

- Arrange extra towel supply and laundry for holiday season.
- Install holiday decorations and mail holiday greeting cards to clients.
- Increase cash register change fund for holiday season.
- Orientation and training of extra holiday employees.
- Regular monthly safety inspection and staff meeting.
- Monthly inventory of grooming supplies and retail pet goods.

SEPTEMBER

- Conduct job performance evaluations.
- Place fall/holiday season advertising.
- Regular monthly safety inspection and staff meeting.
- Monthly inventory of grooming supplies and retail pet goods.

- _____
- _____
- _____

DECEMBER

- Place winter season advertising.
- Regular monthly safety inspection and staff meeting.
- Monthly inventory of grooming supplies and retail pet goods.

- _____
- _____
- _____
- _____

"B" clients are also valuable to your salon. They only differ from "A" clients in the method they schedule their appointments. Telephone them at selected weekly intervals to schedule their next appointment (Chapter Eleven). These members are loyal to your salon but prefer the flexibility of scheduling their next appointment by phone. Frequently, they are busy professionals who don't wish to make commitments too far in advance.

"C" clients are those who decline membership in the Preferred Client Program preferring to schedule the next appointment at their discretion. The goal of management is to bond the client to the salon and motivate them to join the Preferred Client Program. This happens with consistent quality grooming and client service.

Assign the "D" rating to inactive clients. An inactive client is one who hasn't scheduled an appointment in six months or more. Before assigning a "D" rating attempt to contact the client by telephone. If telephone contact fails, mail a Client Response Postcard (Chapter Eleven). The card expresses concern and invites client feedback about the salon's services. Many inactive clients will become active when contacted. Assign the "D" rating if all contact fails. However, do not dispose of these filecards as they may be useful for your mailing list.

Most pet grooming salons offer only standing appointments, and no other alternative. A sound marketing strategy provides several alternatives to meet the needs of clients. Don't wait for them to schedule their next appointment randomly, make it easy to do so by offering options. Always give the client more than one way to say yes! When the choices for an appointment are — yes or no — you have a fifty percent chance of losing. When the choices are — yes, yes, yes, or no — you have a seventy-five percent chance of winning.

When you begin the Madson Management System, convert your present filecards to the Madson Client and Pet History filecards. Circle the appropriate rating and complete every filecard using the instructions in Appendix A. Once completed you are ready to use the filing system to harvest more appointments.

Four filecard boxes are necessary to organize the client and pet history filecards. You can purchase filecard boxes along with dividers at your local office supply store. Divide two of the boxes alphabetically. Divide one by month and one by weekdays. File the client's card in the correct alphabetical section by the first letter of the client's last name. Label the boxes Box #1, Box #2, Box #3, and Box #4. Be sure to label the front of each box clearly with the title written in bold letters.

Place the four boxes together in your client service work area, and near a phone for convenience. Post a copy of illustration 12-2 (instructions for the Madson filecard system) near the boxes for quick reference. File the cards according to the client's rating and the status of their next appointment.

BOX #1 — Clients with scheduled appointments.

Keep all "A" rated (Standing Appointment Client) filecards in Box #1 along with any other clients who have already scheduled their next appointment.

For example, Mrs. Blair prefers to telephone for her next appointment. Her classification is as a "C" rated client. When she calls to make an appointment the receptionist writes her name in the appointment book. She then pulls the filecard from Box #3 and places it in Box #1. Regardless of filecard rating, every client with their next appointment already scheduled has their filecard kept in Box #1.

Note: File the "A" rated filecards back in Box #1 only when they have scheduled their next standing appointment. Present the date and time of the next appointment to the client on the

Pet Groomer's Report and Health Alert (Chapter Eleven). If they change their scheduling method preference, change their filecard rating accordingly.

BOX #2 — Clients to be scheduled.

Box #2 holds the filecards only for Option B clients. These members are called after a pre-selected interval to set up their next appointment. Use the filecard box dividers with monthly divisions and divide the box into twelve sections, one for each month of the year.

When ready to file the "B" filecard after the client's current visit, look at the area marked, "Appointment Schedule Frequency." This shows how many weeks the client prefers to wait between appointments. Add the number of weeks to the date of the current visit to determine the date of the next appointment. Then file the card in the appropriate month. For example, the date of the current appointment is April 12. Mrs. Smith, a "B" rated client, is picking up her poodle. The appointment schedule frequency is eight weeks between appointments. Eight weeks from the current visit on April 12th is June 7th so keep her filecard in the June section of Box #2.

BOX #3 — Random Appointment and Inactive Clients.

Box #3 holds both "C" and "D" rated cards. Since most clients have ratings of either "A" or "B," there is adequate space for the remaining "C" and "D" rated filecards. Divide the box into a "C" and "D" section and file the cards alphabetically. Do not mix them together.

BOX #4 — Current week's appointments.

Divide Box #4 into seven sections, one for each day of the week from Monday to Sunday. On Monday morning the receptionist places the filecards of all the clients with appointments scheduled that week in Box #4. Place the filecards in the section for the day of the week on which their appointment is scheduled. Instruct the receptionist to make a reminder call to each client in Box #4 three days ahead of their appointment date. For example, on Monday the clients with appointments scheduled for Thursday receive a reminder call. On Tuesday, call clients with appointments scheduled for Friday, and continue in that fashion.

The proper organization and maintenance of the client and pet history filecards is vital to the marketing program. Take time to train all employees to use the system properly. Alert them to the illustrated instructions you placed near the four boxes. After adding the receptionist and telemarketer the system will become much easier. Until then, train employees to fill out the filecards and use the filecard system correctly. It is the manager's responsibility to supervise the use of the filecard system. Make certain to use it properly and keep it in order. Misfiled cards waste time and inhibit client service efficiency.

Once you have organized the client and pet history filecards they will become one of your most valuable marketing tools.

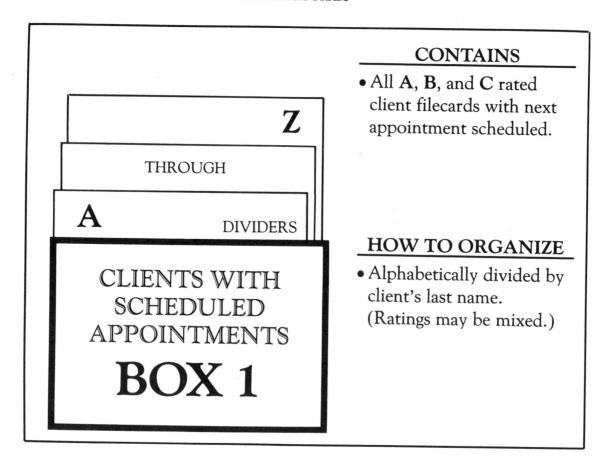

CONTAINS

- All **A**, **B**, and **C** rated client filecards with next appointment scheduled.

HOW TO ORGANIZE

- Alphabetically divided by client's last name. (Ratings may be mixed.)

Z
THROUGH
A
DIVIDERS

CLIENTS WITH SCHEDULED APPOINTMENTS

BOX 1

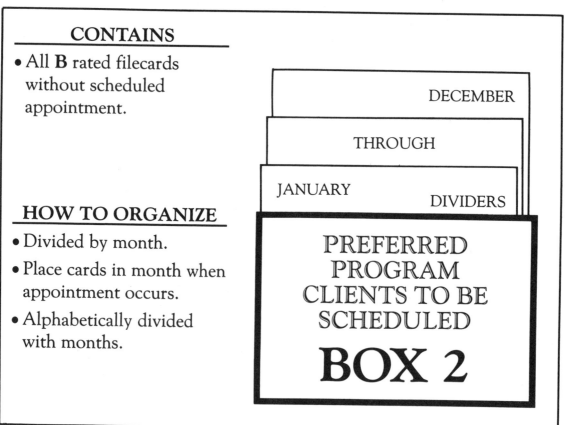

CONTAINS

- All **B** rated filecards without scheduled appointment.

HOW TO ORGANIZE

- Divided by month.
- Place cards in month when appointment occurs.
- Alphabetically divided with months.

DECEMBER
THROUGH
JANUARY
DIVIDERS

PREFERRED PROGRAM CLIENTS TO BE SCHEDULED

BOX 2

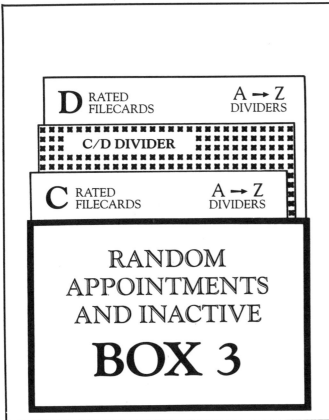

CONTAINS

- All **C** and **D** filecards without appointments.

Note: **D** (inactive) clients who schedule appointments are re-rated to a **C** (or **A/B** if they join the Preferred Client Program).

HOW TO ORGANIZE

- Two sections (**C** and **D**).
- Alphabetically divided within sections.

D RATED FILECARDS   A → Z DIVIDERS

C/D DIVIDER

C RATED FILECARDS   A → Z DIVIDERS

RANDOM APPOINTMENTS AND INACTIVE

BOX 3

CONTAINS

- All filecards for clients with appointments scheduled in the next seven days.

HOW TO ORGANIZE

- Divided by day of week.
- Alphabetically filed in day of the section on which appointment is scheduled.

SUNDAY

THROUGH

MONDAY   DIVIDERS

CURRENT WEEKS APPOINTMENTS

BOX 4

USING THE CLIENT BASE TO MEASURE ACHIEVEMENT

The expansion of the client base is a continuing goal. You must keep precise measurements of it. By following the Madson Management System your client base will expand. Measuring the client base is a crucial procedure in evaluating your marketing success.

The measurement of the salon's client base uses information from the client and pet history filecards. The client base is a major asset and helps to determine the market value of your pet grooming salon. The larger the client base, the greater the salon's market value.

Step One and Step Two of the Business Plan set target increases to achieve before moving to the next step. Take regular counts of the client base to track your success at reaching projected goals. In fact, develop the habit of measuring and recording the size of the client base weekly. The receptionist and manager should collaborate on the weekly calculation as an integral part of their duties.

You measure the client base by counting the number of active client and pet history filecards.

1. Number of "A" rated filecards   _____

2. Number of "B" rated filecards   _____

3. Number of "C" rated filecards   _____

   Client Base (add 1 + 2 + 3)   _____

At the start of each Step of the business plan, measure your salon's "A," "B," and "C" client base. Enter the figure in the box on the Client Base Goal Worksheet labeled, "Starting." To that figure add the client base expansion objective (e.g. 200 new clients for an urban salon in Step One). That gives you the client base expansion goal. Enter the figure in the box labeled "Goal." Record the result of your weekly client base count on the Client Base Goal Worksheet (illustration 12-3). Compare it with the client base expansion goal to track your progress.

The size of the client base is a very useful barometer for management. Making vague guesses about the size of the client base is not effective management. Accurate and regular readings are necessary to evaluate the success of the People and Pet Marketing Program. Steady increases, regardless of their size, are indications of successful implementation.

Your client base is a valuable asset contributing to the worth of your business. Your clients are a type of inventory. You can sell them as part of the business opportunity. The size of the client base contributes to the salon's worth in addition to the revenue from sales and services. A pet grooming salon with 1000 clients is usually worth much more than a salon with 500 clients.

The Madson Management System sets a marketing goal related to the client rating system (illustration 12-4). The goal is to obtain the following percentages of ratings:

CLIENT RATING	AMOUNT
"A" clients	70%
"B" clients	25%
"C" clients	5%
Total	100%

CLIENT BASE GOAL WORKSHEET

Step_____   Starting_____   Goal_____

DATE	A CLIENTS	B CLIENTS	C CLIENTS	TOTAL A + B + C	COMMENTS

These ideal percentages reflect the effective use of the marketing techniques of the Madson Management System. Profit in the pet grooming salon business is dependent on returning clients, and "A" and "B" clients mean repeat business. When you promote the Preferred Client Program, and provide quality pet care services, many "C" clients will upgrade to the higher ratings.

After you record the weekly client base count on the form, calculate your salon's client rating percentages. Follow the instructions on illustration 12-4. Nearly every pet salon is likely to have less than 70% "A" clients when beginning the Madson Management System. When you begin Step One of the Business Plan encourage clients to join the Preferred Client Program. Inform both old and new clients about the program and give them the Pet Care Services brochure describing the service. Within a few months of diligently marketing the Preferred Client Program you will see improvement. As the number of "A" and "B" filecards grow your salon's gross revenue will also increase.

Once you meet the guidelines, maintain the percentages with consistently good client service and additional marketing. Every year you can expect to lose about 3% of the "A" and "B" clients. They will move out of the area or suffer the loss of their pet. Offset these losses by continually striving to increase your client base. And of course, there are always "C" clients to upgrade, and "D" clients to get back. A manager interested in a profitable business never accepts even one client lost to a competitor because of client dissatisfaction.

INCREASING PROFITS USING THE CLIENT RATING

Converting "C" clients to "A" or "B" clients enables you to reach your Annual Profit and Loss Projection goals (Chapter Fourteen). The chart below shows the financial impact on the salon from converting "C" clients to the Preferred Client Program. If the salon converts to 70 percent "A" clients, 25 percent "B" clients, and 5 percent "C" clients, the financial impact on the annual gross revenue will be dramatic!

EXAMPLE   The ABC Pet Grooming Salon

Client Base — 1,000

Average Service Price — $20.00

"A" and "B" clients average eight appointments per year.

"C" clients average four appointments per year.

Ratio of client ratings at start of the Madson Management System: 40% "A" and 60% "C."

No. of Clients		Annual Appts.		Fee	Gross Revenue
400	X	8	X	$20 =	$ 64,000.00
600	X	4	X	$20 =	48,000.00
		Total Annual Gross Revenue			$112,000.00

Converting to the client rating ratio recommended by the Madson Management System: 70% "A," 25% "B," and 5% "C."

70/25/5

CLIENT RATINGS GOAL FORMULA

70% "A" CLIENTS	25% "B" CLIENTS	5% "C" CLIENTS

HOW TO FIGURE CLIENT RATING PERCENTAGES

Make sure your client base totals are current, then calculate your client rating percentages. Follow these formulas and substitute actual figures from your Client Base Goal Worksheet.

1. Number of "A" Clients ($\div$) Total Clients = Percentage of "A" Clients

2. Number of "B" Clients ($\div$) Total Clients = Percentage of "B" Clients

3. Number of "C" Clients ($\div$) Total Clients = Percentage of "C" Clients

EXAMPLE—The Fancy Poodle Salon   Total Client Base–700
"A" Clients–400   "B" Clients–200   "C" Clients–100

1. "A" Clients–400 divided by 700 equals .57 or 57%

2. "B" Clients–200 divided by 700 equals .29 or 29%

3. "C" Clients–100 divided by 700 equals .14 or 14%
                                                         100%

The Fancy Poodle Parlour is well on the way to achieving the 70/25/5 client base percentage goal, but the client relations department should increase efforts to encourage "C" clients to become members of the Preferred Client Program ("A" or "B" ratings).

No. of Clients		Annual Appts.		Fee	Gross Revenue
700	X	8	X	$20 =	$112,000.00
250	X	8	X	$20 =	40,000.00
50	X	4	X	$20 =	4,000.00
		Total Annual Gross Revenue			$156,000.00

Without a single new client the ABC Salon can increase their annual gross revenue by $44,000.00 using the Madson Management System guidelines. These marketing techniques improve the frequency of your present client's appointments significantly increase profits.

THE BUSINESS LOGO

Effective marketing uses imagery for indentification. Without even printing the business' name, the logo should identify your salon from others. A good logo will stick in the mind of people in your market area. A printed name is a printed name, but a logo is a visual symbol of your salon with greater identification recall. It translates everything your business offers into one image.

The logo is part of your business' foundation. Once you have an effective logo, a small business doesn't need to change it. This is a needless expense. The design may be upgraded with more contemporary styling after many years, but its basic appearance and meaning should remain unchanged. Start with a good logo, and constantly promote it as long as you own the business.

My logo is an example of an image, without words, that draws client attention and implies good pet care services. "Leilani" has been representing Madeline's Dog Salon for over twenty-five years. She is on the business' outdoor signs, stationery, advertisements, yellow pages, business cards, and promotional materials. Anywhere the salon's name is promoted, Leilani smiles happily. Her image says a visit to Madeline's is enjoyable, clean, safe, healthy, professional, and loving.

Logos using a pet are most effective for pet grooming salons. Using only the business name, or its initials, is ineffective compared to the impact of an adorable pet. Appeal to the pet owner's love of animals with a pet, or pets, in your logo. The market for cat grooming has grown in the last five years and the trend will continue. Therefore, consider using a cat as well as a dog in your logo.

There are many sources for artwork. You can expect good results from professional artists, but they may be too expensive for your salon's budget. Local art schools are an alternative. Ask if they will allow you to post a flyer on the student's bulletin board offering the logo design job. Ask students who respond to show you a portfolio of their artwork. Choose the artist that seems to understand the character of pets. Alternatively, another business whose logo you admire may provide he name of the illustrator. You might even post a flyer offering the logo design job in your salon. Some clients, or their relatives, may be illustrators.

The cost of the logo need not exceed $150.00. Be sure the artwork is black and white only, and "camera-ready." The typical media used to produce the artwork is black ink and pen. When the original is camera-ready, take it to a print shop or typesetter and have several stats made. Keep them carefully protected in a cool dry place, and undisturbed. Publishers and printers will require a stat to print your logo.

Marketing does require some correspondence, so don't overlook printed stationery. You may have limited need for it, but good stationery makes an important statement about your commitment to be a professional salon. An economical print shop can provide affordable business cards and letterhead. The appearance of the stationery should be neat and simple. Include the company logo as well as the business' name, address, and telephone number. When you post notices to the staff, type the message on the letterhead. The formal look of the statement commands greater attention. Management will find the new letterhead makes correspondence a more enjoyable task, and business cards reinforce your self-image as a professional business owner. A business card also demonstrates pride in your business.

TELEMARKETING — THE REVOLUTION

Telemarketing is sales power. It works for hundreds of different industries, including pet grooming. My telemarketers scheduled an average of eighteen new appointments, or $396.00 gross revenue, per day in a six-day work week. Annualized, telemarketing generated $123,552.00 in new appointments. You too can profit from the power of the Madson telemarketing system. It's contribution to the goals of the management system are enormous. You will want to begin telemarketing with the first step of the business plan.

You conduct telemarketing every day the salon is open for business. The most productive hours to telemarket are weekdays, 4 - 7 p.m.; Saturday, between 11 a.m. - 5 p.m.; and Sunday from 1 - 5 p.m.

In Step One of the Business Plan the owner must cover some of the telemarketing duties. Delegate the remainder to employees, usually pet bathers. During the week, schedule an employee to quit their regular duties by 5 p.m., and then telemarket. Complete a minimum of two hours of telemarketing each day during the week. On Saturdays and Sundays, you should telemarket a minimum of three hours per day. The employee's salary will include remuneration for the hours they telemarket in addition to their regular job duties.

Step Two covers the telemarketing duties by assigning them to the newly hired receptionist. The receptionist performs telemarketing as well as making confirmation calls. Before completing Step Two, business may increase so the receptionist is too busy to effectively handle telemarketing. Don't neglect them. Hire a telemarketer. Even if it is before Step Three.

However, definitely fill the telemarketer position of the support staff when you begin Step Three of the Business Plan. The job description is in Appendix B. The typical pet salon will telemarket with the following schedule:

Day of Week	Hours	Total
Monday – Friday	4 p.m. to 7 p.m.	15 hours
Saturday	10 a.m. to 5 p.m.	7 hours
Sunday	1 p.m. to 5 p.m.	4 hours
	Weekly Total	26 hours

Two part-time telemarketers can work alternate days each week as an alternative to hiring only one telemarketer. Full-service salons open for business seven-days-a-week should employ two telemarketers and telemarket everyday of the week.

Reward a telemarketer who achieves above-average results with intermittent raises or small incentive rewards. An experienced telemarketer will average at least twelve appointments scheduled per day, and more on the longer weekend shift. Multiplied by an average service fee of $22.00, the telemarketer generates $264.00 in appointments each three-hour shift. It is a dramatic improvement in a pet grooming salon's earning power to earn this much each day — and for a modest salary!

The Madson Management System provides a Telemarketing Procedures Form in Appendix C. Make copies of it and maintain an adequate supply of them. Provide a copy to the telemarketer or other employees who telemarket. Demonstrate telemarketing procedures before allowing an employee to make calls. Supervise a new employee's calls for proper completion. Provide a copy of the Telemarketing Procedures Form to every employee for reference.

As stated in their job description, a telemarketer's strongest work attributes are a pleasant personality and good communication skills. The telemarketer's speech must be clear, pleasant in tone, and positive. The telemarketer must be knowledgeable of the salon's services in order to answer client questions. What the telemarketer says establishes an image in the client's mind of the pet salon and its management. Demonstrate the correct procedures to telemarketers and supervise their performance carefully.

Telemarketers complete a Daily Response Report (Telemarketer) for every shift worked. A copy of the report is in illustration 12-5. Make copies of the illustration and keep a supply available. Instructions to complete the report are in Appendix A. Return completed reports to the manager. He reviews and files them with the Manager's Daily Summary Report of Services and Sales (Chapter Thirteen). Make copies of the Daily Response Report-Telemarketer and keep an adequate supply available.

A reasonable goal for an effective telemarketer is to schedule twelve or more appointments each day. Review the completed Daily Response Report-Telemarketer for every work shift. The telemarketer records how many new appointments were scheduled that day. If the telemarketer is below the goal level, determine why. Provide additional training as necessary to achieve the goal.

Provide the telemarketer with these items. The pet salon's appointment book, a calendar, the filecard boxes, copies of the Daily Response Report-Telemarketer, a copy of Instructions to Complete the Daily Response Report-Telemarketer (Appendix A), and of course, a phone. Allow the telemarketer as much uninterrupted use of the phone as possible. Ideally a pet salon should have two or more phones with three lines for effective client service. During the busiest hours of the day each of them have their own line, and one is free for incoming/outgoing calls.

There are three separate areas of telemarketing procedures for serving clients and attracting first-time customers.

Appointment Scheduling Calls to Option B Preferred Clients

Before beginning the procedure, the telemarketer must clearly understand how to file the filecards in Box #2. Review the instructions for filing the "B" rated filecards. They are in this chapter under the heading Marketing With the Client and Pet History Filecards. Once telemarketers are familiar with the filing system, they follow the instructions on the Telemarketing Procedures Form in Appendix C. In order, the telemarketer:

DAILY RESPONSE REPORT-TELEMARKETER

Telemarketer _____   Manager _____

Today's Date _____   Target Date _____

For instructions, see Telemarketing Procedures.

"B" CLIENT NAME	DATE APPT. SCHEDULED	NO ANSWER (enter n/a)	COMMENTS

C.D. NEW	CLIENT NAME	DATE APPT. SCHEDULED	NO ANSWER (enter n/a)	COMMENTS

	# of Pet Sympathy Cards	# of Get Well Cards	# of Client Response Postcards	
TOTALS	"B" CALLS	"C" CALLS	"D" CALLS	"NEW" CALLS	APPTS. BOOKED

1. Determines Option B clients due an appointment scheduling call.

2. Pulls their filecards from Box #2.

3. Contacts them and confirms appointment date and time.

4. Completes the daily response report-telemarketer and returns it to the manager.

5. Re-files filecards in proper order.

Call Option B members two weeks before their next appointment due date. The telemarketer then confirms the actual date and time of the next appointment.

Each work day the telemarketer begins the Daily Response Report by filling in the current date and the target date. If the current date is May 30, the target date is June 12. The telemarketer knows then to call those clients with their next appointment due on or about June 12.

Store Option B client filecards in Box #2.

In the above example, the target date is in June so the telemarketer pulls the filecards from the June section. Review every filecard in the section. On each filecard, the telemarketer refers to the date of the client's last appointment and adds the interval between appointments previously selected. A calendar will hasten the calculation. If the date is the same, or close to the target date of June 12, remove the filecard for a telemarketing service call. If the date is several days or more past the target date, the client is not yet due a call. The filecard remains in the June section of Box #2 until the appropriate time.

When the telemarketer has finished reviewing the filecards in the June section, telemarketing service calls begin. There should be one stack of filecards, all of whose clients are due for an appointment on or about the target date. Using the script on the Telemarketing Procedures Form, the telemarketer calls each client to make an appointment. Make appointments in the salon's appointment book for every client contacted. If a client is not available, place the filecard on the bottom of the stack, and continue with the next filecard. Place the filecards for clients contacted and scheduled in a separate stack. Count and re-file them at the end of the business day.

When scheduling the client's next appointment, the telemarketer also asks the client's how they liked their last service. The telemarketer's Daily Response Report includes space for any comments received. For instance, if a client's pet has died, record that information and mail a pet sympathy card to the owner. Register if a client is moving out of the area. Review the completed Daily Response Report at the end of the workday, and assign follow-up action as necessary. It is the manager's responsibility to resolve every complaint quickly and keep the client satisfied.

When completing telemarketing service calls, count the number of filecards in the stack for clients who have scheduled their next appointment. Enter the number on the Daily Response Report under, "Number of "B" clients scheduled." Then place the filecards in Box #1. Remember, this box includes all filecards for clients who have their next appointment scheduled in the salon's appointment book. At the end of the work shift keep the filecards for uncontacted clients separate. Call them the next day.

After attempting to reach a client for two days with no contact, call their work number. If not reached after three days, the telemarketer should mail a Client Response Postcard to the client. It requests the client to contact you at their earliest convenience to schedule their appointment or advise you of any problems.

Check-up Calls to Option C Clients

You can convert "C" clients to an "A" or "B" client rating. Effective client service and quality grooming will create the change. The telemarketer has the opportunity to convert every "C" client to a higher rating. The telemarketer exhibits the salon's concern for every client. By occasionally placing calls to them the telemarketer has demonstrated the convenience and attention of your services. By politely "checking-up" on the "C" client, the telemarketer makes them feel more important. At their next visit to the salon, these "C" clients are more likely to join the Preferred Client Program, because they have experienced its benefits. In this way, telemarketers assist in the goal to upgrade "C" ratings.

Each business day, after calling "B" clients, request the telemarketer to sort through the "C" filecards for candidates for "check-up calls." When "C" clients haven't been in for three months or more, the telemarketer calls them to "check-up" for potential problems. To complete the call, the telemarketer uses the script for this purpose on the Telemarketing Procedures Form. They are seeking information. Perhaps the client has a complaint, an ill pet, or they may have moved out of the area. Whatever the reason, the result of record the call on the Daily Response Report for follow-up by the manager. The telemarketer also notes the same information on the client's filecard.

Many "C" clients will schedule an appointment at that call. When they do, write the appointment in the salon's appointment book. File the filecard in Box #1 at the end of the shift. The telemarketer counts the number of "C" clients that schedule an appointment, and places that number under, "Number of "C" clients scheduled." Reward telemarketers who schedule new appointments with "C" clients with small bonuses. They are valuable.

If the client doesn't wish to make an appointment, mark the date on the card with the note, "client declined appointment." The filecard is then re-filed in Box #3 for a call in about four weeks.

A "C" client who hasn't been in for six months is a potential "D" (inactive) client. If they cannot reach the client by phone after a few attempts, send a Client Response Postcard (Chapter Eleven) to the client. If there is no response, rate the filecard as a "D" and file it accordingly. The telemarketer notes on the Daily Response Report, how many "C" filecards were modified to a "D" rating. Don't throw "D" filecards out. If you have the client's correct current address, use them for a mailing list. Many "D" clients may eventually return.

The size of the salon's client base decreases when "C" clients are demoted to a "D." Do not consider "D" clients when calculating the size of the client base. You will lose about three percent of the salon's client base each year. Their pets will die or clients move out of the area. Consistent attention to marketing will offset those losses.

Once a year, the telemarketer "cleans out" the "D" cards in Box #3. If a client has not had an appointment for one year remove their filecard from the box and store it. Always keep the stored filecards for at least seven years from the date of the last appointment. In the event of litigation, or an audit, you may need the history of service provided in your collection of filecards.

Calls to Attract New Clients

A good manager actively seeks sources for new customer leads. Below are some suggestions for obtaining names and phone numbers for potential clients in the salon's market area.

1. Develop a working relationship with local real estate offices. They might provide a periodic list of their clients who recently purchased a home in the area. In turn, you can allow them to leave business cards in the salon. Call the names on the list and welcome them to the community. Ask if you can send them a brochure and other promotional materials. Offer them a tour of the pet salon. When they leave give them a small gift such as the salon's calendar or key ring.

2. Contact your area's Chamber of Commerce and Better Business Bureau. Ask if they have any suggestions to obtain lists of names and phones in the salon's market area.

3. Contact the local Humane Society and again ask for suggestions to get names and phones for pet owners.

4. People advertising pets in local newspapers may want the pet groomed before they sell a pet. If the buyer asks where the pet has been groomed, you'll get the referral.

5. Ask the specialty clubs if they will provide a list of members you can call to offer pet care services. They are more likely to cooperate if they know you will offer their members a special discount on the first appointment.

6. Ask your contacts in the pet industry for sources of pet owner listings.

Flag new first-time customers from telemarketing on the salon's market area map. Find their street address on the map, and use a color-coded stick pin to represent telemarketing as their source.

PROFITABLE ADVERTISING

Profitable media advertising promotes your pet grooming salon with a twofold purpose. First, is to cost-effectively attract clients, and secondly, to establish widespread recognition of your business in the community. To accomplish this purpose requires a proficient advertising strategy.

The foremost goal of an advertising strategy is to gain the maximum response for the advertising dollar. In this section you will learn how to set an advertising budget and write an advertising plan that uses it cost-effectively. It does more than teach you how to make ads that appeal to pet owners. It teaches how to select publications serving your market area and schedule the placement of ads at the most opportune time.

Do not advertise on impulse. It isn't profitable to advertise in every publication. Always consult the advertising plan before placing an order for space. If an advertising sales representative drops-in unannounced develop a working relationship with them but delay deciding. Wait until you have reviewed your advertising plan to assess the appropriateness of the representative's proposal.

The cost of advertising can easily become excessive. Spend only the amount budgeted for advertising in the Annual Profit and Loss Projection (Chapter Fourteen). Five percent of the projected annual gross profit is what the Madson Management System advocates as a reasonable budget for advertising. If a pet grooming salon expects a gross profit of $100,000.00 in a given year, the advertising budget is $5,000.00.

Out of this five percent budget spend sixty percent on yellow pages, thirty percent on local publications, and ten percent for neighborhood canvassing.

EXAMPLE   The Poodle Parlor

Annual Projected Gross Revenue $100,000.00

Annual Advertising Budget: 5% = $5,000.00

Ad Location	Budget %	Cost in Dollars
Phonebook-yellow pages	60 %	$3,000.00
Publications	30 %	1,500.00
Neighborhood Canvassing	10 %	500.00
Total	100 %	$ 5,000.00

Using the chart you know exactly how much to spend on various types of advertising.

Radio and television advertising is too expensive for most pet grooming salons. The cost of advertising by radio or television is more effectively distributed to increased telemarketing efforts.

Promotional materials such as the Pet Care Services brochure/mailer are also not included in the advertising budget. The Annual Profit and Loss Projection (Chapter Fourteen) considers their cost an operating expense separate from advertising.

Do some advertising in local charity and non-profit organization programs. This shows your goodwill toward the community. However, limit it to preserve the advertising budget.

Yellow Pages

Your first priority is to arrange for advertising in the yellow pages. Many pet grooming salons spend too much of their advertising budget on the yellow pages, sixty-percent is the maximum to spend. Yellow page advertising is important but not as the sole advertising medium. Don't disregard yellow pages advertising, just keep its cost within budget. Your yellow pages budget should provide for a small ad and a general listing. Always remember, no form of advertising is a substitute for exceptional client and pet care services.

Give the advertising sales rep from the yellow pages your budget for the year ahead. They can then help you determine the most cost-effective size and placement of the ad. In recent years other "yellow pages" have begun to service highly-populated areas. Always place an ad in the area's most established city-wide yellow pages. Neighborhood yellow pages serve some market areas. Use some of your yellow pages advertising budget to place an ad in the edition that serves the immediate area surrounding your business. However, don't exceed the total amount budgeted for yellow pages advertising. Divide the cost between them with the largest portion going to the city-wide yellow pages.

Large ads in the yellow pages may not attract more clients than a modest ad if it has special appeal. A well-designed ad captures the same attention as a competitor's advertisement which only says, "Look at me, I'm big!"

Local Publications

After arranging the yellow pages advertising, gather information from community publications to find the superior value. Make a list of local publications that serve your salon's market area. Send a letter of request for an advertising rate card to every publication on the list. Use the form letter (illustration 12-6) typing the letters on your pet salon's letterhead. Be sure to request all the information stated in the form letter.

When you begin receiving the advertising rate card information watch for announcements of special issues that concern pets. You can expect a better response from pet owners to an ad placed in such an issue.

Read and save sample copies of each publication you receive. You need to get a feel for every publication and its readers. Look for ads that attract pet owners. Do your competitors advertise in the publication? If they do, and are successful, increase your interest in the publication. Ask the publisher's advertising sales representative if they have demographics on their readership which includes the number of pet-owners. Find out if they offer a discount to new advertisers. This request alone can save you hundreds of dollars.

Make a file folder for each publication. Label the folder with the publication's name. Place in the folder a sample copy of the publication, the advertising rate card, and other advertising information.

Put an Ad Response Record (illustration 12-7) in every file folder to chart the response of future ads.

Fill in the information requested on the Advertising Response form for each publication. Include the name of the publication, address, telephone, name of the advertising sales representative, circulation size (number of readers), the issue date, and the cost-per-thousand rate. Follow the method of calculation in the example below to determine the cost per thousand rate. This tells you what it costs you to reach one thousand readers. Obviously, the lower the cost, the better value it is. When new customers, or current clients mention seeing an ad, note this information on the Ad Response Record. By following this system you can evaluate the success of each advertisement and publication.

EXAMPLE ONE   Newspaper #1

Cost of a 1/4 page ad = $250.00

Circulation = 150,000

$250.00 divided by 150,000 = $.001666 per copy

$.00166 multiplied by 1000 = $1.66 per thousand

In this example, $1.66 represents the cost-per-thousand for Newspaper #1. Put the figure on the Ad Response Record.

EXAMPLE TWO   Newspaper #2

Cost of a 1/4 page ad = $200.00

Circulation = 65,000

$200.00 divided by 65,000 = $.00307 per copy

$.00307 multiplied by 1000 = $3.07 per thousand

In this example, $3.07 is the cost-per-thousand for Newspaper #2.

A comparison of these cost-per-thousand rates produces the following information. The cost for Newspaper #2 is $1.41 more per thousand than Newspaper #1. Therefore, an ad in Newspaper #2 will have to bring 1.8 times as many new customers to be of equal value.

Rely on your advertising records to decide if a more expensive publication draws the additional response necessary to justify its extra cost. There is another factor to give consideration.

LETTER OF REQUEST FOR ADVERTISING INFORMATION

Your Salon's Letterhead

Date

To

Dear Advertising Sales Manager:

We are considering advertising our pet care services in your publication. Please send your media package including the following information:

1. Advertising rate card (display and classified).

2. Audited circulation figures with readership demographics.

3. Sample copies to assist in determining size and placement of our advertisements.

4. Space reservation and ad layout deadline dates for the next twelve months.

If you offer special rates, please include detailed information with qualifications.

Also, please place our company on your mailing list and notify us of any future rate and policy changes.

Your cooperation is most appreciated.

Sincerely,

Your Signature
Your Title

The focus of salon advertising is to reach pet owners. It isn't cost-effective to spend money on advertising in areas that have few pet owners. A publication's rate may be higher than others, but if it serves areas concentrated with pet owners the extra expense is worthwhile.

The most profitable strategy for pet grooming salons uses the four seasons of a year. Even if the advertising rep offers very attractive rates for signing long-term advertising contracts, avoid them. Your interest lies in advertising only occasionally each season.

Divide the 30% portion of the advertising dollar allocated for community publications into four allotments, one for each season. If a salon has a $2,100.00 advertising budget for advertising in community publications, allocate $525.00 for each season of the year. This plan spreads the advertising dollar evenly over the year. Keep advertising expenses within each season's allocated portion and you won't run short of advertising capital before the year ends.

Selecting Publications for Advertising

Developing an advertising strategy includes determining which publications will generate enough new client interest to justify the expense. Ads in large, urban newspapers with broad circulations are for pet salons located in the city. Their cost drains most salon's advertising budgets and are not worth the money. You are paying to reach people well outside of your market area. Publications such as local television guides or drug store handouts are also ineffective unless they are well-distributed.

Construct charts, similar to the examples below, which will assist you in deciding. The information used in the charts is in the file folders for local publications prepared previously.

EXAMPLE ONE   Newspaper #1

Season - Spring

Budget maximum - $525.00

Circulation - 150,000

Cost per thousand - $1.66 (1/4 page/$250.00)

Past response - no ads run in paper to date

Pet owners in Circulation - high

No. times run	Size	Cost each	Total
1 x	1/4 Page	$250.00	$250.00
2 x	1/4 Page	$200.00	$400.00
4 x	1/4 Page	$125.00	$500.00

EXAMPLE TWO   Newspaper #2

Season - Spring

Budget maximum - $525.00

Circulation - 65,000

Cost per thousand - $3.07 (1/4 page/$200.00)

Past response - good

Pet owners in circulation - moderate

AD RESPONSE RECORD

Publication _____   Issue _____

Size _____   Page _____

Code _____   Position _____

Cost of Ad _____   Circulation _____   Cost per 1000_____

	DATE	RESPONSES		SPECIAL COMMENTS
		Number Received	Total to Date	
1.				
2.				
3.				
4.				
5.				
6.				
7.				
8.				
9.				
10.				
11.				
12.				
13.				
14.				
15.				
16.				
17.				
18.				
19.				
20.				
21.				
22.				
23.				
24.				
25.				
26.				

No. times run	Size	Cost each	Total
1 x	1/4 Page	$200.00	$200.00
2 x	1/4 Page	$175.00	$350.00
4 x	1/4 Page	$125.00	$500.00

Expect your charts to cause some confusion. The cost to run an ad is less when ran more than once. A more expensive advertising rate may actually be less in some instances.

It costs the same amount, $500.00, to run an ad four times in either newspaper. Even so, assess the effectiveness of the ad by looking at the cost-per-thousand. For an indication of the value of different publications, the cost-per-thousand rate is invaluable. In the two examples, the cost-per-thousand rate varies between newspapers. Ads in Newspaper #2 cost roughly the same as the other newspaper but its circulation is 85,000 readers fewer.

Response from ads in Newspaper #2 has been good in the past, but the number of pet owners in the circulation is apparently low. Newspaper #1 has a high concentration of pet owners in their circulation. Nevertheless, client response is unknown since you haven't advertised in the publication. A test ad in Newspaper #1 looks worthwhile because the high concentration of pet owners suggests a good response.

A manager must interpret advertising data to make decisions. Experience, and accurate advertising records make the difference in creating profit. The experience gained by placing test ads, and measuring their response makes future decision-making easier.

The advertising budget for a pet grooming salon is low in comparison to many other businesses in the community. Yet, most competitor pet grooming salons are in the same situation and have similarly limited advertising budgets. Following the guidelines provided will give you a successful ad. Publications that give you good customer service are attractive, but if you don't get a cost-effective response don't use them. There are key guidelines to keep you within your budget, and get the most response.

1. *Publishers who provide the services of their in-house graphic designer at low cost to secure your business.*
   They create your "camera-ready" advertisement with your specifications, and approval, before publication. Independent artists are typically more expensive. If the in-house designer produces a good quality ad, use their services to reduce artwork expense.

2. *Ads with a size between 1/8th and 1/4th page.*
   Ads less than 1/8th page aren't as likely to catch the reader's attention. However, ads larger than 1/4th page are usually too expensive for a pet salon's advertising budget.

3. *Smaller, more frequent ads versus larger one-time ads.*
   A seasonal ad, run twice about a month apart, provides more exposure. The ad can be reasonably reduced in size and run twice, for about the same cost as the larger ad run one time. Work with the publication's advertising sales rep to get the most exposure for the ad within your budget. Ask for any special incentives the publisher now promotes. Local neighborhood publications often will bend their prices a little to gain your repeat business.

4. *Place the ad in the front, center, or back of the publication.*
   These locations are more expensive but have been proven to get better response.

5. *Place the ad on the right side of the page.*
   Some studies have shown most people read that side first.

Additional guidelines to improve the appearance and placement of advertising are in illustration 12-8.

The Message

To achieve a favorable response from an advertisement it must reflect a specific need of pet owners. The more specific the need targeted, the more productive will be the new client response. Messages can be about many things. They can offer incentives, describe superior pet care services, announce improvements, promote convenience, and many other features likely to attract the pet owner's attention.

Use two advertising techniques for your messages. First, have the message spoken from a pet's point of view. Ads with a unique and clever perspective strengthen the ads retention and the reader is more likely to respond positively. Appealing to a pet owners' loving attachment to his pet will stimulate more response. Encouraging pet owners to have their pets groomed, not for the sake of fashion, but for the health and happiness of their pet is an example. Regular pet salon clients rarely deny their pet care essential to it's well-being. We are proud and fortunate that the pet grooming industry is patronized by people who love and care for animals.

Secondly, the message should urge the reader to act now! This can be in the form of time-limited promotions. Ads which spur people to respond immediately to receive the promised benefits generate more revenue.

Do not discount your pet care services. Make them a better value. Discounts are unnecessary, potentially harmful, and reduce profitability. People who are looking for the cheapest service available will never bond to the salon and become a regular client. The focus of your promotions should be on quality and service, not on price. Use incentives which offer an additional service for the cost of another service instead of discounting the price. Use common sense for incentives. A cut-out coupon good for a complimentary flea dip or nail clipping is very effective, and the cost to the salon is minimal. Measure the response to different incentives and repeat successful ones periodically as you continually test the market.

The ad campaign in the Madson Management System's seasonal advertising approach exemplifies both approaches. It appeals to a pet-owners loving concern for his pet and a sense of urgency to act now. These reminders promote pet care services germane to the coming season. Clients respond well to encouragement to meet the seasonal health and comfort needs of their pet. In spring; encourage pet owners to have their pets cleaned of winter tangles and get ready for the summer. Hot summers? Inspire pet-owners to give their pet the comfort of a short trim. When fall approaches pets need to be cleaned of summer dirt and weeds. Promote this for the sake of the pet as well as the benefit of the owner. A clean, happy pet is more enjoyable and will keep the house cleaner. Winter holidays would not be as festive for pet owners if their pets were not as pretty as the season's decorations. Advocate pet care in this season as an owner's gift to his pet.

A sample of an effective advertisement is in illustration 12-9. It is friendly, informative, lightly humorous, promotes pet health and happiness, and builds client confidence in the salon's professional pet care services. It makes the pet owner feel a visit to the pet salon will be an enjoyable experience, not just another household responsibility. Such advertising will attract significant client response. Then, it is the responsibility of management and staff to meet the client's expectations. The result will be many more new regular clients and increased profits.

IMPROVING AD COPY AND LAYOUT

■ **Can the reader tell at a glance what your ad is about?**
One dominant illustration or headline should portray the essence of your message.

■ **Will the illustration and text print clearly?**
Have the graphic artist prepare the artwork "camera-ready" and ask the print shop as to reproduction quality. Avoid running the body copy in reverse or surprinted over a halftone.

■ **Does the ad include your pet salon's logo?**
If the logo is to become another effective mark that identifies your business from others, you must use it in every advertisement. Don't forget to also include your salon's name, address, and telephone. If your business is difficult to find include a small street map and directions.

■ **Is there enough white space in the ad?**
White space is the most important basic element in designing an ad. Use more white space (the percentage of the ad not devoted to words or illustrations) to increase its attention value.

■ **Does the headline contain benefits or important news?**
You must give a pet owner at least one good reason to want to purchase your salon's pet care services.

■ **Does the text copy convey benefits?**
Spell out in detail what the pet owner will get by using your salon's services. Make them know that your pet care services will do something special for their pets.

■ **Does the illustration display a benefit?**
Help the pet owner to visualize what your services can do for their pet and you'll make more sales. Consider using a photograph of a pet groomed in your salon. Pet owners want to see what you are selling.

■ **Is the illustration large enough?**
"A picture is worth a thousand words," but not if it goes unnoticed.

■ **Is the language simple and direct?**
Read the ad aloud several times. If it sounds unwieldy try using shorter words and sentences.

■ **Does the ad strongly motivate the pet owner to act immediately?**
Every ad should attempt to encourage the pet owner to act now. It's an important part of closing a sale.

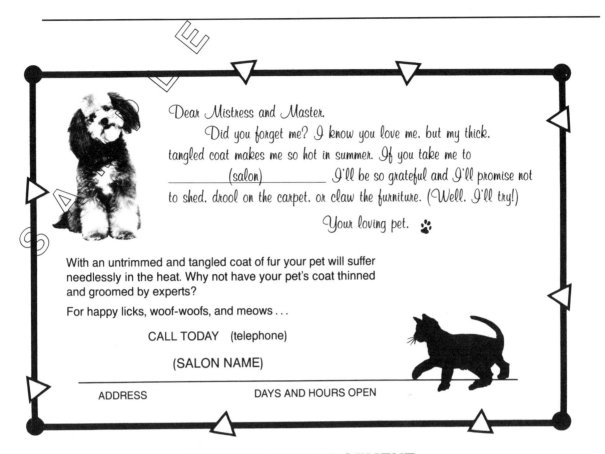

SAMPLE ADVERTISEMENT

12-9

Placing Ads and Tracking Client Response

When ready to place an advertisement contact the publication's advertising sales rep. If you are using their graphic designer provide a copy of your business' logo and a rough drawing of your ideas. Otherwise, have your designer prepare a camera-ready copy of your advertisement. When using the publication's services, be sure to proofread the final ad before publication. Check the location of its placement, the issue in which it will appear, and the accuracy of information. Ads with misinformation can misrepresent you to the public and harm your business.

Most of the response to any advertisement occurs within four weeks. Keep accurate records of the response to every advertisement using the Ad Response Record. In the future, when designing the message for ads, or selecting publications in which to advertise, use response records. They will identify the types of messages and publications which have been the most successful.

The receptionist should ask every new client for their referral source. If an employee forgets to ask, remind the employee of the importance of the information and follow-up and get the answer. Record the answers on the Ad Response Record located in the publication's file folder when advertising is the source. Be certain the description of the client's source is specific. When the client says, "the yellow pages," and the salon advertises in more than one, find out which yellow pages. For other publications, find out in which issue the client saw the ad.

The manager must review the Ad Response Records daily to make sure the receptionist is requesting and recording referral sources. (Note: Referral sources should also be on Client and Pet History filecards).

Allow thirty days after publication to evaluate its profitability. Perform the following calculation from information on the Ad Response Record to accomplish this.

Thirty-Day Response-Evaluation

Cost of Ad Space	# of Responses	Cost per Response
$500.00	98	$5.10

Ninety-eight responses from one ad is a successful response for any pet salon. This level of response will create significant increases in gross revenue. If the new clients spend an average of $22.00 for pet care services, the salon will gross an additional $2,156.00. After deducting the ad cost of $500.00, the salon's net profit from the ad is still a substantial increase of $1,656.00.

Even more impressive is that many of the new clients will return again and become members of the Preferred Client Program. A well-run pet grooming salon will usually have seventy percent, or more, repeat business. A typical client will make seven appointments a year. If seventy percent of the ninety-eight new clients visit the salon six more times in the next year spending an average of $22.00, annual gross revenue from one advertisement is $11,264.00. With similar results from subsequent advertisements potential gross revenue from advertising grows to an astounding $45,056.00 annually.

Use the market area map to track client response to advertisements and the yellow pages. Locate each new client's address on the map and stick a color-coded pin at that point. Assign one color for yellow pages and another for advertisements in publications. Chart every response to provide an accurate analysis of advertising success.

An accurate analysis of new client response is essential to advertise profitably. You can easily evaluate advertising intended to penetrate a specific market by referring to the market area map. Determining which sections of your total market area respond to advertising is as simple as looking for concentrations of color-coded pins.

Determine why various areas respond better to your advertising. Be like a detective looking for clues which assist in designing and placing more profitable ads. Areas with strong response may have high concentrations of pet owners. Or, there may be a lack of pet grooming salons in the neighborhood. Existing pet salons in the area may offer poor services and pet owners are willing to travel to a professional salon. Go for them!

When you discover an ad which gets results, use it again. Consistent, accurate ad response tracking saves needless advertising in unresponsive market areas. Cost-effective marketing does not waste money on advertising in areas not expected to bring a profitable return. Effective interpretation provides the information to distribute the advertising budget for winning advertising strategies.

Neighborhood Canvassing as Advertising

Although not usually a high-response method, door-to-door distribution of advertising can be very effective for pet salons. The key is to isolate those areas with a high concentration of pet owners. In these cases the potential client is more likely to see and read the advertising left at their home. Also, it is more informative because the information is not limited to a small space. The advertising package can contain promotional materials, including the salon's brochure.

With the package, the potential clients have information otherwise requiring a full-page advertisement.

As suggested, assign ten percent of the advertising budget to neighborhood canvassing. Since the material for canvassing is part of the operating budget, the only advertising budget expense is the cost of distribution. If the budget is $500.00, this will pay for about thirteen eight-hour days at $5.00 an hour. You can reach three hundred households in one day. In thirteen days, 3,900 potential clients will receive the salon's promotional materials. If only ten percent of the pet owners respond with one appointment, and spend an average of $22.00, gross revenue will increase by $8,580.00. After deducting distribution expense of $520.00, and the expense of promotional materials (about $.25 each), the net profit is $7,085.00. This doesn't even include revenue increases from new customers who become repeat clients.

Guidelines for the selection of neighborhoods to canvas are below.

1. *The immediate neighborhood surrounding the salon.*
   How many times has a pet owner walked their groomed pet by your salon and you know you are not the groomer?

2. *Neighborhoods with few or no local pet grooming salons.*
   The potential of these areas are among the most significant and the distance to your salon is less pertinent. They have little choice but to travel for quality pet care services. Give them a good reason.

3. *Neighborhoods with high concentrations of pet dogs and cats.*
   On your day off, invest the time to drive through neighborhoods looking for those with many pets.

4. *Apartment buildings allowing pets.*
   Apartment complexes allowing pets provide a bounty of potential clients in one, easily reached, concentrated area.

As with the other marketing methods, track the response to neighborhood canvassing on the market area map.

"SWING-SHIFT" PET CARE SERVICES

You can substantially increase your daily income by adding a swing-shift. Clients leave their pets between 3 p.m. and 5 p.m. and return between 8 p.m. and 10 p.m. Clients with busy work schedules will appreciate the convenience dropping their pet off after work offers. Indeed, an associate of mine reports a $4,000.00 monthly increase in service revenue in her first month offering swing-shift services.

Swing-shift grooming is most appropriate for salons at Step Three of the Business Plan. At this level there are two or more experienced trimmers; one of which will have to work during the new shift hours. As business grows, you can add another trimmer. It is also a good idea to have the manager work 2 p.m. to 10 p.m. The owner/trimmer can open the salon and leave the manager in charge in late afternoon or early evening. Add additional pet bathers to the staff as needed.

About a month before you offer swing-shift services prepare a flyer announcing convenient new hours and the effective date. Have the receptionist distribute one to every client. Update the salon's promotional materials such as the Pet Care Services brochure with the new hours. Also make the new service hours a part of your next advertising in publications.

MARKETING FOR CATS

Cat owners are increasingly patronizing pet grooming salons. I achieved a 15% increase in gross revenue (over $30,000.00) in one year simply by promoting cat grooming. If you do not presently offer, and promote cat grooming in your pet salon, reconsider. It could be a valuable addition to your profit potential. Test the cat grooming market in your area.

There are many methods to test the cat grooming market. Below are some suggestions:

1. *Announce by advertisement your exciting, new, convenient, cat grooming service.*
   Offer an incentive to cat owners for their first visit in local publications.

2. *Ask apartment building managers for permission to place a flyer promoting the salon's cat grooming services on the building's bulletin board.*
   Apartment dwellers have more cats than dogs and less room to bathe them. They will enjoy the convenience of having someone else groom their cats. Most building managers will authorize your request because they know a clean cat is less likely to soil their apartment units.

3. *Post cat grooming service flyers on community bulletin boards in supermarkets, coin laundries, and churches.*
   Use copies of cat grooming ads placed in publications for the flyer copy.

4. *Contact local veterinarians and advise them of your cat grooming service.*
   They know many pet salons only offer dog grooming. Let them know the demand for cat grooming is growing and you have decided to offer it. They may send you many referrals.

5. *Announce the availability of cat grooming to your present clients. Provide an incentive for every cat owner they refer who schedules a visit.*
   A gift certificate worth ten to fifteen percent off their next service fee is sufficient and effective.

6. *Contact Cat Fancy Clubs and request permission to advise their members of your salon's cat grooming service.*
   Offer members a small incentive for their first visit. If officers of the club prove helpful offer a nail-clipping gift certificate for their cat.

Ask new cat owner clients who referred them. Track the referral sources to determine which promotions are working. Emphasize the most successful methods in future promotions. The more you promote cat grooming, the greater will be your share of this expanding market, and the larger your revenues.

DIRECT MAIL MARKETING

The term "direct mail" refers to using the mails for advertising. It involves establishing mailing lists for people who have, or potentially have, an interest in pet grooming. Direct mail is an effective way to keep your clients informed of changes in client services and to offer incentives. When you open the salon an extra day, as in Step One of the Business Plan, send the message out. Plan to increase business in slow periods. About two weeks before a slow period, typically mid-January for many pet salons, offer your clients an incentive. Specify the date the offer expires clearly on the gift certificate. As you become more experienced in marketing, you will learn to which incentives your clients respond.

Preferred Client Program members already have priority holiday scheduling. During the first week of November send a holiday appointment postcard to non-members advising them they can now schedule holiday grooming. Increase the hours and days of the week the salon will be open to accommodate clients during the upcoming holiday season. Encourage them to plan well in advance to avoid disappointment. Include a reminder that members of the Preferred Client Program have priority in selecting their holiday appointments and encourage membership. Membership will grow as clients realize appointment times are scarce and choice appointments are being filled by Preferred Client Program members.

Direct mail is a valuable tool to keep your clients informed and loyal. Communicate with clients between appointments by direct mail to strengthen the bond between them and your salon. Track and interpret client response to direct mail efforts on the market area map.

The salon's mailing list is an asset in other ways also. Besides using the list to mail information to your clients, you can rent it. This is additional gravy income. The more names you have, and the more specific the market, the more valuable your list. When your mailing list contains from 500 to 1,000 names with current addresses, contact a mailing list broker. Find out their interest in renting it for you. If not, ask them to suggest someone who would have interest. Do not sell or rent the list to other pet grooming salons or competitors. Require that a non-compete clause be in the agreement. Make sure both parties sign the agreement.

There are mailing list management services who will make sure your list is rentable. Research the local yellow pages for these companies. Request their price list for mailing list management services. They can computerize your mailing list and print it on pre-sorted mailing labels for cost-efficient, bulk-mail postage. Then when you rent the list, simply call the mailing service house, order the list printed on mailing labels, and deliver it to the renter.

Renters may use the names one time only. Do not allow them to use the names again unless they pay for it. Your attorney can draw up an agreement which prohibits renters from using the list more than once per rental. A method used frequently to catch violators is to place a fictional name and address in your mailing list. If you receive more than one mailing from the renter, you know they have broken the agreement. Contact them immediately and let them know you are aware they violated the agreement, demand payment, and pursue legal action as needed.

REFERRALS

Referrals frequently come from people outside the pet industry. For instance, your bank's president and staff, who know of you and your salon's good reputation, will make referrals. Nearly everyone who loves pets will have interest your salon's services. Use this to your advantage, make people aware of how professional your pet grooming is and you will gain many referrals.

Interact positively with a broad spectrum of contacts in the pet industry. It is a form of advertising and it creates referrals. These include veterinarians, wholesale pet product vendors, trainers, dog and cat clubs, and kennel owners. Nurture your working relationships and be certain to thank them personally for their referrals. They are showing their confidence in you and your business by sending referrals. The process is a two-way street, and it is important to make referrals to them also. However, never recommend only to get business. Since your referrals reflect on you, make certain the service they receive from businesses you recommend will make you look good.

Veterinarians

Building good relationships with veterinarians builds referrals. Show them the Pet Care Services brochure, the Employee Handbook, and the Pet Groomer's Report and Health Alert. This will impress them that you are a professional salon. In particular, discuss the Employee Handbook sections on "Handling the Aged, Ill, and Disabled Pet" and "The Humane Bath." A serious attitude toward professional pet care and safety will gain their trust and cause referrals.

Work cooperatively with local veterinarians requesting special medicated baths for pets they are treating. The pet owner can forward the Pet Groomer's Report and Health Alert to the veterinarian. Follow through by making a call to the veterinarian confirming his instructions and informing him of the pet's response to the medicated bath. The veterinarian will frequently be busy and you don't need to interrupt his schedule. Discuss the details with his staff. He will find out about your professional follow-through and have a positive attitude toward you.

Market the availability of these special care appointments to veterinarians and pet owners. Groom sick, or very fragile pets under veterinary care at times when the groomers can give special attention to them. Book these pets very early, or very late in the day when fewer pets are in the salon and it is quiet. The veterinarian and the pet owner will appreciate this professional grooming service and your salon's reputation will receive a boost. The manager should closely supervise the groomer's performance with all special care pets.

Realtors

Get to know local Realtors and establish a working relationship with them. My salon received hundreds of referrals from Realtors. Many homeowners moving into your area have pets. They are potential clients interested in knowing the finest and most convenient pet grooming salons. Your objective is to be the first salon they visit. The way to stimulate their initial visit is by a referral from their Realtor. New homeowners often ask Realtors for shopping and service business recommendations. If you have established good working relationships with Realtors in your market area, you will win many referrals.

Introduce yourself to Realtors. Supply them with several copies of the Pet Care Services brochure. They can distribute to their clients. Occasionally call them to check on the supply of brochures. Strengthen your working relationship with the Realtors by writing or calling with your appreciation for every referral. Offer a very helpful Realtor one complimentary bath or trim for their pet.

MARKETING RETAIL PET PRODUCTS

Many salon owners complain that retail pet products move slowly because they cannot afford a salesperson. With the Madson Management System, you can. The receptionist's regular contact with your clients makes her the salon's key salesperson. Train the receptionist to sell rather than waiting for clients to buy. You've probably visited beauty salons with hair products gathering dust on the shelves unoffered by the receptionist. You have also probably bought things you weren't planning to because the receptionist was helpful, informative, and had a pleasant personality. When the receptionist courteously interacts with clients with, "Have you seen our latest products?", or "Wouldn't this look wonderful on Fido?", your retail sales will grow. Study sales techniques in sales management periodicals and manuals. Train your receptionist in effective salesmanship. Set a sales goal for the receptionist and offer a reward for achieving it.

The average pet shop customer spends about sixteen dollars on purchases per visit. At this outlay, a grooming salon with retail goods visited by thirty-five clients a day could gross $560.00 in retail sales daily. Even if the average sale was only half that, retail sales would be $280.00 per day. That is $1,680.00 per six-day week, and $87,360.00 annually. This may seem phenomenal, but it is an example of how attending to little things can achieve big things. The difference between salons with large sales and those with few sales is little things. Little things like training the receptionist to sell. Train them effectively and your business will make more money. It's that simple.

The display space required to sell pet products is between 150 and 250 square feet. Highlight the displays with adequate direct lighting. Have the receptionist be responsible to remove dust and pet hairs from the retail display regularly.

DAILY BOOKKEEPING AND RECORD KEEPING PROCEDURES

CHAPTER
13

T he difference between bookkeeping and accounting is that bookkeeping collects financial data while accounting analyzes that data. Accurate and complete bookkeeping records are a vital monitor of your business' performance. If you don't understand the need for accurate records, the possibility of financial success is doubtful. Inadequately kept financial records, or those kept solely to satisfy the Internal Revenue Service, is a common mistake for many small businesses. Thorough and up-to-date financial records furnish feedback allowing evaluation of business activities and permitting adjustments leading to greater financial accomplishment.

The bookkeeping records essential to every pet grooming salon include:

1. A daily summary of cash receipts. This includes totals from sales receipts, payment registers, register tapes, and credit card vouchers.

2. An expense ledger for the salon's checkbook(s) and an expense ledger for payments made in cash.

3. An inventory purchase journal showing shipments received, accounts payable, and cash available for future purchases.

4. An employee pay record listing salaries, hours, and withheld deductions.

5. An accounts receivable record if the salon allows charge accounts. Charge accounts, however, are not recommended.

Additional records necessary for business activity analysis are:

1. Accurate daily, weekly, monthly, and yearly totals of pets groomed.

2. Accurate totals from sales of services and goods, operating expenses, cost of goods sold, and inventory.

3. Income statements, and a current balance sheet.

4. Financial statements suitable for use by the owner, manager, and prospective creditors.

5. Copies of tax returns and reports to regulatory agencies.

MADSON BOOKKEEPING BUSINESS FORMS

The Madson Management System uses three forms to assist you with collecting income, expense, and payroll data. These custom forms complement the management system and provide much of the financial information required by a bookkeeper or accountant. When properly completed they contain an easily accessed wealth of financial information necessary in preparing the salon's financial records. Your accountant and bookkeeper will use them to prepare the Income Statement, and Balance Sheet (Chapter Fourteen). These key bookkeeping forms are:

1. The Weekly Employee Timekeeping Record

2. The Daily Caging and Payment Register

3. The Manager's Daily Summary Report of Services and Sales

The Weekly Employee Timekeeping Record is in illustration 13-1. You may make copies for use in managing your salon's payroll records. The Manager's Daily Summary Report of Services and Sales Envelope and the Daily Caging Payment Register are available separately from The Madson Group.

Weekly Employee Timekeeping Record

Every salaried or hourly employee completes a Weekly Employee Timekeeping Record. At the end of the payroll period, the manager approves the regular hours and overtime on each record before completing payroll. As part of the approval process, closely examine the overtime. Overtime may be a blessing if justified to complete the week's work. However, management should not rely on overtime to get work done. Properly distributed work will keep overtime to a minimum. Poor management is implied if overtime occurs constantly.

Every employee records start and finish times for the hours worked and lunch breaks on the Weekly Employee Timekeeping Record. The manager must check the accuracy of "punch-in" and "punch-out" times.

Groomers list the client's name for every pet they groom on the Weekly Employee Timekeeping Record. It can be useful to have the name of the groomer if questions arise in the future.

The manager submits Weekly Employee Timekeeping Records to the salon's owner for review and approval before completing payroll. The manager should justify any overtime and prepare alternatives when possible.

Once approved, use the Weekly Employee Timekeeping Records to prepare payroll. Then store the forms with the business' permanent records.

Instructions to complete the Weekly Employee Timekeeping Record are in Appendix A.

WEEKLY EMPLOYEE TIMEKEEPING RECORD

Employee Name _____ Week of _____ thru _____

☐ Salary ☐ Hourly ☐ Receptionist ☐ Telemarketer ☐ Pet Bather ☐ Bathing Dept. Supervisor ☐ Asst. Pet Trimmer ☐ Master Pet Trimmer ☐ Manager ☐

	SUNDAY	MONDAY	TUESDAY	WEDNESDAY	THURSDAY	FRIDAY	SATURDAY
	Time In: ____	Time In: ____	Time In: ____	Time In: ____	Time In: ____	Time In: ____	Time In: ____
	Lunch Begin: ____	Lunch Begin: ____	Lunch Begin: ____	Lunch Begin: ____	Lunch Begin: ____	Lunch Begin: ____	Lunch Begin: ____
	Lunch End: ____	Lunch End: ____	Lunch End: ____	Lunch End: ____	Lunch End: ____	Lunch End: ____	Lunch End: ____
	Time Out: ____	Time Out: ____	Time Out: ____	Time Out: ____	Time Out: ____	Time Out: ____	Time Out: ____
1.							
2.							
3.							
4.							
5.							
6.							
7.							
8.							
9.							
10.							
11.							
12.							
13.							
14.							

13-1

FORM 377-1

The Daily Caging and Payment Register

The receptionist completes a Daily Caging and Payment Register every business day. Like a hotel register, it tells which client's pet occupies the cages in the salon. It also registers the service fee and form of payment for each client. The register stays at the front counter throughout the business day. After accepting a client's pet for grooming, enter service information on both the Client and Pet History filecard and the Daily Caging and Payment Register.

Spaces numbered one through fifty-two represent cage numbers. If you haven't yet numbered your cages, do so now to improve efficiency. You may not have fifty-two cages yet, but you will by the time you complete Step Three of the Business Plan. Assign each client's pet a numbered cage. Next to the corresponding number on the Daily Caging and Payment Register, write the client's name, bath or trim information, service fee amount, and promised time out. When clients pick-up their pets, record the form of payment.

At the end of the day, the receptionist and manager summarize bookkeeping and record keeping information on the Daily Caging and Payment Register. The bookkeeping summary information requires total service fees, retail pet products sold, and sales tax collected. Enter every service order on the register. The record keeping summary information requires the total number of trim and bath-only pets completed that day. Use this information to measure the progress toward reaching the salon's financial goals (Chapter Fourteen).

The Daily Caging and Payment Register saved several hundred dollars on one occasion when someone robbed my salon. The police recommended a method to recover some of the stolen money. Using the Daily Caging and Payment Register, we contacted each client who paid by check or charge card. We placed stop payments on checks and charges and had new ones issued. In this manner we reduced the initial loss of over $700.00 to slightly over $100.00. Use the Daily Caging and Payment Register to protect your money.

Instructions for completing the Daily Caging and Payment Register are in Appendix A.

Manager's Daily Summary Report of Services and Sales

This form, when completed, tells the whole story of each business day. It charts vital management and accounting information on a daily basis and becomes a part of the salon's permanent records. It is the most important business form in a pet grooming salon and is essential to the Madson Management System.

The Manager's Daily Summary Report of Services and Sales is in eight sections.

Part One	Cash Receipts and Bank Deposit Record
Part Two	Cash Expense Detail
Part Three	Retail Sales Detail
Part Four	Personnel
Part Five	Pet Services Profile
Part Six	Client Services Profile
Part Seven	Manager Task Report
Part Eight	Official Reports

The eight sections are printed on a 9 X 12 envelope. At day's end, the manager transfers data from four other forms to the cover of the envelope and stores the forms inside.

DAILY CAGING AND PAYMENT REGISTER   DATE_____   DAY OF WEEK_____

CAGE NO.	CLIENT NAME	BA TR	TIME OUT	SVC. FEES	PET PRODS.	TAX	CA, CK. CH, M/V	CAGE NO.	CLIENT NAME	BA TR	TIME OUT	SVC. FEES	PET PRODS.	TAX	CA, CK. CH, M/V
1								27							
2								28							
3								29							
4								30							
5								31							
6								32							
7								33							
8								34							
9								35							
10								36							
11								37							
12								38							
13								39							
14								40							
15								41							
16								42							
17								43							
18								44							
19								45							
20								46							
21								47							
22								48							
23								49							
24								50							
25								51							
26								52							

WHEN COMPLETED, POST TOTALS TO MANAGER'S DAILY SUMMARY REPORT ENVELOPE

	NO. OF TRIMS	NO. OF BATH-ONLY	SERVICE FEES	PET PRODS. SOLD	SALES TAX COLLECTED
TOTALS:					

FORM 355-1

Actual Size: 8.5" x 11"

MANAGER'S DAILY SUMMARY REPORT OF SERVICES AND SALES

DATE _____ DAY OF WEEK _____ HOURS OF OPERATION_____ MANAGER_____

PART ONE—CASH RECEIPTS AND BANK DEPOSIT RECORD
Opening till _____ Next till _____

CASH RECEIPTS	CASH PAID OUT	CASH REGISTER
Services _____	Grooming Supplies _____	Currency _____
Sales _____	Cleaning Supplies _____	Coin _____
Sales Tax _____	Office Supplies _____	Checks _____
On Account _____	Bldg. & Equip. Sup. _____	C/Cards _____
Other _____	Repairs & Maint. _____	Other _____
Total _____	**Total** _____	**Total** _____

BALANCE (Total #1 is equal to Total #2 when in balance)

Total Cash Receipts .... _____

Less Total Cash Paid Out .... _____

    Total #1 .... _____

Accounts Receivable .... _____

(Enclose cash register tape, sales receipts, and cash expense receipts.)

Total Cash Register .... _____

Less Opening Till .... _____

    Total #2 .... _____

Cash: Over_____ Short _____

BANK DEPOSIT

Total Cash Register .... _____

Less Next Till .... _____

Total Bank Deposit .... _____

(Enclose deposit receipts.)

DEPOSIT RECORD

_____ _____

(940/941) _____

Total Deposits _____

PART TWO — CASH EXPENSE DETAIL

Total Cash Paid Out_____

Grooming Supplies:	Office Supplies:
Shampoo _____	Postage _____
Flea Dip _____	Stationery _____
Towels _____	First Aid _____
Cotton _____	Refreshments _____
Other _____	Other _____
Bldg. & Equip. Supplies:	**Cleaning Supplies:**
Air Filters _____	Disinfectant _____
Hardware _____	Detergent _____
Other _____	Glass _____
Repairs and Maintenance:	Wall/Floor _____
Equipment _____	Paper Goods _____
Furniture/Fixtures _____	Other _____

SAMPLE
MADSON BUSINESS FORM

PART THREE — RETAIL SALES DETAIL
Total Pet Products Sold _____ Total Sales Tax Collected _____

#	PET PRODUCTS SOLD	PRICE	TAX	TOTAL	#	PET PRODUCTS SOLD	PRICE	TAX	TOTAL
1.					6.				
2.					7.				
3.					8.				
4.					9.				
5.					10.				

PART FOUR — PERSONNEL REPORT

#	Employee Name	Time In	Lunch Begin	Lunch End	Time Out	Staff Attendance Comments
1.						
2.						
3.						
4.						
5.						
6.						
7.						
8.						

Personnel Management Activities

(Check any applicable)

_____ Training Program	_____ Hiring Interview	_____ Orientation
_____ Practical Exam	_____ Reference Checks	_____ Staff Meeting
_____ Demonstration	_____ Safety Drill	_____ Work Schedule
_____ Job Performance Evaluation	_____ Emp. Agreements	_____ Disciplinary

_____ Have the personnel files been updated regarding these activities?

Actual Size: 9" x 12"

13-3

THE MANAGER'S DAILY SUMMARY REPORT OF SERVICES AND SALES

PART FIVE — PET SERVICE PROFILE

Total # Complete Trim Services_____   Total # of Bath-Only Services_____

	COMPLETE TRIM Small	Large	BATH-ONLY Small	Large	NEW	AGED PETS	ILL PETS	VET CARE
Dogs								
Cats								

PART SIX — CLIENT SERVICES PROFILE

Total # of New Preferred Client Program Members . . . . _____

Total # of Pets Assigned Groom Alert Status . . . . _____

Total # of Medical Advisories Issued . . . . _____

Daily Response Reports

RECEPTIONIST	TELEMARKETER
Appts. Confirmed . . . . _____	Appts. Scheduled . . . . _____
Appts. Changed . . . . _____	# "B" Calls . . . . _____
Appts. Cancelled . . . . _____	# "C" Calls . . . . _____
	# "D" Calls . . . . _____
	# "NEW" Calls . . . . _____
Total Calls . . . . _____	Total Calls . . . . _____

Mailings

Get Well Cards for Pets _____   Pet Sympathy Cards _____

Client Response Postcards _____   Pet Care Brochures _____

Client Status and Follow-up Report

	Client/Pet Name	Referral	Birth	Death	Ill	Moved	Complaint	Comments
1.								
2.								
3.								
4.								
5.								
6.								
7.								
8.								
9.								

PART SEVEN — MANAGER TASK PROGRESS REPORT

(Check any of the following which you updated or completed today.)

_____ Business Plan Objectives   _____ Client Base Goal Worksheet

_____ Action Plan   _____ Weekly Summary of Complete Trims and Baths

_____ Supplies Control Log   _____ Annual Profit and Loss Projection

_____ Request for Tax Id.   _____ Business Plan Evaluation Checklist

_____ Ad Response Record   _____ Manager's Advance Planning Schedule

_____ Cash Reserve Journal   _____ Effective Management Checklist

_____ Meeting(s) with a Professional Advisor/Vendor/Local Official/Other Person(s)

Pet Industry and Community Participation

_____ Seminar _____ Trade Show _____ Civic Activity _____ Guest Speaker _____ Salon Tour

PART EIGHT — OFFICIAL REPORTS

(Check any of the following which occurred.)

Reduced Salon Services

_____ Power blackout/brownout   _____ Water supply cut-off

_____ Telephone out of service   _____ Problem corrected

Accidents/Injuries/Incidents

_____ Pet injury   _____ Employee injury   _____ Client injury

_____ Natural disaster   _____ Robbery   _____ Fire

_____ Place a check mark here when an Emergency Report including names, addresses, telephone numbers for all involved employees, clients, witnesses, pets, veterinarians, medical assistants and clinic/hospital has been completed. Make sure you also include details of emergency transport, names of persons placing emergency telephone calls, and the names of police/fire/insurance officials contacted.

1. The Daily Caging and Payment Register
2. The Daily Response Report (Receptionist)
3. The Daily Response Report (Telemarketer)
4. Emergency Reports

At the close of the day, the manager places bookkeeping data and cash receipts in the envelope and delivers it to the owner.

1. Cash Register Tape
2. Cash Receipts
3. Bank Deposit and Tax Deposit Receipts
4. Credit Card Vouchers

Be especially careful when transporting the envelope. Carry it inconspicuously, and with an escort, whenever you leave the salon. If you lose the contents you can never replace them.

The cash receipts and credit card vouchers allow the owner to prepare the deposit and opening till for the next business day.

The information compiled on a Manager's Daily Summary Report of Services and Sales assists in evaluating daily performance. For example, upon reviewing the report you may find the total appointment confirmations to be very low. This alerts you to pay more attention to the work habits of the receptionist and telemarketer and correct this deficiency. The manager is responsible to transfer this information from the other forms. He must study the data, notice any discrepancies, and make appropriate corrections.

Salon owners will find training a manager accelerated by the Manager's Daily Summary Report. All the activities which provide the information included in the report is the manager's supervisorial responsibility. He can refer to the report to learn about his responsibilities.

Instructions to complete the Manager's Daily Summary Report of Services and Sales are in Appendix A.

THE INFORMATION CENTER

The Information Center is the pulse of an efficient salon operation. The manager and staff can easily find the location of a pet, its time out, and the bather/trimmer assigned to groom it. To prevent the service records of pets being groomed from being scattered about, keep them in the Information Center. The Information Center also provides space to post announcements, timekeeping records, work schedules, and other media intended for the staff.

The Information Center requires wall space measuring twelve feet in length and four feet high. In the space post a blackboard, three filecard racks, and two bulletin boards. Illustration 13-5 has instructions in preparing and using the blackboard, filecard racks, and the two bulletin boards.

Blackboard.   The blackboard makes it easy to locate a pet and its assigned groomer. The blackboard (see fig. 1) organizes service information taken from the Client and Pet History filecard. By cage number and client name it lists every pet in the salon. A quick glance at the client's last name on the blackboard will show in which cage the pet is. Bathers and trimmers initial the board to affirm they are responsible to groom the pet.

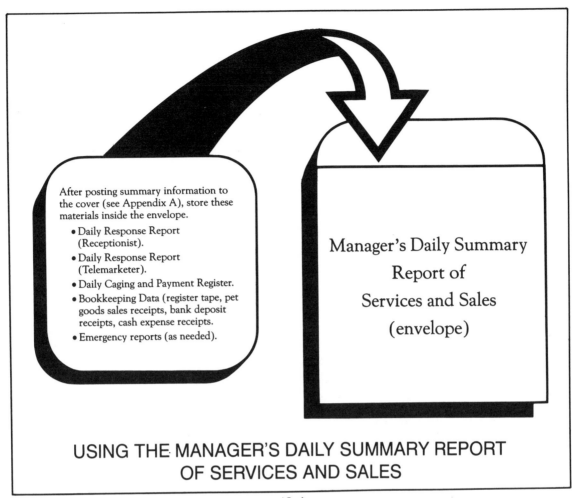

After posting summary information to the cover (see Appendix A), store these materials inside the envelope.

- Daily Response Report (Receptionist).
- Daily Response Report (Telemarketer).
- Daily Caging and Payment Register.
- Bookkeeping Data (register tape, pet goods sales receipts, bank deposit receipts, cash expense receipts.
- Emergency reports (as needed).

Manager's Daily Summary Report of Services and Sales (envelope)

USING THE MANAGER'S DAILY SUMMARY REPORT OF SERVICES AND SALES

13-4

The receptionist writes the client's name and pet's cage assignment on the blackboard after taking a service order.

Filecard racks.   After writing service information on the blackboard, the receptionist places the Client and Pet History filecard with the Pet Groomer's Report and Health Alert in the filecard rack. The filecard remains in the rack until the staff has completed the pet's grooming. The last groomer working on the pet removes it from the filecard rack and returns it to the receptionist when the pet is finished.

Place filecards with complete trim service orders in the rack labeled "Complete Trim." Place bath-only service orders in the rack labeled "Bath-Only." Sort filecards into the rack in order by "Time Out." The filecard with the earliest time out goes at the top of the rack and the latest on the bottom.

When the staff includes two or more master pet trimmers dedicate a "Complete Trim" filecard rack to each.

INFORMATION CENTER

You will need a space 12 feet long by 4 feet high on the wall for the Information Center. Put a blackboard, three filecard racks, and two bulletin boards in the space.

DAILY OPERATIONS

GENERAL INFORMATION

BLACKBOARD	FILECARDS	ANNOUNCEMENTS BULLETIN BOARD	EMPLOYMENT BULLETIN BOARD
See Fig. 1 below	See Fig. 2 below	• Staff Meetings • Memorandums • Policies, Procedures, & Postings • Goal Charts • Informative reading such as trade magazines, newsletters, etc.	•Employee Work Schedule •Timekeeping Records •Safety Reminders •Federal, State, Local Employment Dept. Notices •Emergency Procedures and Telephone Nos. • Reference Copy of Employee Handbook

CAGE	CLIENT NAME	BA TR	TIME OUT	BA INITIALS	TR INITIALS
1	Johnson	BA	1:00	JK	
2	Smith	2-TR	5:00	LK	SM
3	Allen	1-BA 1-TR	6:00		
4	Franklin	TR	3:00	JK	
5					
6	Lewis	BA	2:00	LK	
7					

Fig. 1 BLACKBOARD

Preparation. Using white paint mark the pattern on the blackboard as shown in Fig. 1. There should be one line for each cage in your salon. Title the columns, "Cage," "Client Name," "BA/TR," "Time Out," "BA Initials," and "TR Initials."

Daily Use. Taking information from the Client and Pet History filecards write the "Client Name," "BA/TR" symbol, and the "Time Out" next to each pet's cage number. The bather and/or trimmer initial the blackboard for each pet they groom.

Fig. 2 FILECARD RACKS

Preparation. Label two of the filecard racks "Complete Trim" and the last one, "Bath-only."

Daily. Place the Client and Pet History filecards for pets being groomed in the filecard racks. Put the filecards in the rack ranked by earliest "Time Out" to last "Time Out." When the pet has been groomed return the filecard to the receptionist.

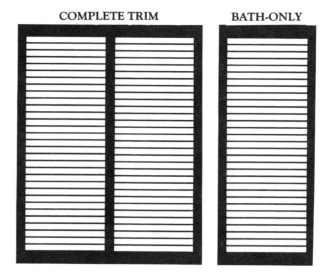

COMPLETE TRIM   BATH-ONLY

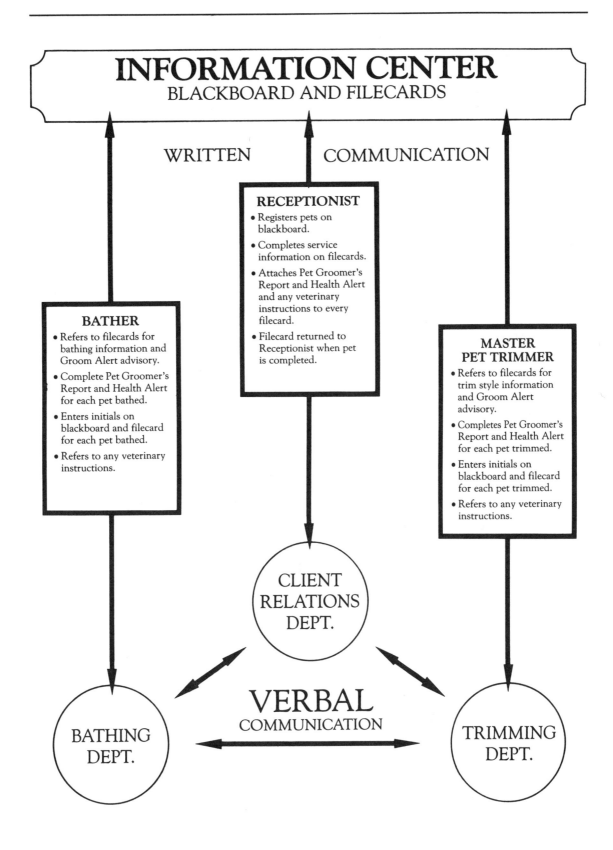

INFORMATION CENTER
BLACKBOARD AND FILECARDS

WRITTEN   COMMUNICATION

RECEPTIONIST
- Registers pets on blackboard.
- Completes service information on filecards.
- Attaches Pet Groomer's Report and Health Alert and any veterinary instructions to every filecard.
- Filecard returned to Receptionist when pet is completed.

BATHER
- Refers to filecards for bathing information and Groom Alert advisory.
- Complete Pet Groomer's Report and Health Alert for each pet bathed.
- Enters initials on blackboard and filecard for each pet bathed.
- Refers to any veterinary instructions.

MASTER PET TRIMMER
- Refers to filecards for trim style information and Groom Alert advisory.
- Completes Pet Groomer's Report and Health Alert for each pet trimmed.
- Enters initials on blackboard and filecard for each pet trimmed.
- Refers to any veterinary instructions.

CLIENT RELATIONS DEPT.

VERBAL
COMMUNICATION

BATHING DEPT.

TRIMMING DEPT.

13-5

CONTROLLING THE SALON'S SUPPLIES INVENTORY

An indirect method to increase profitability is to control the excessive use, and theft, of supplies. You will accomplish this by monitoring supply requisitions and the rate of their consumption using a supplies control log. A further safeguard is to keep the supplies in a locked storage area with only the owner and manager having access.

Make copies of the Supplies Control Log sheet provided in illustration 13-6 and keep an adequate supply available. Use one sheet to monitor the consumption of each supply. For example, use one sheet for clipper oil, one for flea dip concentrate, one for ear powder, and one for floor cleaner. Use a separate sheet for each type of shampoo concentrate also. Use one for standard shampoo concentrate, one for medicated shampoo, and another for baby shampoo. Organize the sheets in a ring binder and call it the "Supplies Control Log."

Label an empty cardboard box "Supplies Control" and have employees place empty supply containers in it. For example, after mixing gallons of shampoo, the bathing department supervisor places empty shampoo concentrate bottles in the box. The manager then removes the items from the control box and records their usage in the Supplies Control Log. The instructions are in Appendix A.

As shipments of supplies arrive, the manager updates inventory levels. The current balance for each supply should balance with an actual count of every stored supply. If not, records haven't been kept properly or someone is taking supplies without proper authorization.

Use the control log to analyze and control use of the supplies. The most costly grooming supply expense is shampoo concentrate. Measure its consumption monthly. For example, imagine a situation where you discover from the log that eight gallons of concentrate were consumed in July. When diluted, the concentrate makes ten gallons of regular shampoo. This tells you that eighty gallons of regular shampoo were consumed in July. You also know that you can bathe an average of ten medium-size pets with one gallon of diluted shampoo. From this you would estimate eight hundred pets had been bathed in July. By reviewing July's financial records, you discover only six hundred pets were bathed, and very few were large breeds. If ten percent of those pets were bathed in medicated or baby shampoo your concern would increase.

This rate of consumption would alert you to several misuse possibilities. The shampoo concentrate is being diluted improperly, pet bathers are using excessive amounts, or it is being carelessly spilled. The situation requires stricter supervision and re-training in proper methods of dilution of concentrate and application to pets. This is the procedure you would follow to analyze consumption data to control waste and theft.

Analyze the rate of consumption for every supply at least once a month. By doing so your operating expenses will be more cost-effective and profits will increase.

INFORMATION RETURN FORM 1099

Many small businesses overlook the requirement to file copies of Form 1099 with the Internal Revenue Service yearly. Failure to do so now can result in a fine of $50.00 for each form not filed. The purpose of the form is to report miscellaneous income paid out by you to individuals without withholding federal employment taxes. Currently, businesses paying $600.00 or more for rent or services to an unincorporated payee must file Form 1099 with the IRS and with the payee. Complete guidelines for determining which businesses or individuals due a Form 1099 are available at your local Internal Revenue Service office. Also, your bookkeeper or accountant can assist you.

You will need the federal tax identification, or social security number of the payee, to complete a 1099. If you don't have these numbers, send a letter of request to them as shown in the sample.

SUPPLIES CONTROL LOG

Product _____ Supplier _____ Reorder Level _____

DATE	DESCRIPTION	PURCHASES	USED	BALANCE

LETTER FOR TAX I.D. NUMBER

Dear

    The Internal Revenue Service requires us to report our payments to you on Information Return Form 1099 (Miscellaneous Income) at the end of each calendar year. To assist us would you please provide your social security or tax identification number in the space provided. (Employer I.D. numbers have nine digits, i.e. 00-0000000).

    In order for us to be in compliance with the law, please complete the statement below and return to us.

    Thank you for your cooperation by _____ .

Legal Name of Business _____

    doing business as   _____
    (if applicable)

Type (check one) ___Corporation ___Partnership ___Individual

    ___Other _____

(Provide one:)
Social Security # _____
    or
Federal I.D. # _____

Business Address _____
                            STREET

                 _____
                         CITY, STATE

                 _____
                    ZIP

Telephone (_____) _____

Signature_____ Date_____

Please return completed form to:

FINANCIAL MANAGEMENT
TO INCREASE PROFITS

Financial planning means planning how to make money in a business and how to spend it. Good financial planning enables you to make more than you spend. The business plan describes the goal and financial planning writes the monetary expression of that goal. Financial planning is management's responsibility and in this chapter you will learn the Madson Management System's recommendations regarding financial planning.

Financially successful owners of a pet grooming business engage in financial planning and unsuccessful owners don't. Running a business without a detailed financial plan in writing is like traveling to an unknown destination without a map. You might get there, but don't bet on it. To succeed in making a profit you must know your financial objectives. This includes estimates of the gross income needed, and the expenses incurred in achieving that income. Financial planning allows you to minimize spending while maximizing income. You cannot have lasting success without it.

Good financial planning begins by estimating how many grooming services you expect to perform in a given time period, and the income you will derive from those services. Make these projections on a daily, weekly, monthly, and annual basis. The annual estimate is in the form of a report called, the Annual Profit and Loss Projection. It determines your salon's operating budget and without a proper budget salon operations are like a "shot in the dark." The annual budget affects literally every aspect of your business.

THE ANNUAL PROFIT AND LOSS PROJECTION

An Annual Profit and Loss Projection is the most vital financial management tool of the Madson Management System. Working out a projection encourages you to think about your business in a realistic way. It also provides measurable financial goals for you to achieve. By doing so, you can often spot problem areas before they drain profits.

Planning does not require a crystal ball and is not a guessing game. Using the guidance of the Madson Management System you can arrive at realistic projections. The time to prepare an Annual Profit and Loss Projection is at the beginning of each year and at each step of the business plan. A copy of the Annual Profit and Loss Projection form is in illustration 14-1. Make copies and keep an adequate supply available.

The Annual Profit and Loss Projection is the "big picture" of your financial goals for gross profit, operating expenses, and net profit. You will achieve those goals by controlling the direction of your salon's finances through effective management. Use the Madson People and Pet Marketing Program to achieve the number of pet services necessary to earn the gross profit projected. Keep the salon's actual operating expenses at, or beneath the limits set on the annual projection. Subtracting the operating expenses from the gross profit provides the net profit or loss. This is your income before taxes.

Begin your financial planning by filling out the Annual Profit and Loss Projection for the past year. That is, use the real figures for the preceding year to give you a basis for projecting increases for the coming year. Determine the increase in pet grooming services you could reasonably handle using the facilities and personnel you have now. Multiply this by the fee for those services. This becomes your projected gross profit. As a rule of thumb, limit projections to an increase of between 10% to 25% of last year's figures. Financial planning is not just determining the number of pets which must be serviced to reach your goals. You must also estimate the increased expenses in reaching this goal.

To demonstrate how to use the Annual Profit and Loss Projection form consider the following example.

EXAMPLE

Last year you earned $100,000.00 in gross revenue (not as difficult as you might think with the Madson Management System). You project an ambitious 25% increase in gross revenue for the coming year. This means a dollar increase to $125,000.00. The objective then is to increase this year's gross revenue by $25,000.00.

Gross Revenue	
This Year's Objective	$125,000.00
Previous Year Total	$100,000.00
Increase	$ 25,000.00

The Annual Profit and Loss Projection is divided by month, so the monthly revenue necessary to achieve a $25,000.00 annual increase is $2,083.00.

$$\frac{\text{Increase} \quad (\$25,000.00)}{\text{Time Period} \quad (12 \text{ months})} \quad \text{equals } \$2,083.33/\text{per month}$$

ANNUAL PROFIT AND LOSS PROJECTION

FROM: Mo. _____ Yr. _____ TO Mo. _____ Yr. _____

LINE	DESCRIPTION	Month 1	Month 2	Month 3	Month 4	Month 5	Month 6	Month 7	Month 8	Month 9	Month 10	Month 11	Month 12
1.	Number of Complete Trims												
2.	Number of Bath-only												
3.	Total Net Sales of Services												
4.	Total Net Sales of Pet Products												
5.	Less Cost of Goods Sold												
6.	Gross Profit Margin												
7.	Operating Expenses												
8.	Payroll Expense–Gross												
9.	Rent Expense												
10.	Advertising Expense												
11.	Taxes-Payroll												
12.	Utilities Expense												
13.	Insurance–Liability & Worker's Comp.												
14.	Insurance–Health												
15.	Supplies–Grooming												
16.	Supplies-Retail												
17.	Office Expense												
18.	Accounting & Legal												
19.	Business/Promotional Forms												
20.	Repairs & Maintenance–Bldg.												
21.	Janitorial Expense												
22.	Towels & Laundry Expense												
23.	Telephone Expense												
24.	Veterinary Expense												
25.	Automobile Expense												
26.	License–Dues & Fees												
27.	Repairs & Maintenance–Equip.												
28.	Publications												
29.	Miscellaneous Expenses												
30.	Bank Charges												
31.	Total Operating Expenses												
32.	Net Profit/Loss Margin (before taxes)												

GRAND TOTALS

No. of Complete Trims	No. of Bath-only	Gross Profit Margin	Operating Expenses	Net Profit/Loss (before taxes)
_____	_____	_____	_____	_____

14-1

This allows a monthly review of the salon's progress in achieving financial goals. You can take appropriate action if the figures are short.

Once the establishing the monthly financial goal you must translate it into pet service objectives. To achieve these objectives state them in the volume of pet services required to reach the goals.

Monthly increase in gross revenue	$2,083.33
Salon's average service fee	$ 20.00
Monthly Increase in Pet Services	**104**

Now you have a tangible, easily measured goal. 104 is the number of pets the salon must groom each month to achieve an annual increase in gross revenue of $25,000.00. Remember, these are additional services. If the salon serviced 400 pets per month in the previous year, it must now service an additional 104 per month to achieve the $2,083.33 increase per month.

Thinking of the increase as 104 additional pets monthly helps accomplish the goal. The staff may not understand what is required of them in achieving a monetary goal. Nonetheless, they can easily understand how increasing the number of pets groomed affects them. By following this process and sharing service goals with your staff (an important part of teamwork) you will take a big step toward attaining your goals.

Salon owners should include in the job agreement the increase in annual gross revenue and service volume expected from the manager. Train the manager in financial planning skills and provide them with copies of past financial plans. Schedule a monthly meeting the first week of each month to review the salon's performance in achieving financial goals. To review the actual financial performance requires financial statements prepared by the bookkeeper/accountant and an Annual Profit and Loss Projection.

Instructions to complete the Annual Profit and Loss Projection are in Appendix A. In preparing your first Annual Profit and Loss Projection consult with your bookkeeper/accountant.

WEEKLY SUMMARY OF COMPLETE TRIM AND BATH-ONLY SERVICES

The Weekly Summary of Complete Trim and Bath-only Services is a method where the manager is able to monitor progress toward service goals. It enables the manager to track the actual number of pets groomed during each work week. You accomplish this by adding the daily service count found on the Manager's Daily Summary Report of Services and Sales Envelopes.

After a few weeks of completing the Weekly Summary, you can compare actual service figures with those on the Annual Profit and Loss Projection. By doing this the manager can assess his success in reaching the salon's financial goals.

FINANCIAL STATEMENTS

Financial statements, sometimes called financials, consist of an Income Statement and Balance Sheet. Preparation of these requires accurately kept daily records. Most of these records are on the Manager's Daily Summary Report of Services and Sales. The rest of it is in the checkbook journal and depreciation record.

WEEKLY SUMMARY OF COMPLETE TRIM AND BATH-ONLY SERVICES

The summary has 52 lines, one for each week in a year. Make photocopies and use one at the start of Step One of the business plan. Complete one line on the summary at the end of every work week.

Compare weekly totals and evaluate the reason for decrease in services. You can also use a copy of the summary to prepare complete trim and bath-only service projections which are kept on the Annual Profit and Loss Projection .

WEEK OF _____ THRU _____	# TR	# BA	WEEK OF _____ THRU _____	# TR	# BA

TR–Complete Trims   BA–Bath-Only

14-2

With these records the bookkeeper/accountant can prepare financial statements and tax returns. If you ever need to approach prospective investors, bankers, or buyers, they will undoubtedly require this financial information.

The Income Statement

The Income Statement, sometimes called a Profit and Loss Statement, summarizes bookkeeping records for a given period. It begins with the adjusted sales totals (service and retail) for the period. Adjust the sales totals for returned checks and credit card refunds. Record the interest earned by funds in the cash reserve (Chapter Three) as revenue. This sum of service and retail sales, interest, and adjustments for returned items is the gross profit for the period.

List the operating expenses incurred in the same time period on the statement. The total operating expenses figure is sum of the itemized operating expenses. Subtracting total operating expenses from the gross profit determines the net profit or loss for the period. This is the owner's income before taxes.

Following are definitions of the terms on the income statement.

REVENUE

Sales-Services   The total of cash receipts for services listed on the Manager's Daily Summary Report of Services and Sales during the time period covered by the Income Statement.

Sales-Taxable/Retail   The total of cash receipts for sales of pet products, including sales tax collected, listed on the Manager's Daily Summary Report of Services and Sales during the time period covered by the Income Statement.

Returned Checks/Credit Card Refunds   The total of all returned checks and credit card refunds during the time period covered by the Income Statement.

Interest   The total interest earned by the Cash Reserve account, or any other business account, during the time period covered by the Income Statement.

Total Income   The total of the four items listed above.

OPERATING EXPENSES

Operating Expenses   The itemized expenses incurred in operating the salon during the time period covered by the Income Statement. Twenty-three categories of operating expenses typical for pet grooming salons are listed.

Total Operating Expenses   The sum of the itemized operating expenses.

Net Profit or <Loss>   Total Income minus Total Operating Expenses equals Net Profit or Loss. This is the owner's income before taxes.

The format for the Income Statement is similar to the Annual Profit and Loss Projection. The latter projects revenue and expenses. That means it attempts to predict them. However, the

Income Statement accounts for the actual revenue and expenses. Each month compare the salon's Income Statement figures with the Annual Profit and Loss Projection. This allows you to assess your success in reaching financial goals.

The Income Statement portrays the financial health of a business over a given time period. It is similar to taking a blood pressure reading of your business. The cash flow, or "blood pressure" of the business, is a gauge of business efficiency. It shows whether a business is reaching income and profit goals. The bookkeeper/accountant prepares it monthly, quarterly, and yearly.

Comparing actual figures for monthly revenue and operating expenses with the monthly projections provides a yardstick to measure your success. The purpose of your evaluation is the comparison of the actual and projected net profit. This is your income before taxes.

The comparison and analysis of the budget (projected) and actual figures also measures your effectiveness with the management system. As your mastery of the management system improves, your projections will improve, and the difference between actual and budget figures will reduce. Understanding why income and expenses are higher, or lower, than projected will help you manage your business more efficiently. Even if you don't meet all your projections, you'll still be ahead because you're paying attention to the right things.

A sample Income Statement especially designed for pet grooming salons is in illustration 14-3. Give a copy of this statement to the bookkeeper.

The Balance Sheet

The Balance Sheet (illustration 14-4) is a more general picture of the business at a single moment in time. This is unlike the Income Statement which is an itemized picture of the business for a longer period. The Balance Sheet shows assets and liabilities, not income and expenses. It states what you have of value and what you owe.

As with the Income Statement, have the bookkeeper/accountant prepare the Balance Sheet monthly, quarterly, and yearly. Subtracting total liabilities from total assets yields a figure which represents your net worth, or owner equity. The higher the net worth, the better your financial success. Total assets must always equal total liabilities plus owner equity.

PROFIT AND LOSS RATIOS

Profit and loss ratios are percentages. Calculate them by averaging information from two or more recent income statements. With these percentages you will be able to determine whether or not you are keeping within the salon's budget. Also, profit and loss ratios will assist you to make accurate projections for operating expenses.

Two sets of operating ratios are on the sample income statement (illustration 14-3). The first set represents the monthly ratio of revenue and expenses, while the second set represents the year-to-date ratio.

Every category of operating expense has its own operating ratio percentage. For instance, utilities is 2.58 percent in the current month and 1.3 percent year-to-date. That means 2.58 percent of every dollar goes for utilities in the current month. The year-to-date ratio shows 1.3 percent of every dollar is for utilities. This comparison reveals the utility expense for the present month is higher than the year-to-date average. What would you do?

ABC PET GROOMING SALON
Income Statement
For the Month June 19-

	CURRENT	%	YEAR-TO-DATE	%
Revenue:				
Sales-Services	$ 8,500.00	97.26	$ 55,750.00	96.98
Sales-Taxable/Retail.........	250.25	2.86	1,775.40	3.09
Returned Checks/				
Credit Cards	<25.00>	<.28>	<110.00>	<.19>
Interest Income	14.00	.16	70.00	.12
Total Income	$ 8,739.25	100.00	$ 57,485.40	100.00
Gross Profit....................	$ 8,739.25	100.00	$ 57,485.40	100.00
Operating Expenses:				
Payroll Expense-Gross	$ 2,774.27	31.76	$ 17,245.62	30.00
Rent Expense	502.99	5.76	3,017.99	5.25
Advertising Expense	379.05	4.34	2,874.27	5.00
Taxes-Payroll.................	243.71	2.80	862.28	1.50
Utilities Expense	224.55	2.58	747.31	1.30
Insurance-				
Liab. & W/Comp...........	145.81	1.69	689.82	1.20
Insurance-Health	45.80	.53	574.85	1.00
Supplies-Grooming	75.82	.88	574.80	1.00
Supplies-Retail	115.81	1.34	574.90	1.00
Telephone Expense	93.93	1.07	430.60	.75
Accounting and Legal	44.90	.52	402.39	.70
Office Expense...............	67.06	.79	288.01	.50
Business/				
Promotional Forms.........	50.90	.59	287.39	.50
Repairs and				
Maintenance-Bldg.	18.75	.22	287.47	.50
Janitorial Expense	38.74	.45	172.48	.30
Towels and				
Laundry Expense	33.94	.40	172.42	.30
Veterinary Expense	13.94	.17	143.66	.25
Automobile Expense	24.17	.28	143.71	.25
Repair and				
Maintenance-Equip.	14.15	.17	115.00	.20
License-Dues and Fees	9.55	.13	114.99	.20
Publications..................	14.56	.17	57.33	.10
Miscellaneous Expenses	4.57	.06	57.53	.10
Bank Charges	3.00	.03	57.58	.10
Total Operating Expenses	$ 4,939.97	57.53	$ 29,892.40	52.00
Net Profit or <Loss>	$ 3,799.28	42.47	$ 27,593.00	48.00
(before taxes)				

ABC PET GROOMING SALON
Balance Sheet
As of October 31, 19-

ASSETS

Current Assets

Cash–Bank (General)	$ 2,356.78	
Cash–Bank (Reserve)	14,940.03	
Cash on Hand	3,570.05	
Accounts Receivable	22.00	
Advances–Employees	<60.00>	
Total Current Assets		$ 20,828.86

Fixed Assets

Furniture & Fixtures	$ 4,400.55	
Equipment	22,550.45	
Accumulated Deprec.	<5,335.77>	
Leasehold Improvements	27,560.07	
Accumulated Amortization	<6,050.50>	
Total Fixed Assets		$ 43,124.80

Other Assets

Deposit–Rental	400.00	
Deposit–Utility	250.00	
Total Other Assets		$ 650.00
Total Assets		$ 64,603.66

LIABILITIES AND OWNER EQUITY

Liabilities

Note Payable	$ 29,245.75	
Note Payable	1,357.88	
Payroll Taxes Payable	576.98	
Sales Tax Payable	37.09	
Total Liabilities		$ 31,217.70

Owner Equity

Capital	$ 25,500.00	
Net Profit or <Loss>	7,885.96	
Total Owner Equity		$ 33,385.96
Total Liabilities and Owner Equity		$ 64,603.66

14-4

By adding the percentages for each category of operating expense you can see the ratios. In this case, 57.53 percent of every dollar goes for operating expenses for the current month and 52.00 percent year-to-date. Subtracting the total operating expense ratio from the Gross Profit ratio yields the Net Profit or Loss ratio. The higher this ratio, the more net profit before taxes.

Illustration 14-5 provides guideline operating expense ratios typical of a profitable pet grooming salon following the Madson Management System.

A bookkeeper or accountant can help you prepare operating ratios by reviewing your salon's actual income statements. As you improve the cost-efficiency of your business you will lower the total operating expense ratio, and increase the net profit.

COMPREHENSIVE BUSINESS INSURANCE

Comprehensive business insurance is too often avoided in the pet grooming field. Your valuable inventory of clients and pets can become a liability. Protect your future with comprehensive business insurance package which includes worker's compensation coverage. It should also cover product liability, premises liability, fire, and malpractice insurance. Malpractice insurance is an investment against a financial loss that could close your pet salon. Make sure your coverage includes pet salon tour groups and pet grooming students. If you provide pick-up and delivery service, be certain your policy covers the vehicle, driver, and transported pets.

If you are now covered by business insurance, make sure it covers all persons that may come into your business. Some policies may have surprising exclusions such as vendors, service repairmen, or non-business visitors. Others may exclude people working as contract labor on commission. This is another good example of the benefit of paying salaries which are characteristic of employees, not contract laborers. You usually will have to pay extra for coverage of contract laborers.

Several years ago groomer insurance was difficult to find. There are now complete packages endorsed by the National Dog Groomers Association of America and by the American Boarding Kennels Association. A good working relationship with your insurance agent is vital for the success of your business. Ask them to keep you informed of any coverage changes before they go into effect.

PROFIT AND LOSS OPERATING RATIOS

Payroll Expense–Gross	30.00%
Rent Expense	5.25
Advertising Expense	5.00
Taxes–Payroll	1.50
Utilities Expense	1.30
Insurance–Liability & Worker's Compensation	1.20
Insurance–Health	1.00
Supplies–Grooming	1.00
Supplies–Retail	1.00
Office Expense	1.00
Accounting & Legal	.70
Business/Promotional Forms	.50
Repairs & Maintenance–Bldg.	.50
Janitorial Expense	.30
Towels & Laundry Expense	.30
Telephone Expense	.25
Veterinary Expense	.25
Automobile Expense	.25
License–Dues & Fees	.20
Repairs & Maintenance–Equipment	.20
Publications	.10
Miscellaneous Expenses	.10
Bank Charges	.10
TOTAL	**52%**

PLANNING FOR THE FUTURE

CHAPTER

15

Puppies and kittens need their owner's care and commitment to develop healthily. Similarly, a pet grooming salon also needs care and commitment to be healthy. Pet salons mature by optimizing their client base, profitability, and pet care services. If they don't, they risk financial stagnation.

Decisions made about your business now affect your lifestyle many years from now. The business activities you engage in today should lead to the position you want to be in when you retire. Have the vision to consider remodeling, expansion, and succession plans. Profitability in the future depends on establishing and implementing long-range objectives, now!

This chapter presents realistic, achievable goals you can accomplish with the Madson Management System. You will have the resources to remodel your salon into a state-of-the-art pet grooming salon or expand into a Pet Center. You can fund a retirement plan, or choose an alternative lifestyle as your salon continues providing revenue. Efficiently engineered space-planning for the salon of the future and a description of its advanced features are in this chapter. Owners of these pet salons and pet centers will be industry leaders setting the pace for the future of pet grooming.

To be in the position to achieve these goals you must exploit the full potential of your market area and optimize your client base.

Most urban/suburban pet salons can obtain 1,500 to 2,000 clients. It is self-defeating to believe you can never achieve this success. It is also untrue. Pet grooming salons in sparsely populated areas may be unable to achieve this number, but they can excel in their area. Competent marketing and client service will attract clients from distances you would not believe possible. Many of my clients travelled up to ninety minutes or more to receive superior service.

Do not limit expectations to the point you fail to see possibilities. Perhaps this is why so many pet salons are not fulfilling their potential. Once, no one in the pet grooming industry thought it possible to have a salon with 3,500 clients. Using my management system I proved them wrong! You too can "take the town" and achieve your fullest potential.

A STATE-OF-THE-ART PET GROOMING SALON

The floorplan and features of a state-of-the-art salon have a purposeful design. The salon's design enhances safety, productivity, comfort, hygiene, client relations, supervision, quality, and retail sales. The salon of the future is capable of serving fifty or more clients and pets. It does this in about one thousand square feet and yields a six-figure gross revenue.

Floors.   The entire salon has a smooth, non-slippery vinyl floorcovering. There are no pebbled surfaces that can trap soil in small crevices.

Walls.   Ceramic tile beginning at floor level and extending to a height of six feet covers the salon's interior. This makes it easy to keep them hygienically clean and glistens with a sparkle sure to impress clients.

Lighting.   Warm fluorescent lighting illuminates the interior of the salon and task lights focus on workstations and product displays. Spot lighting is around each workstation to prevent shadows.

Air Conditioning.   Central air conditioning moderates the heat created by blow dryers keeping pets and people comfortable. Circulation vents are there to cool the "hot" spots.

Electrical.   The electrical system is capable of handling present and future demands for electricity. Emergency power generators are available for use during power outages.

Security.   A central alarm system alerts the police department when someone attempts unauthorized access through any door, basement, window, or roof opening. Security roll-type window coverings provide further protection.

Central Vacuum.   The central vacuum system with outlets in the bathing, trimming, and reception departments simplifies clean-up.

Telephone System.   The salon is serviced by a central telephone system capable of modular expansion for future needs.

Washer and Dryer.   Laundering towels during the business day is easy with the salon's washer and dryer. An overhead rack holds laundry detergent and sterilizing agents.

Dog-run.   The salon's interior includes a dog-run. When pets need to defecate the run is used and immediately sterilized. Very large pets are dried in this area also.

Client Reception Department

Client Entry.   Double doors serve the main entry. However, clients with fearful, ill, hyperactive, oversize, or troublesome pets may use the side entrance. Clients with cats may also enter by the side door to avoid altercations with dogs.

Front Counter.   A spacious, stain resistant, and non-slippery countertop permits service to two clients simultaneously. An attractive display exhibit holds promotional materials.

Safety Gates.   Safety gates flank both sides of the front counter. They open only toward the salon's interior. This prevents pets in the grooming area from entering the reception area, or

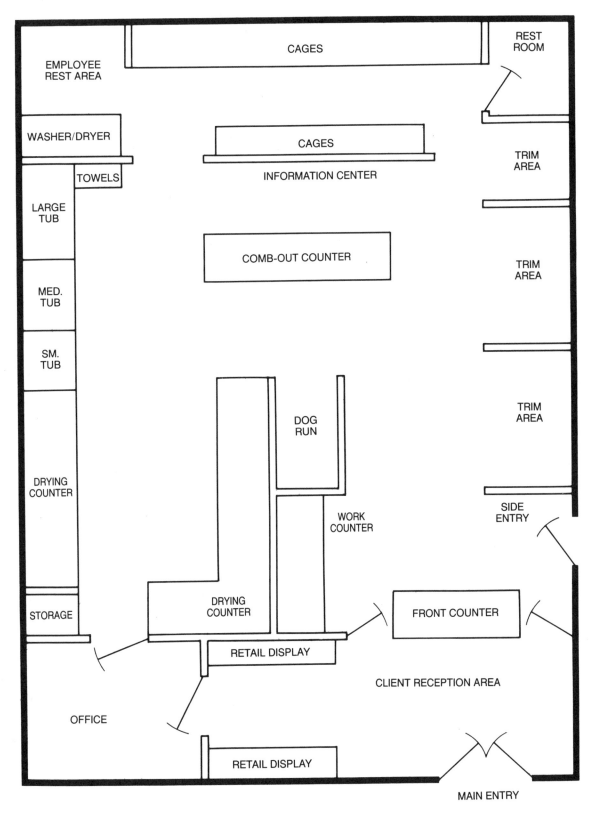

FLOOR PLAN
STATE-OF-THE-ART PET SALON   Scale 1″ = 5′

worse, bolting out the front doors. When two or more clients are present, the two gates keep pets separated minimizing pet fights.

Client Seating.   Ample seating and current reading material is available for clients waiting for their pets. Coffee or tea is available from the refreshment center (Employee Rest Area).

Retail Display.   Well-lit display cases with clear glass doors effectively reveal products and prevent pet hair from accumulating on them. Regular cleaning and neat organization of the retail inventory increases sales.

Work Counter.   A work area behind the front counter holds the filecard boxes, adding machine, and an electronic cash register with battery back-up. The receptionist and telemarketer share this work counter when performing their duties. They have a phone with three lines allowing each exclusive use of one phone and one line.

An under-the-counter lockable storage area holds promotional and office supplies, medicated shampoos, and treatments prescribed by veterinarians.

Trimming Department

Location.   The trimming department location allows the clients to watch trimmer's as they work. Clients enjoy seeing the finish trimming and the proximity allows the trimmers to build better rapport with clients.

The assistant pet trimmer's workstation is next to the master pet trimmer. This facilitates instruction and supervision.

Equipment.   Trimmers use hydraulic grooming tables with four spot lamps illuminating each of them. Each trimming station has its own booster to run clippers more efficiently. Drawers for tools and grooming supplies are in a counter running the length of the trimming department.

Bathing Department

The bathing department is designed to prevent unbathed pets from soiling clean pets as they complete their bath and blow-dry.

Location.   The location of the bathing department near the rear of the salon reduces unwelcome noise and heat in the client reception department.

Comb-out Table.   Here, unbathed pets have an initial brush and comb-out before bathing. Comb-outs create most of the soil and hairballs in a salon. By containing the debris in one area it does not affect clean pets and is disposed of more easily.

Stainless Steel Tubs.   From the comb-out table pets go to one of three stainless steel tubs. The smallest tub is for very small pets, the medium tub for ill pets and medicated baths, and the large tub for all other pets. The tubs are sterilized after each use keeping the work area hygienic.

Special traps in each tub collect pet hair and other debris preventing clogged pipes. A vinyl, non-slip board covers the floor of each tub and each bather's workstation. The vinyl boards with many little holes are on the floor of the tub allowing water to drain. This permits the pet to stand out of the water and protects both pet and bather from slipping. In addition, the boards prevent soap burns caused by standing in soapy water. Be sure the boards have holes small enough to prevent the smallest pet's feet from getting caught.

Ceramic tile covers the walls above the tubs for easy cleaning. A heavy-duty waterproof varnish, such as Enviro-Tex protects the wood framing enclosing the tubs.

A hydraulic lift reduces the risk of backstrain from lifting very heavy pets into the larger tub. In addition, the top lip of the large tub is three feet from the floor.

Central Pump System.   A central pump system dispenses temperature controlled water and three types of shampoos. Hoses from the pump to each tub distribute the water and shampoos.

Drying Area.   From the large tub pets can walk along a non-slip, laminate covered, drying counter to one of four drying stations.

One central, roof-mounted, blow-dryer system provides hot air to four drying stations. Four hoses suspended from an overhead track service each drying station.

Towel Rack.   The towel rack holds an ample supply of clean towels. New towels replace worn ones which become cleaning rags.

Grooming Tools.   Bacticide sterilizes combs, brushes, and ear-cleaning forceps. Sterile glass containers hold cotton balls.

Caging Area

Location.   The placement of cages allows observation of the pets. It is as vital to oversee the safety of pets waiting in their cages as it is to safeguard pets being groomed.

Supplies Storage

A supplies storage area holds the salon's inventory of grooming and cleaning supplies, and maintenance equipment. To control misuse of supplies only the owner and manager have access to keys for the storage area.

Toxic and flammable chemicals are kept in this storage area, as well as shampoo and flea dip concentrates.

Employee Rest Area

Each employee has a locker for personal belongings. The refreshment center, aside from dispensing cold drinks, includes a sink, mini-refrigerator, and microwave to prepare food and hot drinks. A small table with chairs provides seating during lunch.

Office

The manager's office is soundproofed. This is so performance reviews and hiring interviews may be private and undisturbed by noise from the pet salon.

Record Files.   The salon's confidential records are in fireproof file cabinets.

Safe.   The office has a safe to hold the salon's undeposited receipts, and cash register change (called the mainbank).

Exterior

Parking.   At least four, well-lit parking spaces are available.

Lighting.   In addition to lighting in the parking area, the entry to the salon must have adequate lighting controlled by solar switches.

Potty-walking area.   An enclosed, gated potty area enables clients to walk their pets before leaving. Flowering plants refine the area. Sterilizing the area every day prevents it from offending clients and neighbors. A doggie doolie permits convenient and hygienic disposal of pet stools.

EXPANDING INTO A PET CENTER

By accruing substantial equity and having sound personal and business finances you have many options. One is to expand into a Pet Center with its superior profit potential. Your past success gives bankers and investors reason to believe you can make the expansion into a Pet Center a success.

A Pet Center supplies grooming services, pet foods and supplies, and pets, in one central location. People need only make one-stop for their pet shopping needs. Pet Centers in rural areas also offer livestock feed and supplies. A successful Pet Center operation offers its owner one of the highest returns on investment in the pet industry.

Shopping centers use a common principle. They seek a large tenant as the anchor business. This is usually a supermarket because it attracts the widest cross-section of people. Around this anchor are a variety of smaller stores offering the convenience of one-stop shopping. Pet Center owners can profit by using the same principle.

The Pet Center's location and anchor are the two most important considerations before beginning an expansion. The location should be near or in a popular shopping center with high visibility and ample parking. In addition to the shopping center's anchor store, the anchor for the Pet Center is a veterinarian. People will be enticed to the convenience of one-stop pet shopping, grooming, and veterinary care next door to other shopping needs. Convenience and service will be two of the most successful client-attracting features for businesses in the 1990's.

Opening a Pet Center may require more investment capital than you have. However, strong financial standing and an excellent management reputation will attract the attention of bankers and venture capitalists. Before approaching them, you need to have a business plan detailing your strategy for successfully managing the expansion. Bankers and investors require a complete, accurate picture of "where you are" and "where you are going," professionally and financially before making a loan or investment.

Management consultants can assist you in writing a business plan. There are many excellent "how to write a business plan" reference books available. Business management organizations and college extension programs often include business plan writing seminars classes in their curriculum.

Share your vision of the Pet Center in the business plan and show them what it will take to make the vision profitable. Give them the complete details of the capital required. Itemize capital expenditures like the acquisition of the building, inventory, new equipment, hiring and training professional sales staff, and a marketing program to promote the new center. Show the profit and loss projections for the first three years to demonstrate how you will pay back the loan. You are then ready to present the business plan.

Effective working relationships developed during your years working the Madson Management System are now a prime resource for seeking investment capital. Bankers, Realtors, financial advisors, management consultants, attorneys, veterinarians, land developers, and venture capitalists are all possible sources, or leads, for investment capital. Start with your banker. Although he may deny you a loan, he can provide you with leads for alternate sources of investment capital. Also, the veterinarian for the Pet Center is a source of investment capital. He stands to gain clients from your business.

By improving your business knowledge before you expand the salon you will be better prepared for a successful expansion. Do this with seminars and formal education. Study retailing, financial planning, land development, computer systems, and sales management. Have your financial advisors explain the advantages of owning the Pet Center building and include its purchase with your business plan.

FUNDING A RETIREMENT PLAN

If you plan to retire someday, you will want to do so comfortably. The size of your client base is directly proportional to the value of your salon. So, the more your business is worth, the more you will receive for your retirement. If you want to sell your salon, having used the Madson Management System makes this a profitable choice. As your profits increase, you can fund a retirement plan.

The net worth of the pet salon is usually the most significant contributor to the owner's retirement. To maximize the net worth of the business you must install and maintain the Madson Management System. This will teach you how to increase the net worth of your business. This is by expansion of sales and services, purchasing a building for the salon, computerizing the salon's client service and marketing program, and incorporating when appropriate. The assistance of professional advisors including a bookkeeper, certified public accountant, business attorney, and financial planning experts can be invaluable.

CREATING AN ALTERNATIVE LIFESTYLE

Becoming a Full-Time Manager

The owner/trimmer, whose personal finances are in order, may decide to stop trimming and take the position of full-time manager. The expense saved by not hiring a manager offsets the expense of hiring a new trimmer to perform the trims you once completed. You can retire from trimming, but plan to support yourself until you begin deriving the financial benefits of being full-time manager.

The work of a trimmer entails much physical strain. Owners, who stop trimming to become manager will welcome the physical relief. There are other, more pecuniary, benefits. By managing full-time you have the opportunity to develop zero-defect pet grooming operations. Direct your energies to the People and Pet Marketing Program to increase business. Pay strict attention to the fine details of the operation and the overall quality of client and pet care services. Clients appreciate dealing with the owner directly so spend more time at the front counter and develop better rapport with every client. Every pet, on even the busiest days, should receive your "seal of approval" before returning to the client. The client base can dramatically increase by this concentrated effort.

Absentee Ownership

Another exciting option available to you is having your salon run by a full-time manager as you continue to derive an income. This permits a second career, travel, or any of several intriguing alternatives. When the salon has an experienced manager and a history of operating profitably, you have the opportunity to become an absentee owner.

The key to accomplishing this objective is to create a competent manager through proficient hiring and training procedures. You must train the manager in all aspects of the Madson Management System. Allow the manager to run the operation alone several times and evaluate their performance. The manager needs to be able to mirror the owner's operation of the salon before taking on sole responsibility. Owner and manager must cooperate to achieve their goals. They must have shared the vagaries of business before you can be confident of their ability to run the salon in your absence. The manager is the right team member to care for your business. This is because he learned the proper way to manage your salon — from you.

You will still oversee your business, but have more free time. You will supervise the salon's quality and efficiency and act as master of its finances. Your profit will be less compared to when you were working. Nonetheless, it can still provide a regular and steady income and permit you the freedom for which you worked so hard.

Would you like to play golf in the afternoon? Want to go to a matinee, spend more time with your spouse or children, get more involved in a hobby? These are options available to a financially stable pet salon owner with an experienced manager. By following the Madson Management System you will have the luxury of deciding for yourself. This is a luxury most pet grooming salon owners will never have because they lack an effective management system. With an effective system you no longer have to be at the mercy of your business. You can confidently leave the daily management tasks to your manager.Most pet grooming salon owners have never seriously considered hiring a manager to run their operation. Many owners are still tied to the grooming table, not by preference, but because of financial pressure. Using the Madson Management System will one day permit you to create your own lifestyle. This is preferable to having the business control those choices.

Use at least a portion of the time freed from the business by the manager to increase your business management education. Attend seminars and continuing education classes. Regular attendance and active participation in business education improves your prospects for even greater financial success. Benefits can be derived from your pet grooming salon that you never thought possible. The coming years can bring many rewards and much success if you are willing to work diligently. Stay motivated, be responsible, and always monitor every facet of your operation. As the owner of a full-service operation the possibilities are multiple. Work closely with your professional advisors to determine what is desirable for you.

SUCCESSION PLANNING

The time will come when you will own a successful, profitable pet salon and be enjoying a good income from it. Your financial status will include savings and a retirement plan. Your plans for retirement will probably be to collect social security, retirement income, and savings interest to shield you from financial hardship. However, have you prepared the salon to continue without you? You can expect income from it even after retirement by making succession plans well ahead of time.

Many business owners prefer not to make, or even seriously consider succession plans until retirement is near. They usually find chaos at the last minute, and less profitability. Begin to consider your succession options now and work toward them for a more comfortable, profitable retirement.

There are three succession options presented in the following material. Your professional advisors can arrange these plans and offer alternatives. Not all of these options may be applicable to you. However, you will have made significant contributions to them by adopting the Madson Management System.

Selling The Salon to Outsiders

Selling the business to an outsider is usually the least complicated of the succession options. You can walk away from the business with cash and completely sever emotional and financial ties. You can move ahead and never look back. The tactic permitting you to sell for a large profit is making it saleable before it goes on the market.

Using the Madson Management System will make your pet grooming salon attractive to buyers. Buyers will require financial records for the previous three to five years. Because you were using the Madson Management System your financial records for the previous several years of operation will be impressive. This will figure prominently in the market value of your business. Maximum value is given to salons with strong financial statements.

The size of the client base is a major consideration in assessing your salon's market value. A buyer purchases your client list as well as equipment and supplies. The larger your client base, the greater the value of the business. The client and pet history filecards will substantiate the size of the client base.

The market value of a salon is enhanced by a reputation for professionalism, a convenient location, and plenty of client and community goodwill.

When selling, the Madson Management System assists you in allaying buyers fears of being unable to manage as effectively as you. You can put the buyer's fears to rest by providing them with the same management system that enabled you to run the business successfully.

Buyers also purchase expertise. They are fearful of purchasing an operation that relies on the previous owner to continue running properly. The support staff you created by following the Madson Management System will be a further attraction. Keep the staff informed of your intentions to sell the business to prepare them for when they will work for another owner. Your employees will be glad to know they have a good opportunity of retaining their positions after the sale.

Buyers may ask you to accept a contract sale calling for a down payment and monthly payments. This arrangement minimizes your taxes compared to those applied to a large sum capital gain. However, the disadvantage is it keeps you shackled to the business until the final payment. Choose your buyer carefully when you accept a payment plan. Don't accept this arrangement if you don't expect the new owner to run the business profitably. Completely examine the buyer's past pet grooming experience, complete financial background, management abilities, and organizational aptitude before entering the contract of sale. It may be advisable to have your attorney arrange the contract of sale and determine the financial reliability of the purchaser.

An Employee Buyout

Over the many years you own the salon, loyal employees may become like family. If they have developed the leadership to manage the business, an employee buyout may be possible. Competent employees know how to run the operation in the same manner as you. This is beneficial to the clients and community who have relied on your services for many years.

Employees have a vested interest in buyouts. They know an outside purchaser may discontinue their employment. Realistically though, usually only one or two employees take a buyout opportunity seriously enough to accept financial responsibility. Those having the most interest are usually the master pet trimmer or manager with several years experience.

If you choose an employee buyout, an experienced salon manager is likely to ensure a profitable succession. A manager familiar with the Madson Management System will have worked with all aspects of the business with you. Prepare your manager to run the operation without you ahead of time by occasionally giving them sole responsibility to run the business. Then make a performance evaluation.

Most employees will not have the cash to complete the buyout. You will probably have to accept a down payment and payment plan with the same advantages and disadvantages described earlier.

A creative option is an Employee Stock Ownership Plan. Currently in the United States there are about 8,000 of these plans in effect. The ESOP is a legal entity set up by the owner for the benefit of the employees. Most of them will borrow all of the capital to buy your business, pay you off, and then own the business. Consult your attorney for further information.

Bequeathing The Salon to Family Members

If your plans are to turn the business over to your children, prepare them early. They must have leadership and management ability, on-the-job experience, and ideally, some business education. Develop their ability gradually over the years. While attending school they can work during the summer in the salon. As adults, they should take the managerial position at least two to five years before assuming total control. They must have shared your experiences with running the business for many years. Indeed, most children inheriting their parent's business fail to maintain it profitably unless they have substantial on-the-job experience since childhood.

Consult your attorney to structure the turnover carefully over time. By doing so, your children can avoid the huge tax bite applicable when the salon is bequeathed at once.

FORM COMPLETION INSTRUCTIONS

APPENDIX

A

CASH RESERVE JOURNAL

Make copies of the Cash Reserve Journal Sheet (illustration 3-5) on letter size paper. At the top of the cash reserve journal sheet enter the amount of your cash reserve savings goal ($10,000.00 minimum).

Deposits

For each deposit enter: a) DATE = the date the deposit is made; b) DESCRIPTION = the source and date(s) of receipt of the deposit when and how the money was made, (e.g. cash receipts for 5/08/88); c) DEPOSIT = the amount of the deposit; d) BALANCE = the sum of the previous balance and the current deposit.

Interest

To record interest earned, enter: a) DATE = the date the interest was credited to the account; b) INTEREST = the amount; c) BALANCE = the new account balance.

Withdrawals

To record withdrawals, enter: a) DATE = the date of the withdrawal; b) DESCRIPTION = the purpose of the withdrawal; c) DRAWS = the amount of the withdrawal; d) BALANCE = the new account balance.

When the cash reserve journal sheet is used up enter the ending account balance after "Balance brought forward" on a new journal sheet.

When you receive a monthly statement from your bank or savings institution, reconcile it with the cash reserve journal. The ending balance shown on the account statement should be identical to the cash reserve journal balance.

DAILY RESPONSE REPORT (RECEPTIONIST)

Make copies of the Daily Response Report-Receptionist (illustration 11-4) on letter size paper.

The receptionist makes appointment confirmation calls three days in advance of the scheduled appointment. The receptionist records response to the calls on the Daily Response Report-Receptionist.

Fill in the date, day of week, and receptionist's name at the top of the form. After reviewing the completed report the manager signs it in the space titled "Manager."

The receptionist enters the following information for each call.

Client Name. Enter the client's last name.

Appointment Date. Enter the client's scheduled appointment date.

Confirmed? Y/N. Enter a "Y" if the client confirms the scheduled appointment. Enter a "N" if the client declines the scheduled appointment date.

Changed? Y/N. Enter a "Y" if the client changes their scheduled appointment to another date. Enter the new date in the space marked "Comments".

Canceled? Y/N. Enter a "Y" if the client cancels the scheduled appointment and declines to re-schedule. Describe the reasons for cancellation in the space marked "Comments", such as, "pet is ill" or "pet has died."

Comments

The receptionist uses the comments area to communicate client service information to the manager. The manager follows-up on the comments to make sure each client receives personal attention and resolution of any problems.

If a client's pet is ill, or has died, the receptionist sends a "Get Well," or "Pet Sympathy" card to the client.

SUMMARIZING THE RESPONSE REPORT

At the end of the work shift the receptionist fills in summary totals for each of the five summary boxes.

1. *# of Pet Sympathy Cards.* Enter the total of Pet Sympathy Cards sent.

2. *# of Get Well Cards.* Enter the total of Get Well Cards sent.

3. *# of Client Response Postcards.* Enter the total Client Response Postcards sent.

4. *Appointments Confirmed.* Enter the total of confirmed appointments.

5. *Appointments Changed.* Enter the total of appointment changes.

6. *Appointments Canceled.* Enter the appointment cancellation total.

After summarizing the report the receptionist returns it to the manager who checks it for accuracy and initials it.

DAILY RESPONSE REPORT (TELEMARKETER)

Make copies of the Daily Response Report-Telemarketer (illustration 12-5) on letter size paper.

The telemarketer makes appointment scheduling calls to Preferred Client Program — Option B clients. In addition the telemarketer makes calls to "C" clients and potential clients as assigned by the manager. The telemarketer records response to the calls on the Daily Response Report-Telemarketer.

Fill in "Today's Date," the "Target Date," and the name of the "Telemarketer" at the top of the form. The target date is always fourteen days in advance of the current date. After reviewing the completed report the manager signs it in the space titled, "Manager".

The telemarketer enters the following information for each call.

"B" Client Name.   Enter the client's last name.

Date Appt. Scheduled.   Enter the date of the client's next appointment.

No Answer.   Enter the abbreviation "N/A" if the client cannot be reached during the telemarketer's work shift. These clients are called the next business day, or until they are reached.

Comments

The comments area is used to communicate client service information to the manager. The manager follows-up on the comments to make sure each client receives personal attention and resolution of any problems.

If a client's pet is ill, or has died, the telemarketer sends a "Get Well," or "Pet Sympathy" card to the client.

The telemarketer enters the same information as above for "check-up calls" to "C," "D," and potential clients.

SUMMARIZING THE RESPONSE REPORT

At the end of the work shift the telemarketer fills in summary totals for each of the of seven summary boxes.

1. # of Pet Sympathy Cards.   Enter the total for Pet Sympathy Cards sent.

2. # of Get Well Cards.   Enter the total for Get Well Cards sent.

3. # of Client Response Postcards.   Enter the total for Client Response Postcards sent.

4. "B" Calls.   Enter the total for calls to Preferred Client Program-Option B clients.

5. "C" Calls.   Enter the total for check-up calls to "C" clients.

6. "D" Calls.   Enter the total for check-up calls to "D" clients.

7. **"NEW" Calls.**   Enter the total for calls to potential new clients.

8. **Appts. Booked.**   Enter the total for new appointments scheduled.

After summarizing the report the telemarketer returns it to the manager who checks it for accuracy and initials it.

CLIENT AND PET HISTORY FILECARD

The Client and Pet History filecard has two sides. Side A is for the "Client and Pet History," and Side B is for "Pet Care Service History." Periodically update the information.

COMPLETING THE CLIENT AND PET HISTORY — SIDE A

Client History.   Print pet owner's name in the boxes provided. Use one box for each letter and leave an empty box between names. Place a check after Mr., Mrs., or Ms.

Print the rest of the owner information (spouse, street, apt., city, state, zip, home phone, work phone, work phone spouse, emerg. phone, driver no., expiration) in the spaces provided. The reason for the designations is obvious, except perhaps for the driver's license information which is required if you accept personal checks.

Print the client's veterinarian and (veterinary) clinic name and telephone. Provide a complete history of the pet's vaccinations in the "vaccination record" space. This is kept for reference (usually with the client's veterinarian).

Pet History.   Each filecard provides space for two pet histories. For clients with more than two pets use additional filecards and staple them together.

For each pet, indicate its name, breed, color, size, birthdate, and sex.

In the "Groom Alert" area check any of the health conditions or service precautions which apply. If a condition or special handling requirement exists which is not covered, describe it in the space marked "other." On the other side of the filecard check the "Groom Alert" circle to alert groomers to review the Groom Alert information and discuss it with the manager before grooming the pet.

In the "Personality Alert" area check the conditions which apply. Record additional behavior problems in the space marked "other."

Marketing Information.   In the top right corner of the Client and Pet History filecard is a box for marketing information. Circle A,B,C, or D to indicate the client's rating. Use pencil so the ratings may be modified.

Circle the number indicating the appointment frequency between scheduled appointments selected by members of the Preferred Client Program.

Record the referral source of new clients in the "Referred by" space. Record the date of the client's first visit to the salon in the "Client Since" space.

Client Contact History.   A brief history of all calls made to the client is entered in this section. Record mailings to the client such as a Get Well Card, Pet Sympathy Card, and Client Response Card.

For phone calls, record the date, a short description of the purpose of the call, and make a check mark in the "Phone" space. For mailings, record the date, a description of the mailer, and check the "Mail" space.

The Daily Response Reports contain more detailed information.

COMPLETING THE PET CARE
SERVICE HISTORY — SIDE B

This side provides space to record the history of pet care. There is space to record pet care for twelve appointments. Use one line per pet when clients have two or more pets.

In the upper right-hand corner check the appropriate box indicating a preference for bows and/or perfume.

For each appointment complete the following pet care information.

Date. — The date of grooming.

Groom Alert (see front). — If a pet requires special handling place an "X" in the circle. This alerts the staff to review the Groom Alert information on the other side of the filecard and discuss it with the manager before grooming the pet.

Service Description. — The "BA" box is checked for bath-only pets and the "TR" box is checked when the pet receives a bath and trim. Describe the trim-style in the space provided.

Face Style. — The most common grooming error is trimming the wrong face style. Indicating it separately will avoid that problem.

Groom By Initials. — In the space left of "BA" record the initials of the pet bather. The master pet trimmer's initials are recorded to the right of "TR."

Groomer Comments. — Make a brief note of poor health conditions here. A fuller description goes on the Pet Groomer's Report and Health Alert.

Time Out. — Enter the time the client will return for their pet(s).

Total Fees. — Enter the total for services provided.

Total Products. — Enter the total for purchases of retail pet products.

CA/CK/CH/M/V. — Enter the form of payment abbreviation. Note as many forms of payment as needed. (CA = cash, CK = check, M/V = Mastercard or Visa, CH = charges carried by the salon)

PET GROOMER'S REPORT AND HEALTH ALERT

The receptionist fills in three items on the Pet Groomer's Report and Health Alert for every pet groomed. The report is then paper-clipped to the Client and Pet History Filecard and remains with it until given to the pet owner when they pick-up their pet.

Date. — Date of grooming.

Owner. — Pet owner's last name.

Pet. —The pet's name.

Trimmer. — The master pet trimmer grooming the pet initials this space.

Bather. — The pet bather grooming the pet initials this space.

After grooming the pet, the bather and master pet trimmer complete the report with their observations of it's condition. The groomers are not recording a diagnosis, but an objective description of their observations. Train the groomers to advise the manager of all health concerns related to the pet.

Eyes. — Describe any questionable eye conditions such as "appears to be infected," "swollen," or "pet scratching it."

Ears. — Describe any questionable ear conditions such as "foxtails," "poor odor," or "pet scratching it."

Teeth. — Describe conditions such as "tartar buildup" and "bad odor."

Coat. — Check the "matted" space if needed. In the "other" space describe conditions such as "dry" or "oily."

Tail. — Describe conditions in the areas under and above the pet's tail such as "signs of pet chewing" or "swollen." Any questionable conditions observed when dispelling the pet's anal gland are noted in the "anal gland" space; e.g. "appears to be infected or sore" and "unusually bad odors."

Skin. — Check the conditions that apply. If sores or lumps are discovered describe the location. Note other questionable conditions and their location in the space marked "other."

Legs. — In the space for feet use descriptions such as "soreness," "swollen," and "weeds found between pads" and indicate in which feet the condition exists. If knee, hip, or joint problems are suspected, describe the suspect behavior and which area seems affected.

Body. — Note whether the pet is very thin or overweight.

Pet appears to be in good health. — Check the "Yes" space only if no questionable conditions are noted, and there is no observable indication of poor health.

Medical Advisory

The manager is responsible to complete this section of the Pet Groomer's Report and Health Alert when any questionable condition is observed by the groomers. Do not make observations in any way that implies a diagnosis. E.g. when convulsions are observed, indicate them by checking the "yes" space, do not say the pet has epilepsy. The medical advisory merely alerts the pet owner that veterinary attention is recommended. The manager initials the Pet Groomer's Report and Health Alert before it is given to the client.

GIVING THE REPORT TO THE PET OWNER

When each client returns for their pet(s) the receptionist gives them the completed Pet Groomer Report and Health Alert. Direct the client's attention to any questionable conditions and the medical advisory. If the client requests further clarification the receptionist should refer them to the manager.

The receptionist completes the report by writing the client's next appointment on the front cover.

DAILY CAGING AND PAYMENT REGISTER

One Daily Caging and Payment Register is completed for each business day. The receptionist completes the register following the instructions under the heading below, "Completing the Register."

The receptionist will find it necessary to refer to the register throughout the business day, therefore, the register remains at the client reception counter at all times.

At the close of business the receptionist sums up the register's service information following the instructions below under the heading "Summarizing the Register Information." The summarized register is given to the manager to post service information totals to the Manager's Daily Summary Report of Services and Sales.

Completing the Register

Begin the register by filling in the date and the day of the week at the top of the form.

Before entering client service information onto the register, complete each client's filecard and cage number(s) assignment for their pet(s).

For each client there are six pieces of information transferred from the Client and Pet History filecard to the register. Follow the six-step procedure below for each client.

Step 1. — CLIENT NAME

A. *Client with one pet.* Enter the client's last name next to his/her pet's cage assignment.

B. *Client with two, or more, pets in separate cages.* Enter the client's last name next to each cage assignment.

Step 2. — BA / TR

The BA is an abbreviation for a bath-only service and the TR for a complete trim and bath. Enter either a BA or TR for each pet occupying the cage(s).

Step 3. — TIME OUT

Enter the time the client will return for their pet(s).

Step 4. — SERVICE FEES

Enter the total amount of the service fees due. When two or more pets of the same client occupy one cage, enter the combined total of service fees.

If a client has two or more pets assigned separate cages, enter each pet's individual service fee by cage assignment.

Step 5. — PET PRODUCTS

Enter the total amount of pet products sold to the client (do not include sales tax collected).

Step 6. — SALES TAX

Enter the amount of sales tax collected.

Step 7. — CA / CK / CH / M/V

The CA is an abbreviation for cash, the CK is payment by check, the CH for non-credit card charges carried by the salon, and M/V is for mastercard or visa.

Enter the appropriate abbreviation describing the client's form of payment. If a client remits payment in more than one form of payment, enter two or more abbreviations as needed.

WHEN TO USE THE BLANK LINES

There are eighteen blank register lines for use under special circumstances.

Clients providing a portable cage.   When a client provides a portable cage in which the pet will be kept while at the salon, use one of the blank lines to enter the service information. In the blank cage number box write "PC" (portable cage) and then enter the remaining information following the above instructions.

Cages used for two or more clients in the same business day.   Though pets belonging to different clients should never be caged together, a cage may be used for two or more clients in the same day. For instance, Mrs. Smith returns to pick-up her pet in cage eleven at noon. At one o'clock Mr. Johnson brings in his pet which is then assigned the now empty cage eleven.

Since the cage eleven line of information on the Daily Register has been previously filled in with Mrs. Smith's service information, Mr. Johnson's service information will have to be entered into one of the blank lines provided.

Write in the cage number being used for the second client, (number eleven in the example above) and then fill in the remaining information following the instructions for completing the register.

SUMMARIZING THE REGISTER

At the close of business, the receptionist summarizes the information on the completed register. At the bottom of the register there are five boxes for totals of the following:

# of Trims.   Add the number of TR abbreviations in the BA/TR column on the register and enter the total in this box.

# of Bath-only.   Add the number of BA abbreviations in the BA/TR column and enter the total in this box.

Service Fees.   Add the entries in the Service Fee column and enter the total in this box.

Pet Products Sold.   Add the entries in the Pet Products column and enter the total in this box.

Sales Tax Collected.   Add the amount of sales tax collected from each sales receipt and enter the total in this box.

After summarizing the register the receptionist gives it to the manager. The manager checks it for accuracy and then posts summary totals to the Manager's Daily Summary Report for Services and Sales.

Note: The Daily Caging and Payment Register summary totals for service fees, pet products sold, and sales tax collected should be equal the totals shown on the cash register. If not, the cash register tape and caging register must be compared and discrepancies corrected before posting summary totals to the Manager's Daily Summary Report.

WEEKLY EMPLOYEE TIMEKEEPING RECORD

Make copies of the Weekly Employee Timekeeping Record (illustration 13-1) on letter size paper.

Each week, prepare one Weekly Employee Timekeeping Record for each employee with the following information. Fill in the blanks for employee name and the week's starting and ending dates. Check the appropriate box indicating the employee's salary or hourly basis for pay and job title. The records are now ready for the employees to complete them following the instructions below on a daily basis.

Step 1. — TIME ENTRIES

Under the appropriate day of the week, employees enter starting times in the space marked "Time In." Starting and ending times for lunchbreaks are entered in the spaces marked "Lunch Begin" and "Lunch End" respectively. At the end of their work shift, employees enter the time in the space marked "Time Out."

Step 2. — CLIENT NAMES

Under the appropriate day of the week, groomers enter the client name for every pet they complete. Fourteen numbered spaces are provided for these entries per work day.

ANNUAL PROFIT AND LOSS PROJECTION

When you make copies of the Annual Profit and Loss Projection convert the copies to legal size, or larger, to make it easier to use. If you are completing it for the first time do so with the assistance of your bookkeeper or accountant. In the future you will use them only to confirm the accuracy of your projections.

A profit and loss projection need not begin in January. It may begin in any month of the year. Enter the starting and ending dates in top, left corner.

Next, fill in the twelve boxes along the top of the projection titled "Month 1" through "Month 12" with the names of the months. Month 1 is the starting month, and the ending month is Month 12.

Before entering further information, determine how many complete trim and bath-only pets you expect to groom in each of the twelve months covered by the projection. Ten percent increases over the actual service totals of a previous year are reasonable. Use a chart like the one below to organize your projections for complete trim and bath-only services.

PERIOD	COMPLETE TRIM PETS		BATH-ONLY PETS	
MONTH	PRIOR YEAR	PROJECTED YEAR	PRIOR YEAR	PROJECTED YEAR
January	_____	_____	_____	_____
February	_____	_____	_____	_____
March	_____	_____	_____	_____
April	_____	_____	_____	_____
May	_____	_____	_____	_____
June	_____	_____	_____	_____
July	_____	_____	_____	_____
August	_____	_____	_____	_____
September	_____	_____	_____	_____
October	_____	_____	_____	_____
November	_____	_____	_____	_____
December	_____	_____	_____	_____

Under the heading Prior Year (see chart above) fill in the number of complete trim and bath-only pets groomed for each month. If you are just beginning the Madson Management System and have not recorded this information with the Manager's Daily Summary Report of Services and Sales, use your appointment book or other service records to determine the prior year figures.

Using the prior year figures as a guideline, enter your service projections for the coming twelve months. You can expect increases using the Madson Management System. When the chart is complete with your projection figures, you are ready to complete the Annual Profit and Loss Projection.

Line 1. *Number of Complete Trims.*

Enter the projected amount of complete trim pets for each month.

Line 2. *Number of Bath-only.*

Enter the projected amount of bath-only pets for each month.

Line 3. *Total Net Sales of Services.*

A. Multiply the amount on Line 1 by your salon's average complete trim fee.

B. Multiply the amount on Line 2 by your salon's average bath-only fee.

C. Add the figures for A and B together. Enter this amount on Line 3 for each month.

Line 4. *Total Net Sales of Pet Products.*

Enter the projected amount of retail pet products sales for each month. Do not deduct the cost of goods sold from this amount.

Line 5. *Less Cost of Goods Sold.*

If your accounting procedures include the "cost of goods sold" enter the amount on Line 4.

If you do not use "cost of goods sold," the expense for your retail inventory is included on Line 16.

Line 6. *Gross Profit Margin.*

Enter the total from Line 3 and Line 4, minus Line 5 for each month.

Line 7. *Operating Expenses.*

Line 7 is a title line. No amount is entered. Operating expenses are itemized on Lines 8 through Line 30.

Lines 8 through 30. *Itemized Operating Expenses.*

On each line, enter the amount of operating expenses you project for that month.

Line 31. *Total Operating Expenses.*

Total Line 8 through Line 30 for each month.

Line 32. *Net Profit/Loss Margin (before taxes).*

Subtract Line 31 from Line 6.

GRAND TOTALS

Number of Complete Trims. — Add the figures from Line 1 for Months 1 through 12 and enter the total in this box.

Number of Bath-only. — Add the figures from Line 2 for Months 1 through 12 and enter the total in this box.

Gross Profit Margin. — Add the figures from Line 6 for Months 1 through 12 and enter the total in this box.

Operating Expenses. — Add the figures from Line 31 for Months 1 through 12 and enter the total in this box.

Net Profit/Loss Margin (before taxes). — Add the figures from Line 32 for Months 1 through 12 and enter the total in this box.

MANAGER'S DAILY SUMMARY REPORT OF SERVICES AND SALES

The Manager's Daily Summary Report of Services and Sales has eight sections printed on the cover of a nine by twelve inch envelope. Every section is completed daily by the manager.

At the top of report indicate the DATE, DAY OF WEEK, HOURS OF OPERATION, and MANAGER.

PART ONE — CASH RECEIPTS AND BANK DEPOSIT RECORD

Complete Part One after the salon closes for the day.

Opening Till. — Enter the amount of the cash register till at the beginning of the business day.

Next Till. — Enter the amount of the till for the next business day.

Cash Receipts

Services. — Enter the total for "Service Fees" from the Daily Caging and Payment Register.

Sales. — Enter the total for "Pet Products Sold" from the Daily Caging and Payment Register.

Sales Tax. — Enter the total for "Sales Tax Collected" from the Daily Caging and Payment Register.

On Account. — This space is to record payments made on account for those salons who extend credit. Enter the total of payments made on account.

Other. — Enter the total for miscellaneous revenue not included in any other category; such as a pet grooming tutorial fee or a refund from a vendor.

Total Cash Receipts. — The sum of all cash receipts.

Cash Paid Out

Part Two, CASH EXPENSE DETAIL provides the totals for this area. Transfer the totals from Grooming Supplies, Bldg. & Equip. Supplies, Repairs & Maintenance, Office Supplies, and Cleaning Supplies to the spaces provided. For accounts to balance, all cash expenditures paid from cash taken from the register must be recorded in the Cash Paid Out section. Enter the sum of the five cash expense categories in the space marked Total.

Cash Register

After the salon has closed for business count all monies received (including the opening till) and itemize them using the following categories.

Currency. — Total all currency in the cash register and enter it here.

Coin. — Total all coins in the cash register and enter it here.

Checks. — Add the amount of every check received and enter the total.

C/Cards. — Add every credit card charge slip and enter the total.

Other. — Add any other monies not included above.

Total Cash Register. — Enter the sum of all cash register items.

Balance

Total Cash Receipts. — Enter the total from Cash Receipts, Part One.

Less Total Cash Paid Out. — Enter the total from Cash Paid Out, Part One.

Total #1. — Subtract the Cash Paid Out total from the Cash Receipts total to obtain this figure.

Total Cash Register. — Enter the amount from Total Cash Register in Part One.

Less Opening Till. — Enter the amount from Opening Till at the top of the form.

Total #2. — Subtract Opening Till from Total Cash Register to achieve this figure.

Total #1 must equal Total #2 to be in balance. If not, check for errors in your arithmetic and/or the amounts posted from the Daily Caging and Payment Register. If your entries are correct there are two other possible explanations for the imbalance.

Someone has not paid, or has been permitted to charge their fees. If so, enter the amount due in the "Accounts Receivable" space.

Secondly, incorrect change may have been given to someone creating either an overage or shortage. Enter the amount of cash over or short in the spaces provided.

Bank Deposit

Bank deposits should be made each day of business. Do not combine deposits. If receipts are not deposited for Friday, Saturday, and Sunday, make separate deposits for each day on Monday. This process produces a better record of cash receipts and deposits for the bookkeeper/accountant.

The amount of a daily bank deposit is calculated as follows:

Total Cash Register. — Enter the amount from Total Cash Register, Part One.

Less Next Till. — Enter the amount from Next Till (top of the form).

Total Bank Deposit. — Subtract Less Next Till from Total Cash Register to obtain the total bank deposit.

Deposit Record. — Every bank deposit is listed here, including those to other accounts such as the cash reserve account. For every deposit include the amount and the source of the deposit. E.g. $250.00, 9/12/88 receipts.

940/941. — Enter the amount of 940/941 tax deposits made at your bank. Indicate the type and amount of any other tax deposits on this line also.

PART TWO — CASH EXPENSE DETAIL

These categories make it easier for your bookkeeper/accountant to keep accurate expense records in the salon's general ledger. This can lead to tax savings at years end. Obtain a receipt for every cash expenditure. Write a description of the item purchased on the reverse side of the receipt and make sure the date is legible.

Using the receipts from cash purchases categorize them by Grooming Supplies, Bldg. & Equip. Supplies, Repairs & Maintenance, Office Supplies, and Cleaning Supplies. Write in the total for each type of item or service purchased on the lines provided.

Add all the purchases for each category in and place the amount in Total Cash Paid Out. This total will be the same as the total for Cash Paid Out, Part One.

Staple receipts for cash expenditures together and store them inside the Manager's Daily Summary Report of Services and Sales envelope.

PART THREE — RETAIL SALES DETAIL

To complete this section you will need a copy of all of the day's sales receipts and the Daily Caging and Payment Register. If your sales receipts do not describe the items purchased write a description of each item, the price, and the sales tax on the back of the Daily Caging and Payment Register. This procedure is necessary so it is much simpler to change to a system where the receipt describes the purchase.

Total Pet Products Sold. — Enter the total from Total Pet Products Sold from the Daily Caging and Payment Register.

Total Sales Tax Collected. — Enter the total from Total Sales Tax Collected from the Daily Caging and Payment Register.

Using the sales receipts or the itemization from the back of the Daily Caging and Payment Register complete the following.

Pet Products Sold. — Briefly describe the purchase; such as "1 flea collar" or "2 red collars with leashes."

Price. — Enter the amount of the item(s).

Tax. — Enter the amount of sales tax collected.

Total. — Enter the total of the item(s) plus sales tax.

The sum of all "Price" column entries should be equal to the entry made for Total Pet Products Sold. The sum of the "Tax" column should be equal to the entry made for Total Sales Tax Collected.

The data in Part Three will assist the manager in determining which pet products are selling best. It will also be useful when reordering.

PART FOUR — PERSONNEL REPORT

Refer to the Weekly Employee Timekeeping Record to complete this section.

Staff Attendance

Write in the name of every employee, time in, lunch begin, lunch end, and time out from their Weekly Employee Timekeeping Record. Use the comments section for reminder notes such as "left early today for a doctor's appointment" or "arrived late due to traffic accident." Add any comments made to the employee's personnel file.

Personnel Management Activities

Check any of twelve activities printed in this area that you performed today. The line, "Have the personnel files been updated regarding these activities" is to remind you to enter all checked activities in the employee's personnel file.

PART FIVE — PET SERVICES PROFILE

The information in this profile is useful for the People and Pet Marketing Program (Chapter Twelve). It gives an accurate picture of the types of pet care services being used by your clients and which promotional activities are required. The profile may also indicate service problems which can then be corrected. For example, the profile may reveal a higher percentage of bath-only services compared to complete trims. If this happens it may suggest that clients are satisfied with the quality of bath-only services, but dissatisfied with the finish trimming.

Different salons will have different profiles. For instance, the pet service profile for salons that have a reputation with local veterinarians for giving the service provided on the Pet Groomer's Report and Health Alert will have higher percentages of "Vet Care" in their pet service profile. They will also have more referrals from veterinarians.

To complete the Pet Service Profile you will need the Daily Caging and Payment Register.

Total # Complete Trims. — Enter the Total # Complete Trims from the Daily Caging and Payment Register.

Total # of Bath Only. — Enter the Total # of Bath-Only from the Daily Caging and Payment Register.

Using the Client and Pet History filecards enter the following the information for both dogs and cats.

Complete Trim (Small or Large). — Enter the Total # of Complete Trims performed on small/medium and large pets.

Bath-Only (Small or Large). — Enter the Total # of Bath-Only performed on small/medium and large pets.

New. — Enter the total number of first-time customers.

Aged/Ill. — Enter the number of aged or ill pets serviced by special appointment.

Vet Care. — Enter the number of pets serviced under veterinary care which required special handling.

PART SIX — CLIENT SERVICES PROFILE

The Client and Pet History filecard supplies the following totals.

Total # of New Preferred Client Program Members. — Enter the number of clients joining the program.

Total # of Pets Assigned Groom Alert Status. — Enter the number of pets assigned a Groom Alert status.

Total # of Medical Advisories Issued. — Enter the number of Medical Advisories on the Pet Groomer's Report and Health Alert given to pet owners.

Daily Response Reports

The summary totals from the Daily Response Reports for the receptionist and telemarketer are posted in this area.

Mailings

From the Daily Response Reports enter the total number of Pet Sympathy Cards, Get Well Cards, Client Response Postcards, and Pet Care Services brochures mailed by the receptionist and telemarketer.

Client Status and Follow-Up Report

Use the Daily Response Reports and Client and Pet History filecards to complete this section. For the following classifications enter the name of every client and their pet who were contacted by phone or served on the date of the report.
1. A new client referred to the salon.
2. A client whose pet has given birth recently.
3. A client whose pet has died recently.
4. A client whose pet is ill.
5. A client who has moved.
6. A client with a complaint.
7. A client with a special request requiring follow-up.

Referral. — Enter the name of the referral source. It may be another client, veterinarian clinic, or a publication in which you advertise. Be as specific as possible. (Make sure the referral source was correctly included on the client and pet history filecard also). Acknowledge all referrals.

Birth. — If a client's pet has given birth, note it and call them with congratulations. Tell them you are anxious to see the newly arrived pets and provide their first pet care services.

Death. — If a client's pet has died be sure they have been sent a Pet Sympathy Card. For especially loyal clients follow-up with a phone call.

Ill. — If a client's pet is ill make sure they have been sent a Get Well Card for pets. Remind them you provide special handling for ill pets as requested by their veterinarian.

Moved. — Update the filecard address for every client who has moved. If they are not expected to return to the area, assign their filecard a "D" rating and file appropriately. Do not discard it.

Complaint. — When the receptionist or telemarketer receive a complaint, and the manager is unavailable to resolve the situation, it is important to note the complaint on their Daily Response Report. Include the names of clients and contact the client as soon as possible to resolve the complaint.

Comments. — This space is provided for your notes.

PART SEVEN — MANAGER TASK PROGRESS REPORT

Put a check mark next to any of the management system forms which were updated. Next, enter the names of every professional advisor, vendor, local official, or other persons, except staff, with which you had a meeting.

Pet Industry and Community Participation

Check any of the activities listed in which you participated.

PART EIGHT — OFFICIAL REPORTS

Reduced Salon Services

When applicable, check one of the three causes of reduced salon services. When the situation is resolved check the "Problem Corrected" space. Also, note the duration of the event.

Accidents/Injuries/Incidents

Check any situation which occurred. Complete an Emergency Report (Chapter Nine) for any of the above situations. When it has been, check the space next to the report reminder. Make sure it has been completed with the information described in Part Eight. Place the Emergency Report inside the Manager's Daily Summary Report of Services and Sales envelope for review by the owner.

HANDLING OF THE COMPLETED MANAGER'S DAILY SUMMARY REPORT OF SERVICES AND SALES

The following data is placed inside the Manager's Daily Summary Report of Services and Sales envelope.
   1. Daily Response Reports.
   2. Daily Caging and Payment Register.
   3. Cash expense receipts.
   4. Cash register tape and monies.

5. Pet products sold receipts.
6. Bank deposit receipts.
7. Emergency Reports.

Any other data pertinent to the day's business may be placed in the envelope which is to become a part of the salon's permanent files.

SUPPLIES CONTROL LOG SHEET

Dedicate one Supplies Control Log Sheet for each grooming, maintenance, and office supply. For example, use one sheet for each type of shampoo; i.e. baby, regular, and special shampoos).

At the top of the sheet fill in the name of the "Product" and "Supplier." When the supply reaches the "Reorder Level" place an order to replenish it.

As stock is received, record the amount and its usage in Supplies Control Log. DATE = date of purchase, PURCHASES = number of units purchased, USED = record usage as stock is used up, BALANCE = stock remaining, DESCRIPTION = record any comments regarding the stock, e.g. "broken bottle."

The "BALANCE" amount should always be the same as the actual inventory count of the supply.

PERSONNEL FORMS

THE PET SALON MANAGER

The manager is responsible for administrative and financial duties, marketing goals, client relations, and supervision of staff. He reports directly to the owner.

ELIGIBILITY REQUIREMENTS

Previous management experience is desirable. Candidates with client relations or grooming experience in a pet salon are given preference. Promotion of salon staff is given priority whenever possible.

- Ability to train, supervise, and evaluate the performance of staff members.
- Bookkeeping, cash and credit handling, and organizational skills, or the ability to rapidly learn these skills.
- Good verbal and written communication skills with average, to above-average arithmetic ability.
- Good personal hygiene and appropriate dress.
- Pleasant personality capable of working in a team environment.
- A respect and appreciation for pets.

• No medical or physical conditions which would prevent the successful completion of position duties.

If a practical examination is required the applicant will be paid an hourly wage for its duration. Upon selection the applicant is asked to sign introductory period employment and confidentiality agreements. A standard employment agreement is signed after successful completion of the introductory period.

POSITION DUTIES

Owner-Manager Relationship: The manager is responsible to work cooperatively with the salon owner to complete the tasks and achieve the objectives of the business plan and the Annual Profit and Loss Projection. These include increases in; client base, gross revenue, client satisfaction, safety and health standards, staff performance, and operational cost-efficiency. He keeps the owner regularly informed, and as-needed regarding salon operations and maintenance.

Operations: The manager is responsible to maintain a consistently efficient, timely, and hygienic salon operation. He is in charge of the Information Center which organizes each days pet care service orders using the Client and Pet History filecards and makes pet care service assignments to the staff. He maintains equipment and tools, sanitized towels, grooming and cleaning supplies, and business forms. He also orders the retail pet goods inventory.

The manager confirms that all salon documentation is completed in a proper and timely fashion. These reports include the Receptionist Daily Response Report, the Telemarketer Daily Response Report, the Daily Caging and Payment Register, the Pet Groomer's Report and Health Alert, the Client and Pet History Filecards, the Pet Sympathy Cards, Get Well Cards, Pet Birthday Cards, Release and Hold Harmless Agreement, the Pet Care Services Brochure/Mailer, the Client Response Postcard, and the Client Service Questionnaire.

The manager's overall function in operations is quality control and safety. It is the manager's responsibility to ensure that every department head directs their department staff to produce pet care services of the highest standards. He further assures that all services are performed in a safe and humane manner, and promotes emergency preparedness with the staff.

Personnel Administration: The manager solicits, interviews, tests, and hires new employees. He leads orientation procedures, organizes training programs, and keeps performance records. He maintains personnel files, including; federal, state, and local documentation, timekeeping records, and year-end tax forms. He is responsible for employee documents such as job agreements and issues the Employee Handbook to every new employee. He outlines work schedules and distributes payroll.

Financial Administration: The manager is responsible for all financial records including the Manager's Daily Summary Report of Services and Sales. He ensures a cost-effective operation by reviewing financial statements, profit and loss ratios, timekeeping records, retail sales, the supplies control records, and the Annual Profit and Loss Projection versus actual costs.

Communications: The manager ensures that the flow of communications is uninterrupted in the salon. This is accomplished through regular staff meetings, memos, and personal communication.

GENERAL INFORMATION

The Employee Handbook: Every employee is expected to comply with the employee policies and procedures contained in the Employee Handbook. Included are standards of performance for personal appearance, client courtesy, salon cleanliness, humane handling of pets, and safety and emergency procedures.

Job Performance Evaluations: Performance evaluations, the basis for job security, promotions, and pay raises, are given twice a year in _____ and _____ .

Work Schedule: Days and hours: _____.

Working holidays: _____.

Compensation: The position is full ( ) part ( ) time. Compensation is by salary ( ), hourly wage ( ) beginning at $_____ . The actual rate of compensation, based on qualifications and experience, is part of your employment agreement and presented with an offer of employment should you be selected for the position.

Paydays: _____.

JOB PERFORMANCE EVALUATION
Manager

Today's Date:_____   Date of Last Evaluation:_____

Manager:_____   Owner:_____

JOB DUTIES & RESPONSIBILITIES	POOR		SATISFACTORY			GOOD			EXCELLENT	
Skill Level:										
Teamwork	1	2	3	4	5	6	7	8	9	10
Effective Management Checklist	1	2	3	4	5	6	7	8	9	10
Marketing	1	2	3	4	5	6	7	8	9	10
Reaching financial goals	1	2	3	4	5	6	7	8	9	10
Reaching client base goals	1	2	3	4	5	6	7	8	9	10
Short & long-term planning	1	2	3	4	5	6	7	8	9	10
Supervision	1	2	3	4	5	6	7	8	9	10
Staff relations	1	2	3	4	5	6	7	8	9	10
Business relations	1	2	3	4	5	6	7	8	9	10
Delegation	1	2	3	4	5	6	7	8	9	10
Training	1	2	3	4	5	6	7	8	9	10
Performance evaluations	1	2	3	4	5	6	7	8	9	10
Safe work environment	1	2	3	4	5	6	7	8	9	10
Hygienic work environment	1	2	3	4	5	6	7	8	9	10
Cash register proficiency	1	2	3	4	5	6	7	8	9	10
Records maintenance	1	2	3	4	5	6	7	8	9	10
Manager's Daily Summary Report	1	2	3	4	5	6	7	8	9	10
Inventory control	1	2	3	4	5	6	7	8	9	10
Building & equipment maintenance	1	2	3	4	5	6	7	8	9	10

EMPLOYEE POLICIES AND PROCEDURES

Compliance:										
Absence & tardiness	1	2	3	4	5	6	7	8	9	10
Conduct	1	2	3	4	5	6	7	8	9	10
Appearance	1	2	3	4	5	6	7	8	9	10
Client courtesy	1	2	3	4	5	6	7	8	9	10
Cleanliness	1	2	3	4	5	6	7	8	9	10
Pet handling	1	2	3	4	5	6	7	8	9	10
People & pet safety	1	2	3	4	5	6	7	8	9	10
Timekeeping	1	2	3	4	5	6	7	8	9	10

WORK ATTITUDES

	POOR		SATISFACTORY			GOOD			EXCELLENT	
Humane treatment	1	2	3	4	5	6	7	8	9	10
Acceptance of assignments	1	2	3	4	5	6	7	8	9	10
Accepts training	1	2	3	4	5	6	7	8	9	10
Requires minimal supervision	1	2	3	4	5	6	7	8	9	10
Business knowledge growth	1	2	3	4	5	6	7	8	9	10

B-1

MASTER PET TRIMMER

The Master Pet Trimmer (MPT) is a senior level position in the trimming department responsible for final trims, supervision and training, and reports directly to the manager.

ELIGIBILITY REQUIREMENTS

• Substantial pet trimming experience with detailed history and references.

• The ability to perform a minimum ten trims daily on several breeds including poodles, cockers, terriers, and similar long-hair mixes.

• The ability to work in a team environment with an assistant pet trimmer and to supervise the quality and safety of work performed by the APT.

• Good verbal and written communication skills with average arithmetic ability.

• Good personal hygiene and appropriate dress.

• Pleasant personality capable of working in a team environment.

• A respect and appreciation for pets.

• No medical or physical conditions which would prevent the successful completion of position duties.

If a practical examination is required the applicant will be paid an hourly wage for its duration. Upon selection the applicant is asked to sign introductory employment and confidentiality agreements. A standard employment agreement is signed after successful completion of the introductory period.

POSITION DUTIES

When an assistant is not on staff the MPT is responsible to complete pre-clip and finish trims. When an assistant is present his responsibilities are; 1) supervision of safety, quality, and efficiency, and, 2) performing finish trims. All trimming styles must be consistent with the salon's standards.

He ensures that the pet has been properly bathed, examines the condition of the skin and coat, inspects for external parasites, fleas, cuts and sores, and other conditions requiring special attention. He records his observations on the Client and Pet History filecard as well as the Pet Groomer's Report and Health Alert. Conditions requiring the attention of a veterinarian are not reported to the client until the manager has been informed.

Trimming assignments are assigned by the manager. Without an Assistant Pet Trimmer the MPT is expected to complete _____ trims in a typical work day. With an APT he is expected to complete _____ trims daily.

The MPT is also responsible to supervise the proper use and maintenance of salon tools and equipment and to maintain cleanliness in the work area.

Additional duties may be assigned by the manager as needed, which include but are not limited to front counter duties such as making appointments, phone answering, handling payments, and record keeping.

GENERAL INFORMATION

The Employee Handbook: Every employee is expected to comply with the employee policies and procedures contained in the Employee Handbook. Included are standards of performance for personal appearance, client courtesy, salon cleanliness, humane handling of pets, and safety and emergency procedures.

Job Performance Evaluations: Performance evaluations, the basis for job security, promotions, and pay raises, are given twice a year in _____ and _____ .

Work Schedule: Days and hours: _____.

Working holidays: _____.

Compensation: The position is full ( ) part ( ) time. Compensation is by salary ( ), hourly wage ( ) beginning at $ _____ . The actual rate of compensation, based on qualifications and experience, is part of your employment agreement and presented with an offer of employment should you be selected for the position.

Paydays: _____.

ASSISTANT PET TRIMMER

The Assistant Pet Trimmer (APT) is an entry level position in the trimming department and works with the bathing and client relations departments. He reports directly to, and is supervised by the master pet trimmer. With the guidance of the master pet trimmer he can acquire the grooming skills necessary for promotion to master pet trimmer. He is part of a team committed to providing the highest standards of professionalism.

ELIGIBILITY REQUIREMENTS

- Some pet handling experience, preferably in bathing, with references.
- Capable of completing pre-clips daily (pattern style, face, feet, and tail pre-clips).
- Capable of also performing four pet baths daily.
- Successful completion of a training program in pet care, client services, and the assembly line method.
- Good verbal and written communication skills with average arithmetic ability.
- Good personal hygiene and appropriate dress.
- Pleasant personality capable of working in a team environment.
- A respect and appreciation for pets.
- No medical or physical conditions which would prevent the successful completion of position duties.

If a practical examination is required the applicant will be paid an hourly wage for its duration. Upon selection the applicant is asked to sign introductory employment and confidentiality agreements. A standard employment agreement is signed after successful completion of the introductory period.

POSITION DUTIES

Assistant Pet Trimmers are in the first stage of the assembly line doing pre-clips and some baths. A pre-clip consists of trimming a pet's face, feet, tail, and stomach, or the complete removal of a pet's coat per instructions on the Client and Pet History filecard. APT's are responsible to perform all pre-clips consistent with the salon's style and standards. The Master Pet Trimmer completes the pet's movement through the assembly line by performing the "finish" trim.

The APT is responsible to be alert for a "Groom Alert" on the pet's cage or filecard and to refer to the filecard for appropriate information and action.

The APT, and Master Pet Trimmer and Pet Bather when applicable, complete the Pet Groomer's Report and Health Alert for every pet groomed.

Trimming and bathing assignments are given by the Manager. After training and six months experience the APT is expected to complete ___ pre-clips and ___ baths in a typical work day.

The APT is responsible for the proper use and maintenance of the salon's equipment and tools and the cleanliness of the work area.

Additional duties may be assigned by the manager as needed, which include but are not limited to front counter duties such as making appointments, phone answering, handling payments, and record keeping.

GENERAL INFORMATION

The Employee Handbook: Every employee is expected to comply with the employee policies and procedures contained in the Employee Handbook. Included are standards of performance for personal appearance, client courtesy, salon cleanliness, humane handling of pets, and safety and emergency procedures.

Job Performance Evaluations: Performance evaluations, the basis for job security, promotions, and pay raises, are given twice a year in _____ and _____ .

Work Schedule: Days and hours: _____ .

Working holidays: _____ .

Compensation: The position is full ( ) part ( ) time. Compensation is by salary ( ), hourly wage ( ) beginning at $ _____ . The actual rate of compensation, based on qualifications and experience, is part of your employment agreement and presented with an offer of employment should you be selected for the position.

Paydays: _____ .

JOB PERFORMANCE EVALUATION
Trimming Department Positions

Today's Date: _____   Date of Last Evaluation: _____

Employee: _____   Position: _____ Manager: _____

JOB DUTIES & RESPONSIBILITIES	POOR		SATISFACTORY			GOOD			EXCELLENT	
Skill Level:										
Organization	1	2	3	4	5	6	7	8	9	10
Productivity	1	2	3	4	5	6	7	8	9	10
Attention to detail	1	2	3	4	5	6	7	8	9	10
Assembly-line grooming	1	2	3	4	5	6	7	8	9	10
Aged and ill pet handling	1	2	3	4	5	6	7	8	9	10
Groom Alert	1	2	3	4	5	6	7	8	9	10
Filecard maintenance	1	2	3	4	5	6	7	8	9	10
Pet Groomer's Report	1	2	3	4	5	6	7	8	9	10
Equipment maintenance	1	2	3	4	5	6	7	8	9	10
Grooming supply use	1	2	3	4	5	6	7	8	9	10
Supervision	1	2	3	4	5	6	7	8	9	10
Staff relations	1	2	3	4	5	6	7	8	9	10

EMPLOYEE POLICIES AND PROCEDURES

Compliance:										
Absence & tardiness	1	2	3	4	5	6	7	8	9	10
Conduct	1	2	3	4	5	6	7	8	9	10
Appearance	1	2	3	4	5	6	7	8	9	10
Client courtesy	1	2	3	4	5	6	7	8	9	10
Cleanliness	1	2	3	4	5	6	7	8	9	10
Pet handling	1	2	3	4	5	6	7	8	9	10
People & pet safety	1	2	3	4	5	6	7	8	9	10
Timekeeping	1	2	3	4	5	6	7	8	9	10

WORK ATTITUDES

Humane treatment	1	2	3	4	5	6	7	8	9	10
Acceptance of assignments	1	2	3	4	5	6	7	8	9	10
Teamwork	1	2	3	4	5	6	7	8	9	10
Accepts training	1	2	3	4	5	6	7	8	9	10
Staff meeting participation	1	2	3	4	5	6	7	8	9	10
Requires minimal supervision	1	2	3	4	5	6	7	8	9	10

BATHING DEPARTMENT SUPERVISOR

The Bathing Department Supervisor (BDS), salon Manager and Master Pet Trimmer constitute the executive of the pet salon. He works with the trimming and client relations departments to provide high quality care to clients. He reports directly to the manager.

ELIGIBILITY REQUIREMENTS

- Previous pet bathing experience, including references.
- Capable of supervising the efforts of others to insure quality and safety.
- Good verbal and written communication skills with average arithmetic ability.
- Good personal hygiene and appropriate dress.
- Pleasant personality capable of working in a team environment.
- A respect and appreciation for pets.
- No medical or physical conditions which would prevent the successful completion of position duties.

If a practical examination is required the applicant will be paid an hourly wage for its duration. Upon selection the applicant is asked to sign introductory employment and confidentiality agreements. A standard employment agreement is signed after successful completion of the introductory period.

POSITION DUTIES

The Bathing Department Supervisor is responsible to bathe pets and supervise the performance of the bathing department staff to insure that it meets the salon standards of a "humane bath." The BDS insures that all safety and pet handling criteria are followed by the bathing staff. He is also responsible to supervise the proper use and maintenance of salon tools and equipment and to maintain cleanliness in the work area.

He is responsible to maintain an adequate amount of supplies such as, sanitized towels, shampoos, and flea dips. He is also responsible to mix shampoos and dips from concentrates.

The BDS is responsible to make certain that "Groom Alert" instructions are followed by the bathing department staff, and that medicated baths are given according to veterinary instructions.

The BDS is expected to be able to complete _____ baths in a typical work day after three months training and experience, as well as his supervision duties.

Additional duties may be assigned by the manager as needed, which include but are not limited to front counter duties such as making appointments, phone answering, handling payments, and record keeping.

GENERAL INFORMATION

The Employee Handbook: Every employee is expected to comply with the employee policies and procedures contained in the Employee Handbook. Included are standards of performance for personal appearance, client courtesy, salon cleanliness, humane handling of pets, and safety and emergency procedures.

Job Performance Evaluations: Performance evaluations, the basis for job security, promotions, and pay raises, are given twice a year in _____ and _____ .

Work Schedule: Days and hours: _____.

Working holidays: _____.

Compensation: The position is full ( ) part ( ) time. Compensation is by salary ( ), hourly wage ( ) beginning at $ _____ . The actual rate of compensation, based on qualifications and experience, is part of your employment agreement and presented with an offer of employment should you be selected for the position.

Paydays: _____.

PET BATHER

The pet bather works in the bathing department and reports directly to the bathing department supervisor. He is an integral part of the team concept cooperating with the other departments to provide quality pet services.

ELIGIBILITY REQUIREMENTS

- This is an entry-level position but some pet handling experience is preferable.
- Successful completion of a training program in pet care and client services.
- Good verbal and written communication skills with average arithmetic ability.
- Good personal hygiene and appropriate dress.
- Pleasant personality capable of working in a team environment.
- A respect and appreciation for pets.
- No medical or physical conditions which would prevent the successful completion of position duties.

If a practical examination is required the applicant will be paid an hourly wage for its duration. Upon selection the applicant is asked to sign introductory employment and confidentiality agreements. A standard employment agreement is signed after successful completion of the introductory period.

POSITION DUTIES

The Pet Bather (PB) is responsible to bathe pets meeting the salon standards of a "humane bath." He follows Groom Alert instructions and gives medicated baths according to veterinary instructions.

The PB carefully brushes and combs the pet to remove tangles and knots. He then clips and smoothes the pet's nails and cleans the ears. After the bath he uses a blow dryer to fluff and straighten the pet's coat.

The PB inspects the condition of each pet's skin and coat for external parasites, sores, cuts, or any condition requiring special treatment. He reports any suspect health conditions, or behavior problems on the Pet Groomer's report and Health Alert, the Client and Pet History filecard, and to the Bathing Department Supervisor.

He is expected to be able to complete _____ baths in a typical work day after three months training and experience.

The PB is responsible for the proper use and maintenance of the salon's equipment and tools, and the cleanliness of the bathing department.

Additional duties may be assigned by the manager as needed, which include but are not limited to front counter duties such as making appointments, phone answering, handling payments, and record keeping.

GENERAL INFORMATION

The Employee Handbook: Every employee is expected to comply with the employee policies and procedures contained in the Employee Handbook. Included are standards of performance for personal appearance, client courtesy, salon cleanliness, humane handling of pets, and safety and emergency procedures.

Job Performance Evaluations: Performance evaluations, the basis for job security, promotions, and pay raises, are given twice a year in _____ and _____ .

Work Schedule: Days and hours: _____ .

Working holidays: _____ .

Compensation: The position is full ( ) part ( ) time. Compensation is by salary ( ), hourly wage ( ) beginning at $_____ . The actual rate of compensation, based on qualifications and experience, is part of your employment agreement and presented with an offer of employment should you be selected for the position.

Paydays: _____ .

JOB PERFORMANCE EVALUATION
Bathing Department Positions

Today's Date: _____   Date of Last Evaluation: _____

Employee: _____   Position: _____ Manager: _____

JOB DUTIES & RESPONSIBILITIES	POOR		SATISFACTORY			GOOD			EXCELLENT	
Skill Level:										
Organization	1	2	3	4	5	6	7	8	9	10
Productivity	1	2	3	4	5	6	7	8	9	10
Attention to detail	1	2	3	4	5	6	7	8	9	10
Humane bath	1	2	3	4	5	6	7	8	9	10
Aged and ill pet handling	1	2	3	4	5	6	7	8	9	10
Groom Alert	1	2	3	4	5	6	7	8	9	10
Filecard maintenance	1	2	3	4	5	6	7	8	9	10
Pet Groomer's Report	1	2	3	4	5	6	7	8	9	10
Equipment maintenance	1	2	3	4	5	6	7	8	9	10
Grooming supply use	1	2	3	4	5	6	7	8	9	10
Supervision	1	2	3	4	5	6	7	8	9	10
Staff relations	1	2	3	4	5	6	7	8	9	10

EMPLOYEE POLICIES AND PROCEDURES

Compliance:										
Absence & tardiness	1	2	3	4	5	6	7	8	9	10
Conduct	1	2	3	4	5	6	7	8	9	10
Appearance	1	2	3	4	5	6	7	8	9	10
Client courtesy	1	2	3	4	5	6	7	8	9	10
Cleanliness	1	2	3	4	5	6	7	8	9	10
Pet handling	1	2	3	4	5	6	7	8	9	10
People & pet safety	1	2	3	4	5	6	7	8	9	10
Timekeeping	1	2	3	4	5	6	7	8	9	10

WORK ATTITUDES

Humane treatment	1	2	3	4	5	6	7	8	9	10
Acceptance of assignments	1	2	3	4	5	6	7	8	9	10
Teamwork	1	2	3	4	5	6	7	8	9	10
Accepts training	1	2	3	4	5	6	7	8	9	10
Staff meeting participation	1	2	3	4	5	6	7	8	9	10
Requires minimal supervision	1	2	3	4	5	6	7	8	9	10

B-3

RECEPTIONIST

The Receptionist is located in the client relations department and is an important part of the salon team. The Receptionist works with the support staff of the bathing and trimming departments to provide professional pet care to the public. This position reports directly to the Manager.

ELIGIBILITY REQUIREMENTS

- Good verbal and written communication skills with competent arithmetic ability. Cashier experience a plus.
- Good organization skills and attention to detail.
- Socially oriented and enjoy working with people.
- Previous experience preferred, if no previous experience capable of completing Receptionist training.
- Good personal hygiene and appropriate dress.
- Pleasant personality capable of working in a team environment.
- A respect and appreciation for pets.
- No medical or physical conditions which would prevent the successful completion of position duties.

If a practical examination is required the applicant will be paid an hourly wage for its duration. Upon selection the applicant is asked to sign introductory employment and confidentiality agreements. A standard employment agreement is signed after successful completion of the introductory period.

POSITION DUTIES

The Receptionist is expected to learn an extensive set of client relations department procedures. They are; incoming client services, outgoing client services, telephone, cash register duties, and public relations duties.

Incoming Client Services

- Greeting clients.
- Completing and maintaining the accuracy of Client & Pet History filecards and the Daily Caging and Payment Register.
- Receiving pets;

    Assigning cage numbers.

    Securing leashes and collars.

    Accepting service order and inspecting pet's coat for appropriateness of request.

    Informing of pick-up times and fees.

    Beginning the Pet Groomers Report and Health Alert.

- Explaining salon services and grooming styles.

Outgoing Client Services

• Make sure pets are ready to be picked up at time given to client. Notify client of any delays.

• Make sure service order is properly completed.

• Check Client and Pet History filecard and Pet Groomer's Report and Health Alert for accuracy.

• Collect service fees and sales revenue (if any).

• Return pets, collars, leashes, and other belongings.

• Schedule next appointment.

• Promote Preferred Client Program.

Telephone Duties

• Make courtesy appointment reminder calls.

• Send Get Well cards to clients with ill pets and Pet Sympathy cards to clients with deceased pets (information obtained from reminder calls).

• Telephone enquiries are sent Pet Care Services Brochure/Mailer.

• Receptionist's Daily Response Report fully and accurately completed for each call and mailing.

Cash Register Duties

• In addition to collecting receipts and depositing them in the cash register the receptionist keeps payment records on the Daily Caging and Payment Register.

Public Relations Duties

• By informing clients of all salon services, maintaining a professional and personable attitude, providing competent service, and making each client feel they and their pets are valued, the receptionist is a key figure in the success of the salon.

Additional duties may be assigned by the manager as needed.

GENERAL INFORMATION

The Employee Handbook: Every employee is expected to comply with the employee policies and procedures contained in the Employee Handbook. Included are standards of performance for personal appearance, client courtesy, salon cleanliness, humane handling of pets, and safety and emergency procedures.

Job Performance Evaluations: Performance evaluations, the basis for job security, promotions, and pay raises, are given twice a year in _____ and _____ .

Work Schedule: Days and hours: _____.
Working holidays: _____.
Compensation: The position is full ( ) part ( ) time. Compensation is by salary ( ), hourly wage ( ) beginning at $_____. The actual rate of compensation, based on qualifications and experience, is part of your employment agreement and presented with an offer of employment should you be selected for the position.
Paydays: _____.

TELEMARKETER

The Telemarketer is a vital member of the salon team. He uses the telephone to market the salon's services to the public following detailed instructions given by management.

The Telemarketer is a part of the Client Relations department and reports directly to the manager.

ELIGIBILITY REQUIREMENTS

• The ability to successfully complete a training program in telemarketing. Previous experience desirable.

• Good verbal and written communication skills with average arithmetic ability.

• Good personal hygiene and appropriate dress.

• Pleasant personality capable of working in a team environment.

• A respect and appreciation for pets.

• No medical or physical conditions which would prevent the successful completion of position duties.

If a practical examination is required the applicant will be paid an hourly wage for its duration. Upon selection the applicant is asked to sign introductory employment and confidentiality agreements. A standard employment agreement is signed after successful completion of the introductory period.

POSITION DUTIES

The telemarketing procedures are described fully on the Telemarketer's Procedures Form and include telemarketing for, and scheduling appointments. Telemarketers also make "check-up" calls to clients and are responsible for some client correspondence. The Telemarketer must keep accurate records of his activities and make regular reports to the Manager.

After three months training and experience the Telemarketer is expected to schedule an average of _____ to _____ new appointments daily.

Additional duties may be assigned by the Manager as needed, which include but are not limited to front counter duties such as making appointments, phone answering, handling payments, and record keeping.

GENERAL INFORMATION

The Employee Handbook: Every employee is expected to comply with the employee policies and procedures contained in the Employee Handbook. Included are standards of performance for personal appearance, client courtesy, salon cleanliness, humane handling of pets, and safety and emergency procedures.

Job Performance Evaluations: Performance evaluations, the basis for job security, promotions, and pay raises, are given twice a year in _____ and _____ .

Work Schedule: Days and hours: _____ .

Working holidays: _____.

Compensation: The position is full ( ) part ( ) time. Compensation is by salary ( ), hourly wage ( ) beginning at $ _____ . The actual rate of compensation, based on qualifications and experience, is part of your employment agreement and presented with an offer of employment should you be selected for the position.

Paydays: _____.

JOB PERFORMANCE EVALUATION
Client Relations Department Positions

Today's Date: _____ Date of Last Evaluation: _____

Employee: _____ Position: _____ Manager: _____

JOB DUTIES & RESPONSIBILITIES	POOR		SATISFACTORY			GOOD			EXCELLENT	
Skill Level:										
Organization	1	2	3	4	5	6	7	8	9	10
Productivity	1	2	3	4	5	6	7	8	9	10
Attention to detail	1	2	3	4	5	6	7	8	9	10
Filecard maintenance	1	2	3	4	5	6	7	8	9	10
Groom Alert	1	2	3	4	5	6	7	8	9	10
Response Reports	1	2	3	4	5	6	7	8	9	10
Cash Register	1	2	3	4	5	6	7	8	9	10
Pet Groomer's Report	1	2	3	4	5	6	7	8	9	10
Daily Caging & Payment Register	1	2	3	4	5	6	7	8	9	10
Appointment book maintenance	1	2	3	4	5	6	7	8	9	10
Telemarketing procedures	1	2	3	4	5	6	7	8	9	10
Appointment confirmations	1	2	3	4	5	6	7	8	9	10
Client promotion materials	1	2	3	4	5	6	7	8	9	10
Staff relations	1	2	3	4	5	6	7	8	9	10

EMPLOYEE POLICIES AND PROCEDURES

Compliance:										
Absence & tardiness	1	2	3	4	5	6	7	8	9	10
Conduct	1	2	3	4	5	6	7	8	9	10
Appearance	1	2	3	4	5	6	7	8	9	10
Client courtesy	1	2	3	4	5	6	7	8	9	10
Cleanliness	1	2	3	4	5	6	7	8	9	10
Pet handling	1	2	3	4	5	6	7	8	9	10
People & pet safety	1	2	3	4	5	6	7	8	9	10
Timekeeping	1	2	3	4	5	6	7	8	9	10

WORK ATTITUDES

Humane treatment	1	2	3	4	5	6	7	8	9	10
Acceptance of assignments	1	2	3	4	5	6	7	8	9	10
Teamwork	1	2	3	4	5	6	7	8	9	10
Accepts training	1	2	3	4	5	6	7	8	9	10
Staff meeting participation	1	2	3	4	5	6	7	8	9	10
Requires minimal supervision	1	2	3	4	5	6	7	8	9	10

EMPLOYEE HANDBOOK

Name _____

Address _____

Telephone _____

Emergency _____

Days/Hours _____

Owner _____

Address _____

Phone _____

Manager _____

Address _____

Phone _____

Master Pet Trimmer _____

Address _____

Phone _____

Asst. Pet Trimmer _____

Address _____

Phone _____

Bathing Dept. Superv. _____

Address _____

Phone _____

Pet Bather #1 _____

Address _____

Phone _____

Pet Bather #2 _____

Address _____

Phone _____

Pet Bather #3 _____

Address _____

Phone _____

Receptionist _____

Address _____

Phone _____

Telemarketer _____

Address _____

Phone _____

CONTENTS

WELCOME

You have been chosen to join a team characterized by quality workmanship, attentive client services, and humane pet care. As a team member you will participate in, and enhance, the reputation we have earned.

Ours is a growing business and the number of our clients and pets increase annually. Our employees have been a major reason for our growth providing pet owners with professional, caring solutions to their pet care needs. Clients have learned that we staff skilled and friendly personnel.

Your position bestows a special trust on you. Every pet entrusted to your care is precious to it's owner and requires respect and humane treatment. Remain mindful of every pet's value and the consequences of being careless.

Your supervisors want you to be successful and enjoy working for them. They are ready to help with answers to your questions. After all, your performance is one of our best references.

This handbook is provided to you as a quick reference to personnel policies and procedures. Please familiarize yourself with the information, and keep the handbook available for future updates. The salon owner reserves the right to modify, delete, or add to these policies and procedures.

Review the handbook from time to time. When in doubt, ask questions. We're eager to hear from you.

PART ONE — EMPLOYMENT POLICIES

Timekeeping Records

All employees must maintain accurate records of hours worked, including overtime. Overtime must be approved by the manager.

Your rate of pay is confidential. Do not discuss it with others, including clients.

Absence and Tardiness

Punctuality is required! Chronic tardiness can lead to termination. If you expect to arrive late inform the manager in advance by telephone.

If you are unable to work, give the manager as much advance notice as possible so they can cover your duties. Failure to do so is grounds for discipline.

Lunch and Rest Periods

Lunch and break times must be authorized by the manager.

Holidays

Pet grooming salons may be open on certain holidays. Business increases around holidays and extra work assignments may be required. The manager will inform you of the holiday schedule.

Professional Appearance & Behavior

Clients and vendors are often present during the workday. Therefore, the appearance and conduct of our staff is essential to building our clients trust and developing professional pride. Courtesy and graciousness with clients is part of service and required, but these same attitudes are expected with fellow employees and anyone else contacted in the course of business.

Professional behavior includes appropriate business attire. Adhere to common sense guidelines of good grooming and cleanliness. Worn, dirty casual wear is not acceptable. Your appearance not only reflects your attitude toward your work, but also how you feel about yourself.

Your behavior and appearance will be considered when evaluating your job performance. A pleasant attitude, proper attire, good manners, respect for animals, and a professional appearance are expected.

(4)

Personal Use of Salon Resources

All business supplies and equipment are to be used for business purposes only. They are not for personal use.

Personal calls may delay or prevent client services. Both incoming and outgoing telephone calls during business hours are to be restricted to those which are absolutely necessary. Toll calls must be approved by the manager.

Smoking

Smoking is allowed only in areas specified by management. Do not dispose of cigarettes, matches, or ashes in the salon's waste containers. Non-smoker rights take precedent over the rights of smokers.

Memoranda

All memoranda regarding policies, procedures, schedules, and the administration of this business must originate with the manager.

Problem Solving

We hope your association with us will be enjoyable. Nevertheless, we know that misunderstandings and problems may occur. When they arise, you are encouraged to bring the matter to the manager's attention as soon as possible. Most problems can be resolved simply and fairly, or avoided entirely, if we learn of them promptly. If you want a prompt resolution to your problem, please discuss it when it happens.

Confidentiality

During your employment you may become privy to confidential information and possessions. It is our professional responsibility to not disclose any information about a client without the authorization of the manager. All information discovered accidentally or overheard in the business should be regarded as confidential unless it is clear that the information is public.

It is also necessary to protect the business in which you are employed. Exercise discretion in discussing salon operations unless you are authorized to do so by the manager. While it is natural to "talk shop," no confidential information should be given to outsiders.

Upon leaving employment you are expected to return any business possessions. You may also be asked to sign an Employee Confidentiality Agreement.

(5)

Personnel Records

A personnel file is kept for every employee. All employment forms completed by you will be kept in your file as well as any other employment related documents.

All employees are required to complete Form I-9 at the beginning of employment to verify entitlement to work in the United States. You are required to contact the manager if your legal status changes or your employment authorization expires.

Notify the manager also of any changes in your address, telephone, or name. A new W-4 Form is required for address and name changes.

It is your responsibility to have a correct W-4 on file. A new W-4 Form must be completed to change the number of Federal and State Withholding Exemptions. This form is available from the manager.

Discipline & Termination

There are standards of behavior we must all respect. In general, no conduct that is unsafe, inconsiderate, or illegal will be tolerated.

The following are examples of conduct that will lead to disciplinary action or termination.

• Use or possession of alcohol or illegal drugs on business property or reporting to work under the influence of alcohol or illegal drugs may be grounds for termination.

• Theft.

• Inhumane treatment of a client's pet (see Part V).

• Falsification of records, including timekeeping records.

• Willful destruction or waste of property or materials.

• Disorderly conduct.

We ask that you conduct yourself with reasonable and proper regard for the welfare and rights of all employees, clients, and pets and the best interest of the business.

PART TWO — PERSONNEL POLICIES AND BENEFITS

Paydays

Rate of Pay

Your rate of pay is strictly confidential. Adjustment of your rate of pay is to be discussed only with the manager and typically occurs only after job performance evaluations.

Job Performance Evaluations

Performance evaluations are conducted by the manager and take place twice a year. It is an opportunity to acknowledge your contribution to the business' success and to offer suggestions to improve your performance.

Requests for Time Off

Requests for time off for medical and dental appointments, military service, jury duty, or personal leave should be made as far in advance as possible. Requests for time off must be submitted to the manager for approval.

Vacations are scheduled and approved by the manager. It is requested that vacation not be taken during holidays when the demand for pet care services peaks. Vacation period availability will be allotted by order of tenure.

Benefits

You are provided:

_____

_____

_____

_____

_____

(7)

PART THREE — SALON CLEANLINESS STANDARDS

Maintaining high standards of salon cleanliness requires every employee to do their part. A pleasant, hygienic work environment characteristic of professionals promotes morale and contributes to the success of the business.

Maintaining the cleanliness work areas fosters a healthy environment benefiting everyone. If a cleaning need exists outside of your work area bring it to the attention of the responsible employee or the manager. If a pet is soiling its cage it is everyone's responsibility. Furnish immediate assistance and ask others for help.

Procedures

1. Use cleaning solutions according to instructions and place soiled cleaning cloths in a designated container. Note: Always return cleaning solutions to their storage location when finished. Do not place cleaning supplies around pets or in the bathing and trimming departments. They might be confused with grooming supplies resulting in an injury.

2. Always wipe-up liquid spills immediately and caution others to be careful in the wet area. Following the pet bathing safety rules will keep the tub area clean.

3. Do not use a vacuum for wet spills unless the equipment is capable of handling liquids.

4. A cage is not properly cleaned unless you have wiped not only the its floor but also the side, rear, and ceiling panels. Be especially diligent when cleaning corners due to the danger of fungus.

5. Clean the floor of pet hair and other waste frequently. Place refuse in a waste container lined with a trash bag. Before disposing of the bag, tightly seal it to prevent spilling. All waste containers are to be emptied at the end of every business day.

6. The staff of the Bathing Department must keep the wheels of blow-dryers free of pet hair.

7. Pet soilings are to be disposed of immediately. Place fecal matter in a sealed plastic bag before placing it in the waste container. Cloths used to clean pet soilings must be rinsed with a sterilizing solution and placed in a separate holding container.

8. Cleanse counter/table tops and tools after every pet with the appropriate cleaning supplies.

9. Notify the manager of flea or other pest problems immediately.

10. Always leave the bathroom and employee area clean for the next person.

(8)

PART FOUR - CLIENT COURTESY PROCEDURES

Our goal to achieve total client satisfaction requires every employee to courteously receive every person visiting the business, and to answer the telephone in the same polite manner. Without courtesy even the finest pet care services will not satisfy clients and promote the success of the business.

In general

Listen to visitors or callers carefully to determine exactly who they are, and what they need.

When receiving complaints do not dispute them with the client. Politely gather information and advise them you will inform the manager who will resolve the problem.

Always speak clearly so clients can understand you. Use a moderate tone of voice. Be patient and polite even if the client is in a poor mood.

Reception

Try to learn the names of all clients and their pets. Greet clients and pets using their names to make the most favorable impression and of course, smile. Take a minute to sincerely ask how they and their pets have been.

Ask clients if they have any questions. Never assume you know what they want without asking them. Offer the salon's brochure or other informational materials when answering inquiries. Be sure clients know the full range of services the salon provides.

Ask new customers how they were referred to the salon and include the source on their filecard. Then the salon will be able to thank the referral source.

Before clients depart the salon always thank them for their patronage.

Telephone

Telephone calls are usually the first opportunity to make a favorable impression on clients. Always answer the telephone by saying, "This is (salon) , My name is _____, How may I help you?"

In closing the conversation, always thank the caller and quietly replace the receiver on its holder. Always let the caller say good-bye first! This ensures that they are truly finished and avoids the feeling you are anxious to get rid of them.

If a caller wishes to speak to someone else, advise them you will put them on hold and transfer their call. Discreetly notify the person requested they have a call waiting, do not loudly announce the call.

(9)

If someone other than the receptionist answers the call, and the caller requests pet care service information or an appointment, refer them to the receptionist. If the receptionist is not available and you have completed your client service training, assist the caller personally. If not, request assistance from a qualified employee or the manager.

When callers request information carefully note their name, address, and telephone number so promotional materials may be mailed to them and the information can be added to the mailing list.

Be sure to offer compliments to others and support your team.

(10)

PART FIVE - SAFETY

General Safety Rules

Your safety and that of others depends on following the salon's safety procedures. The mark of a successful team is preventing accidents before they happen.

1. Do not lift large pets without assistance. When lifting, bend your legs at the knees keeping your back straight.

2. Wipe up all spills immediately. Alert others to avoid it until it is cleaned.

3. Wear gloves when handling any toxic material.

4. Pick up fallen tools immediately.

5. Do not obstruct the path of others. Keep cords out of the way.

6. Keep all electrical items away from tubs or any wet area.

7. Report any unusual smells, especially burning odors, to the manager immediately. Turn off equipment and look for the source. Until you have found it, do not touch the equipment.

8. Keep aerosol cans away from heat sources; especially dryers, clipper boosters, and water heaters.

9. Check the condition of your equipment and tools regularly. Tighten loose screws or knobs. If maintenance is required, notify the manager.

10. Lubricate clippers and scissors as necessary. Sterilize ear-cleaning hemostats after each use. Empty and clean groomer tool boxes daily.

11. Drain drink containers into sink and wrap food scraps tightly before disposing of them in waste containers.

Pet Safety

Respect for the safety of pets is a priority in this salon. It requires following all of the salon's safety procedures for pets. Handling a pet safely is as important as grooming them well. The salon is a strange environment for pets. They require the reassurance humane pet care procedures provides. Don't risk their lives by taking chances. If you discover conditions not detailed on the Pet Groomer's Report and Health Alert or filecard, contact the manager immediately. Then complete the report according to the manager's instructions. Never attempt to be a veterinarian and make a diagnosis. Merely describe the condition for the pet owner.

1. Before handling any pet check the filecard for the pet's name and Groom Alert information for any special pet-handling concerns. Notice the pet's reaction to you before handling them. Approach them slowly and speak softly using their name.

2. Be aware of other pets while you work. Glance about occasionally to check on them in their cages.

(11)

3. Do not allow pets to run freely about the salon. Pets should be caged or controlled by an employee or owner at all times.

4. Place pets in sanitized cages only, and clean them each time they are soiled. Double check cage door latches after caging a pet.

5. Approach a caged pet from the side and speak its name softly and slowly. Observe its response. Don't startle sleeping pets. Slowly open the cage door and move your hand slowly along the cage floor. Place your hand and arm around the pet's middle and support it from underneath as you remove the pet.

6. If a pet appears aggressive when attempting to remove them from a cage request assistance from the manager.

7. Whenever a pet's behavior seems unusual notify the manager immediately.

8. If you are uncertain how to care for a pet, don't attempt it. Learn the proper procedures before you proceed.

9. When carrying small pets hold them securely providing support underneath their body.

10. Do not carry large pets. Use a short leash, gripping it firmly, and lead them through the salon.

11. While carrying or leading a pet through the salon avoid contact with other pets.

12. Never leave a pet unattended! If you must leave a pet temporarily, place it in a clean holding cage until you return.

13. Whenever a pet is assigned a new cage, advise the Client Relations Department so they can update the service records and make sure the pet's equipment is moved to the new cage.

14. If a pet is nervous, the best remedy is a light massage. Gently massage the pet from the neck to the back to reassure it.

15. Never discipline a pet physically for any reason! Do not yell at it, it makes a bad impression on clients, and is ineffective.

Handling the Aged/Ill/Disabled Pet

Aged/ill/disabled pets require individual consideration. The Groom Alert information on every filecard describes any special handling requirements. Never handle a pet until you review and understand the Groom Alert warnings.

1. Aged/ill/disabled pets with matted coats cannot endure excessive comb-outs. Discuss the situation with the manager. In most cases the manager will contact the client to request permission to remove the coat. After a pet's coat has been removed, keep them warm. Advise the client to keep the pet warm also.

2. Many aged and ill pets have sore gums so don't squeeze their muzzle (stock).

3. Pets with heart ailments as well as many other aged/ill/disabled pets should only be blow-dried on a warm setting. Do not stand pets with heart ailments on their hind legs. Lift their legs and groom them from the inside.

(12)

4. Talk softly and frequently to blind pets to alleviate their fear. Lightly massage them occasionally to diminish their feeling of vulnerability.

5. Aged/ill/disabled pets should be kept warm at all times. If a shampoo or bathing treatment is required to stay on the pet for more than a minute, wrap the pet with two dry towels until ready to rinse. When handling the pet, lift its legs slowly and do not pull them outward. Support the pet by placing your hand underneath them.

6. Some aged/ill/disabled pets should not have flea solutions used on them unless the pet's veterinarian has first given written or verbal approval, and the approval is noted on the pet's filecard. The manager is responsible to determine the appropriateness of using a flea solution on aged/ill/disabled pets. When in doubt, don't.

The Humane Bath

PRE-BATH PROCEDURES

1. First, review the pet's filecard for Groom Alert warnings. See if special pet handling indicators have been marked and described. If the pet is aged, ill, or disabled handle them cautiously. Proceed with the bathing procedure only when you completely understand the Groom Alert information and how it affects the bathing of the pet. If you have any questions notify the manager or bathing department supervisor.

2. If a veterinarian has prescribed special treatment review the instructions. If you have any questions, see the manager before bathing the pet. When the bath is completed, place the treatment in a secure storage area until it is returned to the pet owner.

3. Remove all collars. Flea collars may be toxic when wet.

4. Clean ears and insert cotton to prevent water from entering the ear canal.

5. Clip nails and dew claws and file them smooth.

6. Soak, and carefully remove encrustations around the pet's eyes with warm water only. Place a drop of eye lubricant in each eye.

7. Clean the drying counter.

Bath Procedures

1. Test the water temperature before wetting the pet. Use only warm water.

2. Do not force anal gland expulsions and do not perform them with long fingernails. Report any unusual secretions.

3. Carefully bathe, de-flea (if indicated), rinse, and towel dry the pet's head first. Avoid solutions in the pet's eyes by applying them at least an inch from the eyes and working the suds outward.

(13)

4. When the pet's head is finished, continue to bathe, de-flea, and rinse the pet's body. If the rinse water is very dirty, or red with dead fleas, a second shampoo is usually necessary.

5. Support the pet with at least one hand at all times to prevent it from slipping. Be alert and watch for pets that want to jump out of the tub.

6. Keep shampoo, flea dip, and other treatments away from the pet's eyes and ear canals. Do not leave solution containers in or near the tub where a pet might drink from them.

7. Do not allow the pet to stand in soapy water. Rinse the feet last to completely remove all draining residues. Make sure all dead fleas have been removed.

8. Remove cotton from the ears before drying the pet.

9. Never leave the pet unattended!

Drying Procedures

1. All pets are to be hand-dried. If bathing or drying must be temporarily discontinued, cover the pet with enough dry towels to avoid chills and place them in a holding cage until you return.

2. Do not permit pets in the drying area to be close enough to reach each other.

3. Dry aged/ill/disabled pets on a warm setting only.

4. Return bathed pets to their sanitized cage with a clean, dry towel placed on the floor.

5. Complete the Pet Groomer's Report and Health Alert and present it to the manager for approval.

TELEMARKETING PROCEDURES FORM

APPENDIX

C

T he most desirable qualities for a telemarketer are: 1) a pleasant personality, 2) clear and positive speech, and 3) informative answers to client's questions.

For supplies you will need the appointment book, the filecard boxes, and a copy of the Daily Response Report-Telemarketer.

Appointment Scheduling Calls/Preferred Client Members — Option B.

1. Select Option B clients.

Option B client's select a weekly interval between appointments which is noted on their Client and Pet History filecard. As part of our service the telemarketer calls them two weeks prior to that date to schedule an appointment.

The filecards for Option B clients are in Box #2 filed in the month they have selected for an appointment. For example, Mrs. Jones' last appointment was June 15th, her weekly interval is eight weeks (August 10th is her next appointment so her filecard is in the August section of Box #2), and an appointment scheduling call should be made on July 27th (two weeks prior).

Start each telemarketing session by filling in the dates at the top of the Daily Response Report-Telemarketer (Appendix A). Find the month of the target date in Box #2 and collect all the client filecards whose last appointment was two weeks prior to the target date (the Client and Pet History filecard will specify the last appointment date). Check the previous month to be sure all Option B clients have been reached and keep every Option B client's filecard in Box #2 until they have been contacted.

2. Making calls to Option B clients.

Follow this script for every client called:

"Hello (client's name). **This is** (your name) **of** (salon name). **How are you and** (pet's name)**?"**

"Your next appointment date is (target date). **Is this date convenient for you or would you prefer another date?"**

A. (Is convenient) **"Would you prefer a morning or afternoon appointment?"**

B. (Not convenient) **"Which date would be better for you?"** (client gives date) **"Would you prefer a morning or afternoon appointment?"**

C. (Pet is ill). **"We provide special care appointments every (_____). This is so we can have time to give your pet special attention. If your veterinarian authorizes a grooming for** (pet's name) **we would be pleased to schedule an appointment and provide any services your veterinarian recommends.** (Schedule appointment per instructions. Whether or not an appointment is scheduled, say) **"I'll call you back in a week to see how** (pet's name) **is doing. We all hope for a speedy recovery."** (Note comments on the Daily Response Report and send a Get Well card.)

"Were you pleased with the services you received on your last visit?" (Note client comments on the Daily Response Report).

A. (Yes) **"Thank you, that's good to hear. We'll look forward to seeing you and** (pet's name) **on** (appointment date) **."**

B. (No) **"Will you please describe the problem to me so I can inform the manager."** (listen to complaint) **"Thank you, we will do our best to resolve it to your satisfaction. We value your patronage and enjoy grooming** (pet's name) **."** Note client comments on the Daily Response Report and inform the manager.

3. Record all contacts.

Whether or not you make contact to schedule an appointment, record the date and result (briefly) of every call in the "Client Contact History" section of the Client and Pet History filecard.

4. Client Response Postcards.

Mail a Client Response Postcard to clients you were unable to reach. When a Client Response Postcard is sent put the date of the mailing in the Client Contact History section of their filecard.

5. Re-file filecards.

Filecards for Option B clients who confirm their next appointment are filed in Box #1. Those you were unable to reach are filed back in Box #2.

Check-up calls to "C" clients.

"C" clients have declined membership in the Preferred Client Program. They prefer to call at their discretion when they desire an appointment. They are given equal respect of course. The goal is to encourage them to join the program by providing the type of service which encourages them to become members.

1. Select Option "C" clients.

Check-up calls to "C" clients are made at the manager's discretion. For example, "C" clients who have not had an appointment in the last six months may be selected. You would then pull all "C" client filecards in Box #3 who have not had an appointment in the last six months, and who had not received a check-up call during that period.

2. Check-up calls to "C" clients.

Follow this script for every client called:

"**Hello** (client's name) **. This is** (your name) **of** (salon name) **. I hope you and** (pet's name) **are well. I noticed it's been** (length of time) **since your last appointment. Would you like to schedule a time to groom** (pet's name) **?"**

A. (Yes) **"What would be a good date for you to come in? Would you prefer a morning or an afternoon appointment?"**

B. (No) **"Is there a problem with our service?"**

1. (Yes) **"Will you please describe the problem to me so I can inform the manager."** (listen to complaint) **"Thank you, we will do our best to resolve it to your satisfaction. We value your patronage and enjoy grooming** (pet's name) **."** Note client comments on the Daily Response Report and inform the manager.

2. (Pet is ill) **"We provide special care appointments every (_____). This is so we can have time to give your pet special attention. If your veterinarian authorizes a grooming for** (pet's name) **we would be pleased to schedule an**

appointment and provide any services your veterinarian recommends. (Schedule appointment per instructions. Whether or not an appointment is scheduled, say) **"I'll call you back in a week to see how** (pet's name) **is doing. We all hope for a speedy recovery."** (Note illness on the Daily Response Report and send a Get Well Card.)

3. (Pet has died) **"Please accept the condolences of all of us here. We know this is very sad moment for you. When we can be of service to you again please contact us."** (Note death of pet on Daily Response Report and send a Pet Sympathy Card.)

3. Record all contacts.

Even if you don't make contact record the date and result of the call (briefly) on each client's filecard in the "Client Contact History."

4. Client Response Postcards.

Mail a Client Response Postcard to clients you were unable to reach. When a Client Response Postcard is sent put the date of the mailing in the Client Contact History section of their filecard.

5. Re-file filecards.

Filecards for Option C clients who schedule an appointment are filed in Box #1. Those do not schedule are returned to Box #3.